"In the tradition of Martyn Lloyd-Jones and John Stott, Mark Dever calls the church to rediscover her biblical heritage. Perhaps never in history has the church tried so hard to be relevant to a culture and become less relevant in doing so! While many modern church gurus encourage us to be 'in the world,' Mark reminds us that our calling is to do so without being 'of the world.' This volume is consumed with church 'being' rather than church 'doing.' After all, being comes before doing, for what we ultimately 'do' is always determined by who we 'are.' Let the church *be* the church! Read it and reap!"

—O. S. HAWKINS, President,
  Annuity Board of the Southern Baptist Convention

"For a young pastor wrestling with questions of what success and faithfulness look like for a church, Mark Dever's book is a godsend. It helps you see past the hype and fanfare of numbers, statistics, and the latest methodology. Instead it guides you back to the old paths and the simple, world-changing beauty of God's plan for the local church."

—JOSHUA HARRIS, Senior Pastor,
  Covenant Life Church, Gaithersburg, Md.

"Books that affirm the priority of the church are rare. Books that define the practice of the local church from the pages of Scripture rather than from cultural trends are even more rare. Mark Dever has given us just such a book. Written by a pastor and theologian who has built a strong local church in Washington D.C., this is the best book I have read on this topic of critical importance."

—C. J. MAHANEY,
  Sovereign Grace Ministries

"It is astonishing that the apostle Paul describes the local gathering of Christians as 'the church of God, which he obtained with his own blood' (Acts 20:28, ESV). That raises the stakes of church life and health and mission about as high as it can be. We are dealing with a blood-bought body of people. I do not want human ideas. I want God's word about the church. I turn with hope and confidence to Mark Dever's radically biblical commitment. Few people today have thought more or better about what makes a church biblical and healthy. I thank God for the book and for Nine Marks Ministries."

—JOHN PIPER,
  Pastor for Preaching and Vision, Bethlehem Baptist Church, Minneapolis

"*Nine Marks of a Healthy Church* is required reading for my students in ecclesiology. Even though I do not always come to the same conclusions as the author, the book is one of the few recent serious engagements with trenchantly important ecclesiological issues. This is also a great book for pastors to share with their congregations."

—PAIGE PATTERSON,
  President, Southwestern Baptist Theological Seminary

"A powerful and passionate call for congregations to take seriously their responsibilities, for the glory of God and the saving of lost souls."

—TIMOTHY GEORGE,
  Executive Editor, *Christianity Today*

"In a day when a church is most likely evaluated on her cosmetics, it's vital to know how to assess her true health. They put cosmetics on corpses! Mark Dever gives the biblical criteria for discerning the spiritual well-being of a church, not what it looks like on the outside before the world, but what it is on the inside before God. This is a foundational work which I highly recommend."

—JOHN MACARTHUR,
Pastor-Teacher

"*Nine Marks of a Healthy Church* is one of the very best, most readable, and useful books for learning how to lead a church into spiritual change. Its focus is not on church growth but on church health, which is the proper goal of a God-centered ministry. Each chapter gives the biblical rationale and offers practical suggestions for preaching, evangelism, discipleship, or some other aspect of church life. These principles and practices have been tested in Dever's own dynamic ministry as senior pastor of a thriving urban congregation."

—PHILIP GRAHAM RYKEN,
Senior Pastor, Tenth Presbyterian Church, Philadelphia

"Postmodern America is awash with spirituality—but not with authentic Christianity. Clear evidence of this fact is seen in the loss of a biblical ecclesiology in so many sectors. Reformation is always directed to the church—and we must pray to see the church reformed in our age. Mark Dever points toward a truly biblical recovery of the New Testament church in his manifesto, *Nine Marks of a Healthy Church*. Every page is loaded with thoughtful analysis and careful consideration. It belongs in the hands of every faithful pastor and all those who pray for reformation in this age."

—R. ALBERT MOHLER,
President, The Southern Baptist Theological Seminary

"Books on the church are a dime a dozen. This one is different. Only rarely does a book on the church come along that marries responsible biblical and theological reflection to godly, experienced, good judgment and practical application. This book is one of them. If you are a Christian leader, be careful of the work you are now holding in your hand: it may change your life and ministry."

—D. A. CARSON,
Research Professor of New Testament, Trinity Evangelical Divinity School

"The future of biblical Christianity in the Western world is inextricably bound to the future of the local church. Mark Dever knows this, and his *Nine Marks of a Healthy Church* is a biblical prescription for faithfulness."

—J. LIGON DUNCAN III,
Senior Minister, First Presbyterian Church, Jackson, Miss.

NINE MARKS OF A HEALTHY CHURCH

FOREWORD *by* JOSHUA HARRIS

9 NINE MARKS *of a* HEALTHY CHURCH

NEW EXPANDED EDITION

MARK DEVER

CROSSWAY BOOKS

A PUBLISHING MINISTRY OF
GOOD NEWS PUBLISHERS
WHEATON, ILLINOIS

Nine Marks of a Healthy Church

Copyright © 2004 by Mark Dever

Published by Crossway Books
        a publishing ministry of Good News Publishers
        1300 Crescent Street
        Wheaton, Illinois 60187

New expanded edition; revised and expanded edition published 2000;
first edition published 1997 by Founders Press.

Cover design: Josh Dennis

First printing 2004

Printed in the United States of America

Library of Congress Cataloging-in-Publication Data
Dever, Mark.
  Nine marks of a healthy church / Mark Dever ; foreword by Joshua
Harris.—New expanded ed.
    p. cm.
  Includes bibliographical references and indexes.
  ISBN 13: 978-1-58134-631-2
  ISBN 10: 1-58134-631-X (trade pbk.)
  1. Church—Marks. I. Title.
  BV601.D48   2004
  250—dc22
                           2004014950

DPI		15	14	13	12	11	10	09	08	07	06
17	16	15	14	13	12	11	10	9	8	7	6	5	4

CONTENTS

FOREWORD

For a young pastor wrestling with questions of what success looks like for a church, this book is a godsend. I'm almost thirty and I see many Christians my age—pastors and laypersons alike—struggling to understand God's purpose and plan for the local church.

How is the church supposed to act? What does it mean for a church to be faithful? And how can you tell whether or not you're succeeding?

Today the most visible role models are the Jack Welches of Christendom—the high-powered pastors of super-sized churches whose success in building large congregations has made them sought-after sources of counsel. I've read some of their books. I've gone to a few of their conferences and listened to their tips on how my church can grow and excel. I've learned a few things. And the evangelistic zeal and passion for excellence that many of these pastors and their churches display has inspired me.

But I'm always left with questions and very deep reservations about the course they have taken—and that they encourage me to follow in. All of their advice and methodology seems premised on the belief that bigger is better. If there's a crowd, then what you're doing is working. The fact that a lot of people are attending is the proof that what they're doing is right and blessed by God.

It's hard to argue with numbers. Faced with attendance in the tens of thousands, mega-complex buildings, and budgets bigger than those of some small countries, it's not easy to question whether this is really such a good idea. "Of course it's a good idea!" the evidence seems to scream. "Look how BIG it all is!"

But is size the measure of success? We all know the right answer is no, but I wonder how many of us truly believe it deep down—or how many of us know what to use to measure success in its place.

The fact that something about this book's title and description has drawn you in enough to crack the cover and begin reading makes me think you might be asking the same questions I have asked. Maybe you're uneasy about the shallowness of the modern church. Maybe you're looking for another measuring stick for true health. But whether you're a pastor looking for a blueprint to build your church or simply a Christian asking what matters most in a church, I believe this book can help you.

Mark Dever loves the local church. He pastors a healthy, growing church in Washington, D.C. He has nothing against big churches. He is passionate about evangelism and reaching the lost. But he's not enamored with size and growth. He wants to see God glorified. He wants to see the church faithfully representing the Gospel, not mirroring the culture. His study of God's Word, his knowledge of church history, and his insightful thinking about church make him a valued source of wisdom. Stay home from the next flashy how-to church conference and read this book instead.

Mark isn't worried about being hip or trend-setting. He wants to be faithful to God's Word, and he's courageously committed to the Gospel. And it's precisely these qualities that today's church so desperately needs. In this book Mark shows us from Scripture the characteristics of a healthy church. He helps us see past the hype and fanfare of numbers, statistics, and the latest methodology. He guides us back to the old paths and the simple, world-changing beauty of God's plan for the local church.

Mark Dever is a pastor and friend whom I deeply respect. You can trust the counsel he gives in these pages.

—Joshua Harris
Senior Pastor, Covenant Life Church,
Gaithersburg, Md.

PREFACE
TO THE NEW EXPANDED EDITION

Ten Years of Nine Marks

TEN YEARS ON

As I'm writing this preface to the new expanded edition of *Nine Marks of a Healthy Church,* I'm also about to celebrate ten years pastoring the same congregation. To some reading this sentence, that sounds like an eternity; to others, it may seem as if I've just begun. To be honest, to me it feels a bit like both.

I confess that pastoring a church sometimes feels like difficult work. There have been times when my tears have not been tears of joy, but of frustration, or sadness, or even worse. The people who are least happy and who leave have often been those who have required the most time, and who have talked the most to others as they have gone. And sometimes their talk has been neither edifying nor encouraging. They have little thought of how their actions affect others— the pastor, the pastor's family, those who have loved them and worked with them, young Christians who are confused, others to whom they talk wrongly. There are things I work for that don't work out, and things I care about that nobody else does. Some hopes go unfulfilled, and occasionally even tragedies intrude. It is in the nature of sheep to stray and of wolves to eat. I guess if I can't deal with that, I should just get out of under-shepherding.

But most of my work is, to be honest, exhilarating! I thank God for those many times when I have known tears of joy. In God's grace, the number of people leaving the congregation unhappy has been dwarfed by the number of people leaving with tears of gratitude, and by those coming in. We have known growth in our congregation that hasn't been dramatic when considered in any one year, but which staggers me when I pause and look back. I've seen young men become converted and then eventually go into the ministry. While I'm writing this, two of the men now on our pastoral staff were first friends of mine when they were non-Christians. I studied the gospel of Mark with them. By God's grace, I saw both of them come to know the Lord, and I now sit and listen to them preach the everlasting Gospel to others. My eyes moisten even while I write these words.

The church as a whole has prospered. It seems clearly healthy. Strains in relationships are dealt with in godly ways. A culture of discipleship seems to have taken root. People go from here to seminary, or to their work as architects or businessmen with more resolve in both their work and their evangelism. We've seen many marriages and young families begun. We've seen political types instructed in their worldviews; Christians in all walks of life helped in their understanding of the Gospel; and discipline exercised to try to disabuse those who may be self-deceived. Pain has been exceeded by joy. God's grace toward us seems only to increase with every life encountered.

As God's Word has been taught, the congregation's appetite for good teaching has increased. A palpable sense of expectation has developed in the congregation. There is excitement as the congregation gathers. Older saints are cared for through their difficult days. One dear man's ninety-sixth birthday was celebrated by a bunch of the younger people in the church taking him to McDonald's (his favorite restaurant)! Wounded marriages have been helped; wounded people have found God's healing. Young people have come to appreciate hymns, and older people the vigorous singing of choruses. Countless hours have been given in quiet service to the building up of others. Courageous choices have been prayed for, made, and celebrated. New friendships are being made every day. Young men who have spent time with us here are now pastoring congregations in Kentucky and Michigan and Georgia and Connecticut and Illinois. They are preaching in Hawaii and Iowa. Missions giving has gone from a few thousand dollars a year to a few hundred thousand dollars a year. Our compassion for the lost has grown. I could go on. God has obviously been good to us. We have known health.

MY SURPRISING CHANGE

I didn't intend all of this when I came. I didn't come with a plan or program to bring all this about. I came with a commitment to God's Word, to give myself to knowing, believing, and teaching it. I had seen the blight of the unconverted church member, and was particularly concerned about that, but I didn't have a carefully worked out strategy to deal with the problem.

In God's providence, I had done a doctorate focusing on a Puritan (Richard Sibbes) whose writings about the individual Christian I loved, but whose concessions on the church came to seem increasingly unwise to me. Unhealthy churches cause few problems for the healthiest Christians; but they are cruel taxes on the growth of the youngest and weakest Christians. They prey on those who don't understand Scripture well. They mislead spiritual children. They even take the curious hopes of non-Christians that there might be another way to live, and seem to deny it. Bad churches are terribly effective anti-missionary forces. I deeply lament sin in my own life, and sin's corporate magnification in the life of so many churches. They seem to make Jesus out to be a liar when He promised life to the full (John 10:10).

This all became more central to my life when, in 1994, I became the senior pastor of the congregation I now serve. The responsibility weighed on my mind. Texts such as James 3:1 ("judged more strictly") and Hebrews 13:17 ("must give an account") loomed larger in my mind. Circumstances conspired to emphasize to me the importance with which God regards the local church. I thought of a statement by John Brown, who, in a letter of paternal counsel to one of his pupils newly ordained over a small congregation, wrote,

> I know the vanity of your heart, and that you will feel mortified that your congregation is very small, in comparison with

those of your brethren around you; but assure yourself on the
word of an old man, that when you come to give an account
of them to the Lord Christ, at his judgment-seat, you will
think you have had enough.[1]

As I looked out over the congregation I had charge of, I felt the
weightiness of such an accounting to God.

But it was ultimately through preaching expositional sermons,
serially going through book after book, that all of the Bible's teachings on the church became more central to me. It began to seem
obviously a farce that we claimed to be Christians but didn't love each
other. Sermons on John and 1 John, Wednesday night Bible studies
going through James for three years, conversations about membership and church covenants all came together.

The "each other" and "one another" passages began to come alive
and enflesh the theological truths that I had known about God caring for His church. As I've preached through Ephesians 2–3 it has
become clear to me that the church is the center of God's plan to display His wisdom to the heavenly beings. When Paul spoke to the
Ephesian elders, he referred to the church as something that God
"bought with his own blood" (Acts 20:28). And, of course, on the
road to Damascus earlier, when Saul was interrupted on his course
of persecuting Christians, the risen Christ did not ask Saul why he
persecuted these Christians, or even the church; rather, Christ so
identified with His church that the accusing question He put to Saul
was, "why do you persecute me?" (Acts 9:4). The church was clearly
central in God's eternal plan, in His sacrifice, and in His continuing
concern.

I've come to see that love is largely local. And the local congregation is the place which claims to display this love for all the world
to see. So Jesus taught His disciples in John 13:34-35, "A new command I give you: Love one another. As I have loved you, so you must
love one another. By this all men will know that you are my disciples,
if you love one another." I have seen friends and family alienated from
Christ because they perceive this or that local church to have been

such a terrible place. And, on the other hand, I have seen friends and family come to Christ because they have seen exactly this love that Jesus taught and lived—love for one another, the kind of selfless love that He showed—and they've felt the natural human attraction to it. So the congregation—the gathered people of God as the sounding board of the Word—has become more central to my understanding of evangelism, and of how we should pray and plan to evangelize. The local church is God's evangelism plan. The local church is God's evangelism program.

Over these last ten years, the congregation has also become more central to my understanding of how we are to discern true conversion in others, and how we are to have assurance of it ourselves. I remember being struck by 1 John 4:20-21 when preparing to preach on it: "If anyone says, 'I love God,' yet hates his brother, he is a liar. For anyone who does not love his brother, whom he has seen, cannot love God, whom he has not seen. . . . Whoever loves God must also love his brother." James 1 and 2 carries the same message. This love doesn't seem to be optional.

More recently, this consideration of the centrality of the congregation has brought about in my thinking a new respect for the local congregation's discipline—both formative and corrective. We've had some painful cases here, and some wonderful recoveries; and all of us are clearly still works in progress. But it has become crystal clear that if we are to depend upon each other in our congregations, discipline must be part of discipleship. And if there is to be the kind of discipline that we see in the New Testament, we must know and be known by others, and we must be committed to one another. We must also have some trust of authority. All the practicalities of trusting authority in marriage, home, and church are hammered out on the local level. Misunderstanding these matters and coming to dislike and resent authority seems very near to what the Fall was all about. Conversely, understanding these matters seems very near to the heart of God's gracious work of reestablishing His relationship with us— a relationship of authority and love together. I've come to see that relationship with a local congregation is central to individual discipleship. The church isn't an optional extra; it's the shape of your following Jesus. I've come to understand that now in a way I never did before I came to this church. And I think that I'm seeing something of the health that God intends us to experience in a congregation.

WHAT THIS BOOK IS NOT

I should just say another word about what this book is not. Let me front-load your disappointment. This book leaves out a lot. Many of our favorite topics may not be covered. Re-reading this book now, after a few years of others reading it too, I am even more aware of much I have not said. Friends have said to me, "What about prayer?" or "Where's worship?" John Piper asked, "Mark, why isn't missions in this?" I don't really like to disappoint friends who've taken the time to read the book; and I certainly don't like disappointing John Piper! But this book is not an exhaustive ecclesiology. We've been given good ideas for "more marks" that we could add. And a second edition might seem just the time to do this.

But we've decided not to. I continue to think that common errors in these particular nine matters are responsible for so much that goes wrong in our churches. It seems to me economical, strategic, faithful, and simply correct to continue to try to focus the attention of Christians on these particular matters. More missions, persevering prayer, wonderful worship—all will be best encouraged, I think, by tending better to these basic matters. Nobody is going to believe in the need that missions presupposes if they're not taught about that need from the Word. No one is going to go if they don't have an understanding of God's great plan to redeem a people for Himself. And they won't do missions well if they don't understand the Gospel.

If people do begin to think more carefully about conversion, it will affect their prayers. If we are more biblical in our practice of evangelism, we will find ourselves giving more of our prayer time to praying for non-Christians, and we will realize more of why we must pray for people to be converted. If we come to understand more about biblical church membership, we will find our corporate prayer times more central, better attended, more invigorating to our faith, and more challenging and re-ordering to our priorities.

If we begin to appreciate again the significance of church discipline, our times of corporate worship will be infused with more of a sense of awe at God's grace. If we find ourselves in churches that are increasingly marked by discipleship and spiritually flourishing members, the excitement and anticipation for singing praises and confessing sins together will grow. If we work to be led by those who meet the Bible's qualifications, we will find joy and confidence in our times together growing, we will be more free and enlivened in our times together, and our obedience will be more consistent.

This book isn't a complete inventory of every sign of health. It is intended to be a list of crucial marks that will lead to such a full experience.

AN OUTWARD-LOOKING CHURCH

If I had to add one more mark to what you're about to read, it wouldn't be missions or prayer or worship; but it would touch on all of those things. I think that I would add that we want our congregations to be outward-looking. We are to be upwardly focused—God-centered. But we are also, I think, supposed to reflect God's own love as we look out on other people and on other congregations.

This can show itself in many ways. I long for our congregation to integrate better our vision for global missions and our efforts in local evangelism. If we have a commitment to help evangelize an unreached people group abroad, why haven't we done a better job in trying to find members of this people group in our metropolitan area? Why aren't our missions and evangelism better integrated?

We do pray in the pastoral prayer each Sunday morning for the prosperity of the Gospel in other lands and through other local congregations. We're just now bringing someone on staff to help us plant another church. We as a church help to sponsor 9Marks Ministries, and through them work with many other churches for their benefit. We have "Weekenders" at which we welcome guest pastors and elders, seminarians and other church leaders. We have internships for those preparing for the pastorate. We have curriculum we write and talks we give. All of this is for the building up of other congregations. As a pastor, I am certain that I need to realize that, under God, the local church is responsible for raising up the next generation of leaders. No Bible college, course, or seminary can do this. And such raising up of new leaders—for here and abroad—should be one of the goals of our church.

Looking back, I'm encouraged by how I've seen God's work here and in so many other congregations. In this congregation's life together I've seen evident, increasing, joyful, God-glorifying health.

Some people don't think this image of "health" is a good one. They may think that it's too man-centered, or too therapeutic. But as I've considered this, it seems to me more and more that health is actually a very good image for soundness, wholeness, correctness, and rightness.

Jesus talked of the health of our bodies as an image of our spiritual state (see Matt. 6:22-23 [Luke 11:33-34]; cf. 7:17-18). He said that, "It is not the healthy who need a doctor, but the sick" (Matt. 9:12 [Mark 2:17; Luke 5:31]). Jesus brought soundness to people's bodies to point to the soundness He offered for their souls (see Matt. 12:13; 14:35-36; 15:31; Mark 5:34; Luke 7:9-10; 15:27; John 7:23). The disciples in Acts continued the same health-giving Christ-exalting ministry (Acts 3:16; 4:10).

Paul used the image of the church as Christ's own body, and he described its prosperity in organic images of growth and health. For example, Paul wrote that "speaking the truth in love, we will in all things grow up into him who is the Head, that is, Christ. From him the whole body, joined and held together by every supporting ligament, grows and builds itself up in love, as each part does its work" (Eph. 4:15-16). Paul described correct doctrine in Titus 2:1 as "sound" or "healthy" doctrine. John greeted fellow Christians by telling them that, "I pray that you may enjoy good health and that all may go well with you, even as your soul is getting along well" (3 John 2).

None of this is to say that we can know it's God's will for His children to experience good physical health in this life, but simply to say that health is a natural image that God Himself has sanctioned for that which is right and correct. As I said above, some Christians, out of concern over a wrongly therapeutic culture, shy away from using such images. But the abuse of the language shouldn't detract from its appropriate use. And with such understanding of health—its connection to life and prosperity; the objective norms of what is good and right that are presumed in it; the joy involved in it; the care to be taken over it—we can easily see the wisdom in our desiring to pursue the spiritual health of our own souls, and to work for healthy churches. It is to that end that this book was first written. And it is to that end that I pray that God will now use it in your life, and in the life of your church.

—Mark Dever
Washington, D.C.
June 2004

INTRODUCTION

Author and theologian David Wells reported some very interesting findings of a survey taken in seven seminaries in 1993. One in particular struck me: "These students are dissatisfied with the current status of the church. They believe it has lost its vision, and they want more from it than it is giving them." Wells himself agreed: "Neither their desire nor their judgement in this regard is amiss. Indeed, it is not until we experience a holy dissatisfaction with things as they are that we can plant the seeds of reform. Of course, dissatisfaction alone is not enough."[1]

Dissatisfaction, indeed, is not enough. There is dissatisfaction with the church on every hand. Bookstore shelves groan under the weight of books with prescriptions for what ails her. Conference speakers live off the congregational diseases that always seem to survive their remedies.[2] Pastors wrongly exult and tragically burn out, confused and uncertain. Christians are left to wander like sheep without a shepherd. But dissatisfaction is not enough. We need something more. We need positively to recover what the church is to be. What is the church in her nature and essence? What is to distinguish and mark the church?

FOR YOU HISTORIANS

Christians often talk about "marks of the church." In his first published book, *Men with a Message*, John Stott summed up the teaching of Christ to the churches in the book of Revelation this way: "These then are the marks of the ideal Church—love, suffering, holiness, sound doctrine, genuineness, evangelism and humility. They are what Christ desires to find in His churches as He walks among them."[3]

But this language has a more formal history as well, which must be acknowledged before engaging in the task of a book-length consideration of "Nine Marks of a Healthy Church."

Christians have long talked of the "marks of the church." Here, as in so much of the church's thinking—from earlier definitions of Christ and the Trinity to Jonathan Edwards's musings upon the work of the Spirit—the question of how to distinguish true from false has led to a clearer definition of the true. The topic of the church did not become a center of widespread formal theological debate until the Reformation. Before the sixteenth century, the church was more assumed than discussed. It was thought of as the means of grace, a reality that existed as the presupposition of the rest of theology. In Roman Catholic theology the phrase "the mystery of the church" is the more typical expression, referring to the depth of the reality of the church, which can never be fully explored. Practically, the church of Rome linked its claim to being the true, visible church to the succession of Peter as the bishop of Rome.

With the advent of the radical criticisms of Martin Luther and others in the sixteenth century, however, discussion of the nature of the church itself became inevitable. As one scholar explains, "The Reformation made the gospel, not ecclesiastical organization, the test of the true church."[4] Calvin questioned Rome's claims to be the true church on the basis of apostolic succession. "Especially in the organization of the church nothing is more absurd than to lodge the succession in persons alone to the exclusion of teaching."[5] Since that time, therefore, the *"notae," "signa," "symbola," "criteria,"* or "marks" of the church have been a necessary focus of discussion.

In 1530, Melanchthon drew up the Augsburg Confession, which in Article VII stated that "this Church is the congregation of the saints in which the gospel is rightly taught and the sacraments are rightly administered. And for that true unity of the Church it is enough to have unity of belief concerning the teaching of the gospel and the administration of the sacraments."[6] In his *Loci Communes* (1543), Melanchthon repeated the idea: "The marks which point out the church are the pure gospel and the proper use of the sacraments."[7] Since the Reformation, Protestants have typically viewed these two marks—the preaching of the Gospel and the proper administering of the sacraments—as delineating the true church over against imposters.

In 1553 Thomas Cranmer produced the Forty-two Articles of the Church of England. While not officially promulgated until later in the century as part of the Elizabethan settlement, they show the thinking of the great English Reformer concerning the church. Article 19 read (as it still does in the Thirty-nine Articles): "The visible Church of Christ is a congregation of faithful men in which the pure word of God is preached and the sacraments be duly administered, according to Christ's ordinance in all those things that of necessity are requisite to the same."[8]

In John Calvin's *Institutes of the Christian Religion,* the issue of the distinction of the false from the true church was taken up in book IV. In chapter 1, section 9, Calvin wrote, "Wherever we see the Word of God purely preached and heard, and the sacraments administered according to Christ's institution, there, it is not to be doubted, a church of God exists."[9]

A third mark of the church, right discipline, has often been added since then, though it is widely acknowledged that this is implied in the second mark—the sacraments being rightly administered.[10] The Belgic Confession (1561), Article 29, said,

> The marks by which the true Church is known are these: If the pure doctrine of the gospel is preached therein; if she maintains the pure administration of the sacraments as instituted by Christ; if church discipline is exercised in punishing of sin; in short, if all things are managed according to the pure Word of God, all things contrary thereto rejected, and Jesus Christ acknowledged as the only Head of the Church.[11]

Edmund Clowney has summarized these marks as "true preaching of the Word; proper observance of the sacraments; and faithful exercise of church discipline."[12]

We can see in these two marks—Gospel proclamation and observance of the sacraments—both the creation and the preservation of the church—the fountain of God's truth and the lovely vessel to contain and display it. The church is generated by the right preaching of the Word; the church is contained and distinguished by the right administration of baptism and the Lord's Supper. (Presumed in this latter mark is that church discipline is being practiced.)

THE CHURCH TODAY REFLECTS THE WORLD

This book is a lesser thing than a consideration of these marks of the church. I accept the traditional Protestant understanding of the true church being distinguished or marked off from the false by the right preaching of the Word and the right administration of the sacraments. What I am about in this book is attempting to speak to some marks that set off healthy churches from true but more sickly ones. Therefore this book does not attempt to say everything that should be said about the church. To use theological language, it is not a full ecclesiology. To use an image, it is more a prescription than a course in general anatomy of the body of Christ.

Certainly no church is perfect. But, thank God, many imperfect churches are healthy. Nevertheless, I fear that many more are not—even among those that would affirm the full deity of Christ and the full authority of Scripture.

What has landed us in this predicament? Many causes are suggested.

Various cultural conditions that infest the church have been noted. Carl Braaten has expressed his alarm over the entry into the churches of a subjective, ahistorical neopaganism.[13] Os Guinness, in his provocative little book *Dining with the Devil,* has suggested that the problem is secularization. Guinness writes that even theologically conservative churches that self-consciously oppose secularism are nevertheless themselves often unwitting bastions of a secularized version of Christianity, and that, "The two most easily recognizable hallmarks of secularization in America are the exaltation of numbers and of technique."[14]

One of the most common scapegoats has been the institutions that prepare people for the ministry. Richard Muller has described something of what he has seen of the seminaries' defaulting on their stewardship:

> Seminaries have been guilty of creating several generations of clergy and teachers who are fundamentally ignorant of the materials of the theological task and prepared to argue (in their own defense) the irrelevance of classical study to the practical operation of ministry. The sad result has been the loss, in many places, of the central, cultural function of the church in the West and the replacement of a culturally and intellectually rich clergy with a group of practitioners and operations-directors who can do almost anything except make sense of the church's theological message in the contemporary context.[15]

This book, then, is a plan for recovering biblical preaching and church leadership at a time when too many congregations are languishing in a merely notional and nominal Christianity, with all the resulting pragmatism and pettiness. The purpose of too many evangelical churches has fallen from one of glorifying God simply to growing larger, assuming that that goal, however achieved, must glorify God.

One problem, theologically and even practically, with such a lowering of our vision is the self-defeating pragmatism that results:

> If the aim of the church is to grow, the way to do it is to make people feel good. And when people discover that there are other ways to feel good, they leave the church they no longer need. The relevant church is sowing the seeds of its own irrelevance, and losing its identity to boot. The big question today has become how to get the baby boomers back, what techniques and methods will do the trick. Polls are taken on what baby boomers want and churches are competing to make sure they get it.[16]

Neopaganism and secularization, pragmatism, and ignorance are all serious problems with churches today. But I am convinced that the problem most fundamentally lies in the way Christians conceive of their churches. Too many churches misunderstand the priority that they are to give to God's revelation and to the nature of the regeneration He offers therein. Reevaluating these must be a part of any solution to the problems of today's churches.

POPULAR MODELS OF THE CHURCH

Three models of the church are seen today in my own association of churches (Southern Baptist Convention) and in many other church associations as well. We might summarize these models as liberal, seeker-sensitive, and traditional.

Drawing with bold lines for a minute, we might conceive of the liberal model as having F. D. E. Schleiermacher as its patron saint. In an attempt to be successful in evangelism, Schleiermacher tried to rethink the Gospel in contemporary terms.

We might find something of the same goal in the seeker-sensitive model, seen in the writing and ministry of Bill Hybels and his associates at Willow Creek and the many churches associated with them. The impulse has been, once again, one of evangelism. They have tried to rethink the church with the goal of evangelism always in mind—from the outside in, again, in an attempt to make the Gospel's relevance obvious to all.

The patron saint of the traditional evangelical churches could be said to be Billy Graham (or perhaps one of several other great evangelists of the present or preceding generation). Again, the motive is to be successful in evangelism, as the local church is seen as fundamentally a stationary evangelistic rally. Actually, the "traditional" evangelical church in America is much like the seeker-sensitive model, only to an older culture—the culture of fifty or a hundred years ago. So instead of Willow Creek skits, the First Baptist Women's Trio is regarded as the thing that will draw nonbelievers in.

While there are very important doctrinal distinctions between these various kinds of churches, upon reflection all three are seen to have some important commonalities. All three are in large part influenced by the assumption that evident relevance and response is the key indicator of success. The social ministries of the liberal church, the music of the seeker-sensitive church, the programs of the traditional evangelical church all must be seen to be working well and working *now* to be considered relevant and successful. Depending on the type of church, success may mean so many fed, so many involved, or so many saved, but the assumption the three kinds of churches share is that the fruit of a successful church is readily apparent.

From both a biblical and a historical standpoint, this assumption seems incalculably dangerous. Biblically, we find that God's Word is replete with images of delayed blessing. God, for His own inscrutable purposes, tests and tries His Jobs and Josephs, His Jeremiahs, and even Jesus Himself. The trials of Job, the beating and selling of Joseph, the imprisonment and mocking of Jeremiah, the rejection and crucifixion of Jesus all remind us that God moves in mysterious ways. He calls us more fundamentally to a relationship of trust with Him than to a full understanding of Him and His ways. The parables of Jesus are full of stories of the kingdom of God beginning in surprisingly small ways but growing finally to a glorious prominence. Biblically, we must realize that the size of what our eyes see is rarely a good way to estimate the greatness of something in the eyes of God.

Historically, too, this is an important moment for recovering the truth that looks can be deceiving. In a culture sopped with Christianity and filled with biblical knowledge, in which God's common grace and even His special grace are spread widely, there may be many obvious blessings. Biblical morality may be affirmed by all. The church may be widely esteemed. The Bible may be learned even in "secular" schools. In such a time, it may be hard to distinguish between the apparent and the real.

But in a society where Christianity is being widely and rapidly disowned, where evangelism is often considered inherently intolerant or even officially classified as a hate crime, we find our world changed. The culture to which we would conform in order to be relevant becomes so inextricably entwined with antagonism to the Gospel that to conform to it must mean a loss of the Gospel itself. In such a day, we must re-hear the Bible and re-imagine the concept of successful ministry not as necessarily immediately fruitful but as demonstrably faithful to God's Word.

Great missionaries who have gone to non-Christian cultures have had to know this. When they have gone to places where there were no obvious "fields white unto harvest" but only years and even decades of rejection, they must have had some other motivation to keep them going. If William Carey would be faithful in India or Adoniram Judson in Burma, it could not be because their immediate success showed them that that they were being obviously relevant. It could only be because the Spirit of God in them encouraged them to obedience and trust. Rural pastors labor in churches amid declining populations, and they do so at the call of God. We today, in the secular West, must recover a sense of satisfaction in such biblical faithfulness. And we must recover it particularly in our lives together as Christians, in our churches.

NEEDED: A DIFFERENT MODEL

We need a new model for the church. Actually, the model we need is an old one. Even though I'm writing a book about it, I'm not quite sure what to call it. "Mere"? "Historic"? "Biblical"?

Simply put, we need churches that are self-consciously distinct from the culture. We need churches in which the key indicator of success is not evident results but persevering biblical faithfulness. We need churches that help us to recover those aspects of Christianity that are distinct from the world, and that unite us.

What follows is not intended so much as a full portrait of this new (old) model of the church but as a timely prescription. It focuses on two basic needs in our churches: the preaching of the message and the leading of disciples.

PREACHING THE MESSAGE

The first five "marks of a healthy church" we will consider all reflect the concern to preach rightly the Word of God. MARK ONE is about preaching itself. It is a defense of the primacy of expositional preaching as a reflection of the centrality of God's Word.

Why is the Word central? Why is it the instrument of creating faith? The answer would seem to be that the Word is so central and so instrumental because the Word of the Lord holds out the object of our faith to us. It presents God's promise to us—from all kinds of individual promises (throughout the Bible) all the way to the great promise, the great hope, the great object of our faith, Christ Himself. The Word presents that which we are to believe.

Then, as MARK TWO, we consider the framework of this message: biblical theology. We must understand God's truth as a coherent whole, coming to us first and foremost as a revelation of Himself. Questions of who God is and of what He is like can never be considered irrelevant to the practical matters of church life. Different understandings of God will lead you to worship Him in different ways, and if some of those understandings are wrong, some of those ways in which you approach Him could be wrong as well. This is, after all, a major theme in the Bible, even if it is almost entirely neglected these days.

In MARK THREE we consider the heart of the Christian message as we seek a biblical understanding of the Gospel. How many other messages are churches hawking as the saving Good News of Jesus Christ? And yet how discerning are we in how we understand the Gospel ourselves, how we teach it, and how we train others to know it? Is our message, though larded with Christian pieties, basically a message of self-salvation, or is there something more in it? Does our Gospel consist only of universal ethical truths for our daily lives or are there once-for-all, historical, special saving actions of God in Christ at the root of it?

That brings us to the reception of the message, MARK FOUR: a biblical understanding of conversion. One of the most painful tasks pastors face is trying to undo the damage of false converts who have been too quickly and thoughtlessly assured by the evangelist that they are indeed Christians. Such apparently charitable activity may lead to short bursts of excitement, involvement, and interest; but if an apparent conversion does not result in a changed life, then one begins to wonder at the unwitting cruelty of convincing such people that, because they once prayed a prayer, they have fully investigated all the hope that God has for them in life. "If that failed," we may leave them to think, "then Christianity has nothing more to offer me. No more hope. No more life. I tried, and it didn't work." We need churches to understand and teach what the Bible teaches about conversion.

That brings us to the specific work of spreading the Gospel message. MARK FIVE sets forth a biblical understanding of evangelism. If, in our evangelism, we imply that becoming a Christian is something that we do ourselves, we disastrously pass on our misunderstanding of the Gospel and of conversion. John Broadus, well-known New Testament scholar and preacher of the nineteenth century, wrote a catechism of Bible teaching and in it posed the question, "Does faith come before the new birth?" And he answered, "No, it is the new heart that truly repents and believes."[17] Broadus understood that in our evangelism we must be partners with the Holy Spirit, presenting the Gospel but relying on the Holy Spirit of God to do the true convicting and convincing and converting. Are your church's or your own evangelistic practices in line with this great truth?

LEADING THE DISCIPLES

The other nexus of problems in today's churches has to do with the right administration of the borders and markers of Christian identity. More generally put, they have to do with problems in leading disciples.

First, in MARK SIX, there is the question of the whole framework for discipleship: a biblical understanding of church membership. In this past century, Christians have all but ignored biblical teaching on the corporate nature of following Christ. Our churches are awash in self-centered narcissism, hyper-individualism thinly veiled in everything from some "gift inventories" to "targeted churches" that "aren't for everybody." When we go back to 1 John or even the gospel of John, we begin to see that Jesus never intended us to be Christians alone, and that our love for others who aren't just like us is taken to be indicative of whether we truly love God.

There are also problems today in our churches with even the basic definition of what it means to be a disciple. So in MARK SEVEN we explore a biblical understanding of church discipline. Is there any behavior that churches should not tolerate? Are any teachings in our churches "beyond the pale"? Do our churches indicate a concern for anything beyond their own institutional survival and expansion? Do we evidence an understanding that we bear the name of God and live either to His honor or to His shame? We need churches to recover the loving, regular, and wise practice of church discipline.

In MARK EIGHT we examine Christian discipleship and growth. Evangelism that does not result in discipleship is not only incomplete evangelism but is entirely misconceived. It is not that we need to do more evangelism, rather that we need to do it differently. We don't simply need to remember to tell people to come to church after we have prayed the prayer with them; we need to tell them to count the cost before they pray that prayer!

Finally, in MARK NINE we see that we need to recover in our churches a biblical understanding of church leadership. Leadership in the church should not be granted as a response to secular gifts or position, to family relationships, or in recognition of length of service in the church. Leadership in the church should be invested in those who seem to evidence in their own lives and who are able to promote in the life of the congregation as a whole the edifying and sanctifying work of the Holy Spirit.

The end and purpose of all this is the glory of God as we make Him known. Throughout history, God has desired to make Himself known. This is why He delivered Israel from Egypt in the Exodus, and why He delivered them again from the Babylonian Exile. It was for His own glory, to make Himself known. Scores of passages in Scripture tell of God's desire to make Himself known (e.g., Ex. 7:5; Deut. 4:34-35; Job 37:6-7; Ps. 22:21-22; 106:8; Isa. 49:22-23; 64:4; Ezek. 20:34-38; 28:25-26; 36:11; 37:6; John 17:26). He has created the world and has done all that He has done for His own praise. And it is right and good that He should do so.

Calvin used to call this world the theatre of God's splendor. Others have referred to history as one great parade culminating in the glory of God. Mark Ross has put it this way:

> We are one of God's chief pieces of evidence. . . . Paul's great concern [in Ephesians 4:1-16] for the church is that the church manifest and display the glory of God, thus vindicating God's character against all the slander of demonic realms, the slander that God is not worth living for. . . . . God has entrusted to His church the glory of His own name.[18]

All who read these words—those who are church leaders and those who are not—are made in the image of God. We are to be walking pictures of the moral nature and righteous character of God, reflecting it around the universe for all to see—especially in our union with God through Christ. This, therefore, is what God calls us to and why He calls us to it. He calls us to join together with Him, and together in our congregations, not for our glory but for His own.

THIS BOOK

This book comes from a series of sermons. According to George Barna, sermons should be easier to understand, less abstract, more spontaneous, shorter, filled with more stories of the preacher's personal experience, and should even allow for the participation of the audience.[19] Barna is not alone in suggesting that we do something to mitigate the one-sidedness and the bare appeal to reason that marks so much preaching, particularly expositional preaching. David Hilborn, in *Picking Up the Pieces,* has suggested the same thing.[20]

Permit me to suggest that the one-sidedness of preaching is not only excusable but is actually important. If in our preaching we stand in the place of God, giving His Word by His Spirit to His people, then surely it is appropriate that it be one-sided—not that it should be one-sided in the sense that the one preaching is never to be questioned; but, in the event of preaching itself, the univocal character of God's Word comes as a monologue to us, not hoping to elicit interest and participation but requiring that we respond. Something of this character must be retained. All of this does not mean that the sermon must be deliberately boring, obscure, or abstract; and I hope that, in these sermons masquerading as chapters, something of a serious engagement with the great truths of the Bible and with the context today will come through. This is the model that we must follow wherever we may be.

WHAT'S COMING UP . . .

MARK ONE:
EXPOSITIONAL PREACHING

Expositional Preaching

The Central Role of the Word of God

The Role of God's Word in Bringing Life

The Role of God's Word in Sanctifying

The Role of the Preacher of God's Word

EXPOSITIONAL PREACHING

✝

This is how I began my sermon one Sunday morning in January, not too long ago:

> So, how's it going? Did you get enough sleep last night? Did you have trouble finding a good parking place this morning? Were the doors clearly marked? Did the people welcome you as you came in? Did the building seem nice and neat? I wonder, did the church's name make it more difficult for you to decide to come in? Or, maybe that was part of the reason why you decided to come in.
>
> And when you did come in, were the people friendly and welcoming? Any trouble dropping the kids off? And what do you think about the stained glass? I know I have the best view of it, but it's really pretty, isn't it? Then again, maybe it's a little too traditional for you.
>
> Are the pews comfortable? Do you have a good view of all the activities from where you are sitting? Can you see clearly? Can you hear okay? Is it warm enough for you right now? Do you feel pretty comfortable?
>
> And how about the bulletin? Nice, clear, simple, pretty straightforward, wouldn't you say? Not too complicated. Maybe a little too staid. Did you notice all the announcements in it? And did you see all the programs listed in the church card? There are a lot of them, aren't there? Probably

more than you've even read. Of course, it's easy to read, but I guess the print is kind of small, isn't it? And there aren't any pictures. I mean, it's so type-heavy. That probably tells you a lot about the church, doesn't it? You think this is probably the kind of church where they'd rather have the thousand words than the picture, right?

And what about the people sitting around you? Are they the kind you like to go to church with? Yeah, I know you're too nervous to look around you right now, but you know who they are. What do you think? Are they the right age? Are they the right race? Are they the right social class? Are they just like you?

And what about the service so far? I mean, was it too difficult switching between the two hymnals? You know, most churches just use one and here you've got two; you've got to go to the green one and then sometimes the beige one. Has the leader seemed informed, yet not know-it-allish? Competent, yet not overbearing? There weren't too many announcements in the service, were there? I don't think so this morning. Have the prayers been involving? Have they engaged your heart and mind?

It is a bit unusual these days to read so much Scripture in church, isn't it? You don't often find that done.

And of course, there's the music. You know, we're still trying to get some things worked out, as you can tell—contemporary or traditional, classical or more modern, liturgical or more informal. As with every other church in America this very morning, there are probably some people who have come to this church in the past who this morning are out looking at other churches because they would like a different musical experience. And, you know, there are probably some people who are still here, in part, because they like this musical experience.

And how's it been for you with the offering? Can you believe that? They actually took up an offering in public with visitors and all! That is the kind of thing they tell you in seminary these days you should never do. How did it make you feel? Did it make you feel that the church is full of a bunch of money-grubbing people who just want to get from you when you come?

What are you doing here? Whether you've been coming to this church for fifty years or this is your first Sunday—why do you come?

And now, of course, well, you know what's coming now. Maybe it has already begun: the sermon! For some people, this is what you just have to sit through to get to the good bit—maybe some more singing, or meeting and talking to people afterwards.

The preacher does have a very difficult job, doesn't he? The preacher has to be someone that you feel you could relate to and talk with and let your hair down with or trust in some measure. But he needs to seem holy, too. But not too holy. You know, he needs to be knowledgeable, but not too knowledgeable. He needs to be confident, but not too confident. He needs to be compassionate, but not too compassionate. And his sermon? Well, his sermon needs to be good enough, relevant enough, entertaining and engaging enough, and certainly short enough.

There is so much to consider when you are evaluating a church, isn't there? Have you ever really stopped to think about it? There are so many different things to think of and, as much as Americans move these days, we have to evaluate churches. It happens all the time. We have to ask ourselves what makes a really good church.

In my study I have shelf after shelf and stack after stack of books about exactly this question: What really makes a good church? And you would be amazed at how widely the answers vary. They range from friendliness to financial planning to pristine bathrooms to pleasant surroundings to vibrant music to being sensitive to visitors to plentiful parking to exciting children's programs to elaborate Sunday school options to the right computer software to clear signage to homogeneous congregations. You will find books written and sold that advocate all of those things as the key to a good church.

So, what do you think? What makes for a healthy church? You need to know that. If you are a visitor today, looking around for some church where you can come regularly and to which you can commit yourself, you need to consider this question. Even if you are already a member here, you need to consider this question—you might move, you know. And even if you don't ever move again, you need to know what constitutes a healthy church. If you're going to stay in the church and be a part of building it and shaping it, don't you need to know what you're trying to build? What you want it to look like? What you want to aim for? What should be foundational?

Be very careful how you answer these questions. As I said, you'll find experts who will tell you the answer is everything from how religion-free your language is to how invisible your membership requirements are.

So, what do you think? Are secure nurseries and sparkling bathrooms, exciting music and look-alike congregations really the way to church growth and church health? Is that really what makes a good church?

And so I began the series of sermons that has become this book—*Nine Marks of a Healthy Church*. The purpose of this book is to ask and answer the question, What distinctively marks a really good church?

In this series of studies I suggest nine distinguishing marks of a healthy church. You can find them listed in the table of contents. These nine marks certainly are not the only attributes of a healthy church. I'm not suggesting that for a moment. They're not even necessarily the most important things that could be said about a church. For example, I address only in passing the topics of baptism or communion, even though these are essential aspects of a biblical church, commanded by Christ Himself. This book is not a complete ecclesiology. It is merely trying to focus on certain crucial aspects of healthy church life that have grown rare among churches today. Though they may often be misunderstood, baptism and the Lord's Supper have not vanished from most churches; but many of the attributes that we will consider in these pages *have* disappeared from many churches.

Of course, there is no such thing as a perfect church, and I certainly don't mean to suggest that any church I ever pastor will be a perfect church. But that doesn't mean our churches can't be more healthy. It is my goal to encourage such health.

EXPOSITIONAL PREACHING

The first mark of a healthy church is expositional preaching. It is not only the first mark; it is far and away the most important of them all, because if you get this one right, all of the others should follow. This is the crucial mark. If you want to read only one chapter of this book, you've picked the right one. This is the one you should read first, before all of the others. This will help you to understand what pastors are to give themselves to, and what congregations are to demand of them. My main role, and the main role of any pastor, is expositional preaching.

This is so important that, if you miss this one and get all the other eight marks right, in a sense these others would be just so many accidents. You would have just happened to get them right. They may be discarded or distorted, because they didn't spring from the Word and they're not continually being reshaped and refreshed by it. But if you get the priority of the Word established, then you have in place the single most important aspect of the church's life, and growing health is virtually assured, because God has decided to act by His Spirit through His Word.

So what is this all-important thing called expositional preaching? It is usually talked about in contrast with topical preaching. A topical sermon is like this chapter—it takes a subject and talks about it, rather than taking a particular text of the Bible as its subject. The topical sermon begins with a particular matter that the preacher wants to preach about. The topic could be prayer or justice or parenting or holiness or even expositional preaching. Having established the topic, the preacher then assembles various texts from various parts of the Bible and combines them with illustrative stories and anecdotes. The material is combined and woven together around this one topic. The topical sermon is not built around one text of Scripture but around this one chosen theme or idea.

A topical sermon can be expositional. I could choose to preach on a topic and just pick one passage of Scripture that addresses exactly this concern. Or I could preach with a number of texts that address this same theme. But it is still a topical sermon, because the preacher knows what he wants to say and he is going into the Bible to see what he can find to say about it. So, for example, when I preached a version of this material as a sermon, I largely knew when I set out what I wanted to say. When I preach expositionally, this is not usually the case. In preparing my normal expositional sermon, I am often a bit surprised by the things I find in the passage as I study it. Generally, I do not choose series of expositional sermons because of particular topics that I think the church needs to hear about. Rather, I assume that all of the Bible is relevant to us all of the time. Now, I trust that God may lead to some particular books, but very often when I'm working on a text and reading through it in my quiet times the week before preaching, and working with it very seriously on Friday, there will be things that I find in it that I didn't expect to find at all. I will sometimes be surprised by the point of the passage and therefore by what must become the point of my message.

Expositional preaching is not simply producing a verbal commentary on some passage of Scripture. Rather, expositional preaching is that preaching which takes for the point of a sermon the point of a particular passage of Scripture. That's it. The preacher opens the Word and unfolds it for the people of God. That is not what I'm doing in this chapter, but it is what I normally intend to do when I step into the pulpit on Sunday.

Expositional preaching is preaching in service to the Word. It presumes a belief in the authority of Scripture—that the Bible is actually God's Word; but it is something much more than that. A commitment to expositional preaching is a commitment to *hear* God's Word—not just to affirm that it is God's Word but to actually submit yourself to it. The Old Testament prophets and the New Testament apostles were given, not a personal commission to go and speak, but a particular message to deliver. Likewise Christian preachers today have authority to speak from God only so long as they speak His message and unfold His words. As loquacious as some preachers may be, preachers are not commanded simply to go and preach. They are commanded specifically to go and preach the Word. That's what preachers are commanded to preach.

Many pastors happily accept the authority of God's Word and profess to believe in the inerrancy of the Bible; yet if they do not in practice regularly preach expositionally, I'm convinced that they will never preach more than they knew when they began the whole exercise. A preacher can take a piece of Scripture and exhort the congregation on a topic that is important but that isn't really the point of that particular passage. You can pick your Bible up right now, close your eyes, open it to a certain place, put your finger down on a verse, open your eyes and read that verse and you can get a great blessing from it for your soul but still not necessarily learn what God intended to say through that passage. What they say about real estate is true in understanding the Bible: the three most important factors are location, location, location. You understand a text of Scripture where it is. You understand it in the context in which it was inspired.

A preacher should have his mind increasingly shaped by Scripture. He shouldn't just use Scripture as an excuse for what he already knows he wants to say. When that happens, when someone regularly preaches in a way that is not expositional, the sermons tend to be only on the topics that interest the preacher. The result is that the preacher and the congregation only hear in Scripture what they already thought when they came to the text. There's nothing new being added to their understanding. They're not continuing to be challenged by the Bible.

In being committed to preach a passage of Scripture in context, expositionally—that is, taking as the point of the message the point

NINE MARKS OF A HEALTHY CHURCH

of the passage—we should hear from God those things that we didn't intend to hear when we set out to study the passage. God surprises us sometimes. And, from your repentance and conversion to the latest thing the Holy Spirit has been teaching you, isn't that what it means to be a Christian? Don't you again and again find God challenging you and saying some things you would never have thought about a year ago, as He begins to unearth the truth of your heart and the truth of His Word? To charge someone with the spiritual oversight of a church who doesn't in practice show a commitment to hear and to teach God's Word is to hamper the growth of the church, in essence allowing it to grow only to the level of the pastor. The church will slowly be conformed to the pastor's mind rather than to God's mind. And what we want, what as Christians we crave, are God's words. We want to hear and know in our souls what He has said.

THE CENTRAL ROLE OF THE WORD OF GOD

Preaching should always (or almost always) be expositional because the Word of God should be at its center, directing it. In fact, churches should have the Word at their center, directing them. God has chosen to use His Word to bring life. That's the pattern that we see in Scripture and in history. His Word is His own chosen instrument for bringing life.

At a reception the conversation turned to a book that had just been published. I had read it, because I was about to give a speech on the topic of the book. My host, a Roman Catholic, had also read it—for a review he was writing. I asked him what he thought.

"Oh, it was very good," he said, "except it was marred by the author's repeating that old Protestant error that the Bible created the church, when we all know," said my Roman Catholic friend, "that the church created the Bible."

Well, I was in a bit of quandary. It was his gathering and I was a guest. What should I say? I saw the whole Protestant Reformation flash before me!

I decided that if he could politely be so openly dismissive, then I could be as forthright and honest as I wished. So I just came right out and said, "That's ridiculous!" Trying to be as pleasantly contradictory as I could, I continued, "God's people have never created God's Word. From the very beginning God's Word has always created His people! From Genesis 1, where God literally creates all that is, including His people, by His Word; to Genesis 12, where He calls Abraham out of Ur by the word of His promise; to Ezekiel 37, where God gives Ezekiel a vision to share with the Israelite exiles in Babylon about the great resurrection to life that would come about by God's Word; to the supreme sending of God's Word in Jesus Christ, the Word made flesh; to Romans 10, where we read that spiritual life comes to us by the Word—God has always created His people by His Word. It has never been the other way around. God's people have never created God's Word."

Now, I can't remember exactly what happened in the rest of that conversation, but I remember that part very clearly because it helped to crystallize for me the absolute centrality of the Word.

Let's follow this path through the Scriptures and see what it tells us about the centrality of God's Word in our lives, and then consider what that means for the nature and importance of preaching in our churches. I want to draw your attention to three points: The role of the Word in bringing us life; the role of the Word in sanctifying us; and, therefore, what role the preacher of God's Word should have in the church.

The Role of God's Word in Bringing Life

Let's start at the beginning, where the Bible starts. Let's look at Genesis 1. There we see that it was by His Word that God created the world and all the life in it. He spoke, and it was so. If we keep reading, we see the grim story of what happened next. In Genesis 3 we read of the Fall. There we see that our first parents sinned, and that when they sinned they were cast out from God's presence. They quite literally lost sight of God. But in God's great grace they did not lose all hope. Though God was vanishing from their sight, He mercifully sent His voice to them so that they could hear the word of promise. In Genesis 3:16 God cursed the serpent. He warned him that the offspring of the woman would crush him. That little word is the first word of hope Adam and Eve had in the aftermath of their own sin.

Reading on, we come to Genesis 12, where we find that it was by God's Word that Abraham was called out of Ur of the Chaldeans. The word of God's promise recorded in the first few verses of Genesis 12 was used by God as the attractive force, the drawing promise, literally calling Abraham out of Ur to follow after God. And so you see, God's people were created—they became visible—by hearing that word of promise and by responding to it—by coming out after it. God's people were created by God's Word.

Abraham never set up a committee to craft God's Word. No, he was made the father of God's people because God's Word came specially to him and he believed it. He trusted God for what He said. He believed Him. And we know the story of how the children of Abraham expanded in the Promised Land, then went down into Egypt, eventually falling into slavery there for centuries. Just when that bondage looked so permanent, what did God do? He sent His Word. We see in Exodus 3:4 that God began with Moses, calling out to him. A burning bush was an extraordinary thing to see, but a burning bush in and of itself wouldn't tell Moses anything. Even learned scholars disagree on the symbolism of the burning bush. The key is that God spoke out of the bush. He gave His words to Moses. He called out to him by His Word. God's Word came not just to Moses and his descendants but to the whole nation of Israel, calling them to be His people.

Moving on to Exodus 20, you find that God gave His law to His people, and by accepting God's law they became His people. It was by God's Word that the people of Israel were constituted as God's special people.

As we go on through the Old Testament we see that God's Word plays both a seminal and a discriminating role, as some people hear it and others refuse to hear it. Consider, for example, the story of Elijah in 1 Kings 18: "After a long time, . . . the word of the LORD came to

Elijah: 'Go and present yourself to Ahab, and I will send rain on the land'" (v. 1). The phrase "the word of the LORD came" or its equivalents occurs more than 3,800 times in the Old Testament. The Word of the Lord came as He created and led His people. God's people were those who heard God's words of promise and responded in faith. In the Old Testament, God's Word always came as a means of faith. It was, in a sense, a secondary object of faith. God, of course, is always the primary object of our faith—we believe in God—but that doesn't mean very much if it is not defined. And how do we define who God is and what He calls us to do? We have basically two options for doing this: We could make it up; or our God could tell us. We believe that God has told us. We believe that God has Himself actually spoken. His Word is to be trusted and relied upon with all the faith that we would invest in God Himself.

So we see in the Old Testament that God led His people by His Word.

Do you see why the Word of God is central as an instrument in creating faith? It is so because it presents God and His promises to us—from all kinds of individual promises throughout the Old and New Testaments, all the way to the great promise, the great hope, the great object of our faith, Christ Himself. The Word shows us what we are to believe.

For the Christian, the speed of sound (the Word that we hear) is in a sense greater than the speed of light (the things we can actually see). It is as if, in this fallen world, we perceive the future first by our ears rather than by our eyes.

In the great vision of Ezekiel 37 we see most remarkably that life comes by the Word of God:

> The hand of the LORD was upon me, and he brought me out by the Spirit of the Lord and set me in the middle of a valley; it was full of bones. He led me back and forth among them, and I saw a great many bones on the floor of the valley, bones that were very dry. He asked me, "Son of man, can these bones live?"

I said, "O Sovereign LORD, you alone know."

Then he said to me, "Prophesy to these bones and say to them, 'Dry bones, hear the word of the LORD! This is what the Sovereign LORD says to these bones: I will make breath enter you, and you will come to life. I will attach tendons to you and make flesh come upon you and cover you with skin; I will put breath in you, and you will come to life. Then you will know that I am the LORD'" (vv. 1-6).

This is one encouraging vision! If you have ever been called to pastor a church that looks like it might be on its last legs, or if you can recall your own feelings of spiritual hopelessness before you found salvation, then you can see why this is a great passage of hope.

In verses 7-10 we see what happens when Ezekiel responds in obedience to the vision:

I prophesied as I was commanded. And as I was prophesying, there was a noise, a rattling sound, and the bones came together, bone to bone. I looked, and tendons and flesh appeared on them and skin covered them, but there was no breath in them.

Then he said to me, "Prophesy to the breath; prophesy, son of man, and say to it, 'This is what the Sovereign LORD says: Come from the four winds, O breath, and breathe into these slain, that they may live.'" So I prophesied as he commanded me, and breath entered them; they came to life and stood up on their feet—a vast army.

Then God interprets this vision for Ezekiel. He says that these bones stand for the whole house of Israel, who says "our hope is gone" (v. 11). God's answer to Israel, as it was to the dry bones, is that "I will put my Spirit in you and you will live" (v. 14). And how does He do this? How does God put His Spirit in Israel so that they will live? He does it *by His Word*. To make the point crystal clear, God calls Ezekiel to start preaching to this bunch of dry bones, and through that preaching of the Word God brings life to the bones. God has Ezekiel speak His Word to them while they are dead, and as he does so, they come to life!

The vision of the dry bones reflects the way God called Ezekiel to speak to a nation that wouldn't listen to him. It also reflects the way God Himself spoke into the void and created His world—by the power of His Word. We are reminded, likewise, of what happened when God's Word came into the world in the person of Christ: ". . . and though the world was made through him, the world did not recognize him" (John 1:10). And yet through that Word, through the Lord Jesus, God has begun creating His new society on earth.

God told Ezekiel to speak to the dry bones. Life came through breath; the Spirit traveled through speech; and that Word of God, His breath, gave life. Do you see the close connection between life, breath, spirit, speech, and word? It is reminiscent of a number of times in Jesus' own ministry. Think, for instance, of that time when, "Some people brought to him a man who was deaf. . . . He looked up to heaven and with a deep sigh said to him, . . . 'Be opened!' At this, the man's ears were opened" (Mark 7:32, 34-35). Jesus spoke to a deaf man, and his ears were opened. Life came back into His ears! Jesus called His people to Himself in just the way that Ezekiel prophesied: "I will give you a new heart and put a new spirit in you; I will remove from you your heart of stone and give you a heart of flesh" (Ezek. 36:26).

This is the glorious reality that we Christians have experienced. As I said to a Jehovah's Witness worker some months back, we Christians know that in and of ourselves we are spiritually dead, and that we need God to initiate His life in us. We need Him to reach down and rip out our old, stony hearts and put in us new, fleshy hearts of love toward Him—hearts that are soft and pliant to His Word. That's what we need, and that's just what Jesus Christ does for us. He is creating a different *kind* of people, a people who show the life of God in them as they hear His Word and as by His grace they respond to it.

This brings us, of course, to the supreme picture of God's Word bringing life:

> In the beginning was the Word, and the Word was with God,
> and the Word was God. . . . Through him all things were made;
> without him nothing was made that has been made. In him
> was life, and that life was the light of men (John 1:1, 3-4).

It is in Christ that the Word of God has fully and finally come
to us.

Jesus modeled that great reality in His own ministry. At the very
beginning of His ministry, when His disciples told Him that many
people were looking for Him because they wanted Him to do some
more miracles and to heal them, Jesus replied, "Let us go somewhere
else . . . so I can *preach* there also. *That* is why I have come" (Mark 1:38,
emphasis added). If you keep reading Mark's gospel you'll find that
Jesus knew that He had come fundamentally to lay down His life for
our sins (see 10:45); but in order for that event to be understood, He
first had to teach.

I don't mean to give the impression that Christianity is only a
bunch of words—but words are important. As you read through the
Bible you see that God acts, but He doesn't stop there. After He acts,
God speaks. He interprets what He has done so that we can understand it. God doesn't allow His acts to speak for themselves; He
speaks, in order to interpret for us His great saving acts.

This "verbal" nature of God really fits in with the way He has
made us, doesn't it? Consider our human relationships. How do we
come to know each other? We can get to know each other through
just watching. Husbands and wives can learn about each other
through physical intimacy. But there is a profound part of our knowing each other that can come about only through some kind of cognitive communication. Words are important for our relationships.

You tell me you've got a great relationship with your dog (he's
man's best friend, after all!), and that you love your dog, though he
could never speak to you or cognitively communicate with you. You
come home, you say, and he wags his tail. He rushes to you. He wants
to lick you. You look in his eyes and see they're oh-so-sympathetic.

He understands all of life and will never desert you. You figure this is love, so who needs words?

Well, words are important. If you go home today and your dog looks up at you and casually says, "So how was church today?" I submit that that is going to change your relationship with your dog! That's going to show you exactly how important words are in relationships.

Because we have separated ourselves from God by our sin, God must speak if we are to know Him. This is why the work of one of the members of our church, Carl F. H. Henry, has been so important. In his *magnum opus*, the six-volume *God, Revelation and Authority*, he makes exactly this point—that God will not be known if He does not speak, and we cannot know Him if He has not spoken a word that we can rely on. God must reveal Himself. That's the point of the Bible. Because of our own sins, we could never know God otherwise. Either He speaks or we are forever lost in the darkness of our own speculations.

We see this clearly throughout the New Testament. Consider Romans 10:17: "Consequently, faith comes from hearing the message, and the message is heard through the word of Christ." This "word of Christ" is the great message of the Gospel: that God has made us to know Him, but that we have sinned and separated ourselves from Him; that therefore God in His great love has come in the person of Jesus Christ, who has lived a perfect life, taking on our flesh and our infirmities; that He died on the Cross specifically as a substitute for all of those who would ever turn to Him and trust in Him; and that He has been raised by God from the dead as a testimony that God has accepted this sacrifice; and that He calls us now to repent and to trust in Him, even as Abraham trusted in the Word of God as it came to him in Ur of the Chaldeans so many centuries ago.

Paul writes just before this, in Romans 10:9, "If you confess with your mouth, 'Jesus is Lord,' and believe in your heart that God raised him from the dead, you will be saved."

Trusting in and relying on the truth of God's raising Jesus Christ is the way to salvation, the way to inclusion in the people of God. And so we see, once again, that God has always created His people by speaking His Word. And His greatest Word is Christ. As the writer to the Hebrews began his letter,

> In the past God spoke to our forefathers through the prophets at many times and in various ways, but in these last days he has spoken to us by his Son, whom he appointed heir of all things, and through whom he made the universe (Heb. 1:1-2).

Living as we do after the Fall but before the Heavenly City, we are in a time when faith is central, and so the Word must be central—because God's Holy Spirit creates His people by His Word! We can create a people by other means, and this is the great temptation of churches. We can create a people around a certain ethnicity. We can create a people around a fully-graded choir program. We can find people who will get excited about a building project or a denominational identity. We can create a people around a series of care groups, where each feels loved and cared for. We can create a people around a community service project. We can create a people around social opportunities for young mothers or Caribbean cruises for singles. We can create a people around men's groups. We can even create a people around the personality of a preacher. And God can surely use all of these things. But in the final analysis the people of God, the church of God, can only be created around the Word of God.

Asked about his accomplishments as a Reformer, Martin Luther said, "I simply taught, preached, wrote God's Word: otherwise I did nothing. . . . The Word did it all."[1] The Word of God brings life.

The Role of God's Word in Sanctifying

We must also consider the role of God's Word in sanctifying us. The Word of God must be central to our lives as individuals and as a church because God's Spirit uses the Word to create faith in us (as we have seen) and because He also uses the Word to make us grow. We won't explore this point as carefully as the last, but it is just as clear in Scripture. As Jesus replied to Satan, quoting from Deuteronomy, "Man does not live on bread alone, but on every word that comes from the mouth of God" (Matt. 4:4; quoting Deut. 8:3). We know also those famous words of the psalmist, "Your word is a lamp to my feet and a light for my path" (Psalm 119:105).

When we look at the history of Israel and Judah in the Old Testament we find this again and again. During the reign of King Josiah, in the declining days of Judah (2 Chron. 34), the Law—the written Word of God—was rediscovered and read to him. Josiah's response was to tear his clothes in repentance and then to read the Word to the people. A national recovery came as God's Word went out. God uses His Word to sanctify His people and to make them more like Himself.

This is what the Lord Jesus taught, too. In His High Priestly Prayer He prayed, "Sanctify them by the truth; your word is truth" (John 17:17). And Paul wrote that "Christ loved the church and gave himself up for her to make her holy, cleansing her by the washing with water through the word . . ." (Eph. 5:25-26).

We need God's Word to be saved, but we also need it to continually challenge and shape us. His Word not only gives us life; it also gives us direction as it keeps molding and shaping us in the image of the God who is speaking to us.

At the time of the Reformation the Roman Catholic Church had a Latin phrase that became something of a motto: *semper idem*. It means "always the same." Well, the Reformed churches, too, had a "semper" motto: *ecclesia reformata, semper reformanda secundum verbum Dei*. "The church reformed, always being reformed according to the Word of God." A healthy church is a church that hears the Word of God and continues to hear the Word of God. And such a church is composed of individual Christians who hear the Word of God and continue to hear the Word of God, always being refashioned and reshaped by it, constantly being washed in the Word and sanctified by God's truth.

For our own health, individually as Christians and corporately as a church, we must continue to be shaped in new and deeper ways by God's agenda in our lives, rather than by our own agendas. God makes us more like Himself through His Word, washing over us, refreshing us, reshaping us.

That brings us to a third important point.

The Role of the Preacher of God's Word

What about the role of the preacher of God's Word? If you are looking for a good church, this is the most important thing to consider. I don't care how friendly you think the church members are. I don't care how good you think the music is. Those things can change. But the congregation's commitment to the centrality of the Word coming from the front, from the preacher, the one specially gifted by God and called to that ministry, is the most important thing you can look for in a church.

In *Dining with the Devil,* Os Guinness cited an article from *The New Yorker* magazine lamenting the "audience-driven" nature of much preaching today:

> "The preacher, instead of looking out upon the world, looks out upon public opinion, trying to find out what the public would like to hear. Then he tries his best to duplicate that, and bring his finished product into a marketplace in which others are trying to do the same. The public, turning to our church culture to find out about the world, discovers there is nothing but its own reflection."[2]

That's not the way it should be. Preachers are not called to preach what's popular according to the polls. What good is that? People already know all that. What life does that bring? We're not called to preach merely moral exhortations or history lessons or social commentaries (though any of those things may be a part of good preaching). We are called to preach the Word of God to the church of God and to everyone in His creation. This is how God brings life. Each person who is reading this book—and I, the one who has written it—is flawed and has faults and has sinned against God. And the terrible thing about our fallen natures is that we are greedy for ways to justify our sins against God. Every single one of us wants to know how we can defend ourselves from God's charges. Therefore we are in desperate need to hear God's Word brought honestly to us, so that we don't just hear what we want to hear but rather hear what God has actually said.

All of this is important, remember, because God's Holy Spirit creates His people by His Word.

This is why Paul told Timothy to "form a committee." Right? Of course not! He never said that. You'll never find a preacher in the New Testament told to form a committee. "Take a survey"? No! Paul never told anyone to take a survey either. "Spend yourself in visiting"? No! He never told a preacher to do that either. "Read a book"? No! Paul never told young Timothy to do any of those things.

Paul told Timothy, straight and clear, to "Preach the Word" (2 Tim. 4:2). This is the great imperative. This is why the apostles earlier had determined that, even though there were problems with the equitable distribution of financial aid in Jerusalem, the church would just have to find others to solve their problems, because, "We . . . will give our attention to prayer and the ministry of the word" (Acts 6:4). Why this priority? Because this Word is "the word of life" (Phil. 2:16). That is the great task of the preacher: to "hold out the word of life" to people who need it for their souls.

There are today some criticisms of such expositional preaching. Some suggest that today we need a less rational, more artistic, less authoritarian and elitist, more communal and participatory way of communicating God's truth than this ancient method of one person standing up front and talking in a monologue to others. We need video clips, they say, and dialogues and liturgical dance. And yet there's something right and good about this ancient method that makes it appropriate, perhaps even especially appropriate, for our culture today. In our isolatingly subjectivist culture where everyone's just into their own thing, in this anti-authority culture where everyone is confused and confusing, there is something appropriate about us all gathering together and listening to one who is standing in the place of God, giving His Word to us as we contribute nothing to it other than hearing and heeding it. There is an important symbol in this process in and of itself.

Of course there will come a day when faith will give way to sight and sermons will be no more. And let me tell you there is no one who looks forward to that more than I and most of my fellow-preachers. When you don't need faith anymore because you can see the Lord— that's the climax of the Bible. "They will see his face" (Rev. 22:4). And at that point this old cane of faith can be cast aside as we run and see Him with our own eyes.

But we're not there yet. We're still laboring under the results of the sins of our first parents and of our own sins. On that day, faith will finally give way to sight, but for now we are in a different time—but by God's grace this is not a time of total despair. He gives us His Word and He gives us faith. We are in a day of faith. And so, like our first parents before us, like Noah and Abraham, the Israelites and the ancient apostles, we rely on God's Word.

What does all this mean for our churches? Simply that the preaching of the Word must be absolutely central. It shouldn't surprise you to hear that sound, expositional preaching is often the fountainhead of growth in a church. Let a good expositional ministry be established and watch what happens. Forget what the experts say. Watch hungry people have their lives transformed as the living God speaks to them through the power of His Word. As it was in Martin Luther's own experience, such careful attention to God's Word is the way to salvation and is often the beginning of reformation. As Paul said, "Since in the wisdom of God the world through its wisdom did not know him, God was pleased through the foolishness of what was preached to save those who believe" (1 Cor. 1:21).

God's Word is the word we need to hear today. We live in a strange day, when even Christians who claim to be born again and churches that claim to be evangelical ignore God's Word.

Are you in a job where you get a lot of phone calls? Some of those

BIBLICAL THEOLOGY

I had made a statement in a doctoral seminar about God. Bill responded politely but firmly that he liked to think of God rather differently. For several minutes, Bill painted a picture for us of a friendly deity. He liked to think of God as being wise, but not meddling; compassionate, but never overpowering; ever so resourceful, but never interrupting. "This," said Bill in conclusion, "is how I like to think of God."

My reply was perhaps somewhat sharper than it should have been. "Thank you, Bill," I said, "for telling us so much about yourself, but we are concerned to know what God is really like, not simply about our own desires."

The seminar was silent for a moment as they took in this potential breach of politeness on my part, but they were also taking in the point. I made some appreciative noises toward Bill, and we got on with our discussion about the nature and character of God as revealed in the Bible.

What do you think God is like? Not, what do you *like* to think God is like, but how do you put together the God of Christmas with the God of the great judgment of the final day? What is your understanding of God and of what He is like? To some of you, this whole discussion may sound nonsensical. Why expend any energy at all over what various people believe about an invisible being?

I can understand that kind of skepticism over the importance of this topic. Regardless of our religious confession these days, who can dispute that in many ways religious beliefs seem irrelevant to our world? On television we see Roman Catholics fawning over the pope in St. Louis while ignoring his teachings about contraception and abortion. Southern Baptists, who used to be known for decrying illicit sex, drugs, and rock and roll music—lest they lead to dancing, drinking, or playing cards—are now portrayed in a national magazine as antinomian Christians who have made peace with an anything-goes morality.

This inattention to belief fits our culture's impatience with detail. In society today, beliefs have been domesticated. We no longer fight about them. We don't really argue about them. We may not even care about them anymore. After all, we think, so many beliefs are merely passing fashions or momentary expressions of individual wants or desires. Americans create designer religions and smorgasbord faiths—"Oh, I'll take a little of this from Hinduism, a little of this from Christianity, a little of this from my grandmother (I don't remember what she was)"—and put it all together as their own individual, unique religion. Today people *believe* to be true simply what they *desire* to be true.

Long-held Christian beliefs about everything from the nature of God to morality have been reshaped and have become unimportant to many people. They have been jettisoned in the name of making Christianity more relevant, more palatable, more acceptable to today's hearer.

How relevant are your own beliefs to your daily life? When you last sat in church, how much did you examine the words of the prayers you heard? How much did you think about the words of the songs you sang? Or how about the words you heard from Scripture? Does it really matter to you if what you said or sang in church was true?

How much does it really matter, anyway? If I attend church, and I'm friendly, and I feel encouraged, and if I give my time to being there and even give my money, how much does it really matter if in my heart of hearts I really don't believe all this stuff that the people around me say, and maybe even that I say? How important are religious beliefs?

To the best of my knowledge, my only famous relative is Samuel F. B. Morse, inventor of the telegraph code that bears his name. He was, I am told, my mother's mother's father's mother's cousin. (And don't tell me his parents didn't have any brothers or sisters!) In February 1999, after being in use more than ninety years, Morse Code was dropped as the official means of communication for ships, in favor of an on-board satellite system. It is, of course, necessary to have some kind of overall framework for ships to navigate by, whether it is the North Star or global positioning satellites.

Such frameworks are important, not just for ships but for us as individuals and as churches. We need to have what literary types would call a "metanarrative"—a meaning. There has been not only negligence of but even hostility toward such overarching meanings. This hostility isn't something new that's come in with postmodernism; it has been around for a long time. Karl Popper, more than fifty years ago, wrote his great work *The Open Society and Its Enemies*.[1] He devoted the last chapter specifically to denying the idea that history has any meaning at all. Popper wanted to discourage people from saying that history has a meaning because he was convinced that it was dangerous to say that. Popper knew this because he himself was an Austrian Jew and had fled from the Nazi occupation of Vienna. The Nazis, like the Marxists, justified their actions in terms of the purpose they saw in history.

As I reflect on Popper's book and on this theme of biblical theology—the theology of the whole Bible—I see a demonic irony in the postmodern claim that such overarching meanings oppress us. The postmodernists' word to express this is "totalizing," as in "these are totalizing metanarratives." By that they mean that these metanarratives oppress us by making us see everything from their point of view. Yet the story God tells us in the Bible is a story of liberation. Isn't it amazing that exactly what God intends to liberate us from—our culture—is now calling all such "metanarratives" oppressive? God's "metanarrative" doesn't oppress—it liberates!

In the previous chapter we considered the importance of expositional preaching. Our concern, however, should not be only with how we are taught, but—more importantly—with specifically what we are taught. We should want pastors who will preach from the Word of God, but we should also carefully listen to what the pastor says and decide whether or not what he says is according to the Word of God. We need not just someone who claims to preach from the Word, but someone who substantially does that—whose sermons are in line with what the Word of God actually teaches. That is especially important when it comes to what is taught about the nature and character of God Himself. One of the chief marks of a healthy church is a biblical understanding of God in His character and His ways with us.

In this chapter, therefore, we will seek to discover the main lines of the great story of the Bible. If we can hear and see those main lines more clearly, then we will understand the God of the Bible more clearly. We can summarize the main story line of the Bible simply under five words; this is what the Bible teaches us about God: that He is *creating;* that He is *holy;* that He is *faithful;* that He is *loving;* and that He is *sovereign.*

Listen to each one of these five truths as we look at the Bible's presentation of them, and see if you can imagine the difference it would make if any of these things were not true.

THE GOD OF THE BIBLE IS A CREATING GOD

First, beginning where the Bible begins, we see that God is a creating God—creating the world and creating a special people in the world.

The Bible is sometimes represented as a collection of noble ethical sentiments. But when people describe it like that I can only assume that they have never read it. If you have read the Bible at all you know that it is really full of history. Much of the Bible is a long story about what goes on with God and the world He has made. I know that some people are bored by history the minute you mention the word, but the story of the Bible is an amazing story. It begins with nothing and then nothing becomes something. That's the most amazing thing ever conceived of. Then, after nothing has become something, God makes the first inanimate creation. And then comes animate life. Then finally God makes man and woman in His own image.

We find the story of the Garden of Eden, and then the story of the Fall. And then we see that things go downhill from there. It is all disintegration, from Cain down to Noah. And then there comes the Flood, and after Noah there is disintegration again, down to the time of the Tower of Babel.

Then God calls Abraham. And here begins the very special story of God creating a particular people for Himself. After a brief time of prosperity, Israel falls into centuries of slavery, and then there is the Exodus, when they are let out of slavery, are given the Law, and enter the Promised Land.

There is the time of confusion under the judges, then the kingdom is established under Saul and David. David's son Solomon takes the throne upon David's death, and then Solomon's son Rehoboam takes the throne. Next we find the nation divided into two, the northern kingdom and the southern kingdom. Idolatry becomes more and more common. God through the Assyrians destroys the northern kingdom of Israel in 722 B.C. and then destroys the southern kingdom of Judah through the Babylonians a little more than a century later. So the Hebrews are exiled to Babylon for several decades, until they return to Judah and rebuild Jerusalem and the temple.

And that's where the Old Testament leaves off, with the story of this remnant of the Israelites, needy, rather pitiful, being reduced to complete, utter dependence.

So you see the Old Testament gives us, not some disembodied theology about God, not simply a list of philosophical ideas, but a very specific, earthy revelation of who God is and of what He is like.

Many of you know what it's like to get a resumé from a prospective employee. It is one thing to look at a resumé; it is another thing to actually work with a person. That's why prospective employers call the references—to know what it is like to actually interact with this person. In the Old Testament, God hasn't just sent us a resumé of some abstract truths about Himself. No, we have an account of what it is like to actually live with God, what it is like to know and interact with Him. In this history, we see much of what it means to be God's people, and we see much of what God is like.

We need to understand the truth that the Bible presents about God and about us. Sound teaching in our church must include a clear commitment to the teachings of the Bible, even if those teachings are often neglected. If we are to learn the sound doctrine of the Bible, we must come to terms even with the doctrines that may be difficult or even potentially divisive but that are foundational for our understanding of God. You see, theology is not merely an abstruse, abstract, academic affair. Biblical theology is a mark of a healthy church.

One thing that quickly becomes apparent in our brief Bible survey of God as Creator is that He created and chose a particular nation of people as His special people. Some may respond that God's so choosing was in some way unfair. There are a couple of problems, however, with such a response. First, "unfair" is not a category we should apply to God. Second, even if it is a category we would allow of God, I suggest that you and I are not the ones to apply it. You and I have too much of our own self-interest involved to be so arrogant as to determine that we can decide when God, the Creator of the Universe, is being fair or unfair.

The history recorded in the Bible shows us very plainly that God is a creating God and that He is an electing God. Even if we cannot fully understand everything that is involved in this, it is undeniable that this is what the Bible teaches. It may have implications that we don't fully understand, but no small matters issue from this if we decide that our salvation ultimately comes from God rather than from ourselves.

It affects how we understand God. It affects how we understand ourselves.

We must acknowledge that God is the Great Initiator, the Great Giver, the Creator of the World, the Creator of His People, the Author of our Faith. That is what God is like.

THE GOD OF THE BIBLE IS A HOLY GOD

The Bible also clearly presents God's passion for holiness. The God of the Bible is a holy God.

If we are to understand the whole story of the Bible, not only must we understand that God is a creating God, but we must also understand that He is not a morally indifferent God, as some people have thought Him to be—as if God built the clock, wound it up, and then just walked off and let it run. That's not the way it is. God is not unconcerned with His creation. No, when you read the pages of the Bible you see that there is a God who has a passion for holiness.

When our church family celebrates the Lord's Supper, we hear the words that Jesus said: "This cup is the new covenant in my blood" (Luke 22:20). This language of covenant is straight out of the Old Testament. Sometimes theologians say that this language sounds sort of cold or dry, but the idea of covenant is not like that at all. It is not just a legal relationship. When you go to the Old Testament you find that the language of covenant is the language of personal relationship. Consider your own life. The covenant commitments that you make are the most important, deep, tender relationships in your life. The marriage relationship, especially, is a covenant relationship where you commit before God to love and to care and to give. And when we read in the Bible about God's passion for holiness, it is within the context of His covenant with us—it is within the context of His commitment to having a relationship with us.

God's passion for holiness, however, causes a problem as He seeks a relationship with us. For instead of being holy, we humans sin—and yet we are called to relate to a holy God. In English we have the word *atonement,* which literally means "at-one-ment." Atonement was needed because we somehow needed to be reconciled to—to become at one with—this holy God. We as sinners had separated ourselves from God and so we needed to be reconciled to Him. According to the Bible, everyone is a sinner. And so everyone has this problem: How can I relate to God?

We need reconciliation because sin separates us from God

(Prov. 15:29; Isa. 59:2; Hab. 1:13; Col. 1:21; Heb. 10:27). According to the Bible, all people are sinners (1 Kings 8:46; Ps. 14:3; Prov. 20:9; Eccles. 7:20; Mark 10:18; Rom. 3:23) and are not able to deal with sin themselves (Rom. 3:20; Gal. 2:16). Sin, as broken divine commandments, needs some reparation.

In the Old Testament this idea of atonement is linked with sacrifice as the way God provides for us to make reparation and to restore our relationship with Him. That doesn't mean pitifully trying to propitiate some volcano, like something that you've read of in a book or seen in a movie. It isn't like that at all. The Old Testament idea of sacrifice does not involve human efforts to win God's favor. Rather, it is God's own revelation to His people of how we can come to know Him, of how we can find our way to Him in spite of our sin. The living God has spoken, providing a way of reconciliation.

The idea of sacrifice seems to be innate in the Bible. Cain and Abel offered sacrifices. The Passover lamb (Ex. 12) was to be offered as a sacrifice. It was to be without defect and was to be slaughtered. Its blood was to mark the houses God would save. The lives of the firstborn (who represented the whole family) would be required. God said, ". . . when I see the blood . . ." (Ex. 12:13). The object of this sacrifice was clearly God's satisfaction.

We find sacrifice again and again in the book of Leviticus, teaching people that sin was defiling; that sin cost life; that sin separated us from God. You can even see this in the construction of the temple. A Holy God must be separate from a sinful people. These sacrifices showed us that holiness was needed and that, because we didn't have holiness, we needed some kind of atonement, some way of reconciliation with God. These sacrifices pointed to the restoration of the people's relationship with God. All the offerings had to be voluntary, costly, the offerer's own, accompanied by confession of sins, according to God's prescriptions.

There was an important distinction between biblical sacrifices and other ancient sacrifices. Biblically, sacrifices were not to be brought by the grateful but by the guilty; they were not brought by the ignorant but by the instructed. The life of the animal victim, symbolized by its blood, was required in exchange for the life of the guilty human worshiper. The sacrifices showed that sin is serious and that it costs life. All the offerings had to be voluntary and costly—the offerer's own property. Perhaps God was implanting in His people's minds symbolically the idea of the innocent being given in place of the guilty. These sacrifices taught that sin was defiling. That's why the temple was designed as it was, with the restricted access to the Holy of Holies showing how sin hinders access to a holy God. These sacrifices showed that purification was needed, and that sin is so serious that death is needed to atone for it—that salvation and forgiveness are costly.

You see that especially in the Day of Atonement, the one day of fasting prescribed for all of Israel. The Day of Atonement centered on a special sin offering for the whole nation. It served as a reminder that all the other regular sin offerings did not completely atone for sin (see Lev. 16). The high priest, as representative of the people, entered the Holy of Holies one day of the year for access to God; and this atonement had to be made in the very presence of God. The high priest bore the blood of the goat, the sin offering (cf. Heb. 9:7). First he made atonement for himself—because he himself had to be clean—then for the people. And when he brought that blood into the Holy of Holies, who could see it? Only God. The point of this sacrifice, the point of the atonement, is for God to be reconciled to us.

It is particularly interesting that this sacrifice of atonement is repeated annually. You see, other nations would go into frenzies of sacrifices whenever they thought things were going badly for them. But Israel is taught from the very beginning that, regardless of how good or how bad their circumstances, they must annually make this sacrifice—as if to remind them that they are continuously in a state of sin, that sin separates people from God, that they can never offer a perfect sacrifice, and that it is God Himself who provides the way of access to Him as He forgives our sins.

Well, what does all this mean for us? I think it very practically raises the question, What kind of people are we? Are we as bad as these people in the Old Testament must have been to have this huge system of sacrifices set up for them? What do you think? Are people basically bad or good? That will determine much of what you think a church needs to do. If you think people are basically good, then a church is simply a place where we seek encouragement or perhaps the enhancement of our self-esteem. We need simply to take the good that's in us and build on it. However, if you think something is much more radically wrong with us humans, if you think that we are spiritually dead, guilty before God and separated from Him, then there is something different that churches must do. In that case, churches need to present the Gospel clearly. Churches need to tell people how to find forgiveness for their sins and how to find new life.

We will "do church" differently, depending on how we understand God and ourselves. To be biblical, we must know that God is a holy God and that we, by nature, are dead in our sins and transgressions and justly stand under His condemnation.

THE GOD OF THE BIBLE IS A FAITHFUL GOD

God is a creating God, a holy God, and He is also a faithful God. This brings me to a question that seems really to be the riddle of the Old Testament. In Exodus 34:6-7, the Lord is speaking to Moses and He says the most amazing thing, especially given what we've just thought about—that God is this great Creator who made the world and that our sin then caused a rupture in His creation. Considering God's passion for holiness, how does all of this fit with what He says to Moses in Exodus 34:6-7? The Lord is revealing Himself and His character, and He says,

> "The LORD, the LORD, the compassionate and gracious God, slow to anger, abounding in love and faithfulness, maintaining love to thousands, and forgiving wickedness, rebellion and sin. Yet he does not leave the guilty unpunished . . ."

If you stop and think for a second, the last couple of phrases don't seem really to fit together very well. How could this be? "Abounding in love and faithfulness, maintaining love to thousands, and forgiving wickedness, rebellion and sin," and yet, "he does not leave the guilty unpunished."

If we want to understand the God of the Bible, we're going to have to understand this passage. This is the promise of hope for the redemption of God's people. The biblical picture is not simply of an uncaring God of grim condemnation. God is not only holy and just in His unwavering commitment to oppose and punish sin; He is also faithful to His promises. Throughout history, God planned and promised to reveal His glory to His people. And He did. But how could the Lord "forgive wickedness" and yet, as He says here, "not leave the guilty unpunished"? What's the answer to that mystery?

The answer to that mystery wasn't found in these Israelites, but in God and His promise—particularly in His promised person. In the Old Testament, we see that hope requires an atoning sacrifice, a propitiation to assuage the righteous wrath of God. We see that it requires a substitution of suffering and death on the part of the innocent for the deserved punishment of the guilty. And it would seem to require some relationship between the offerer and the victim.

In the time of Christ, people were not wondering whether or not a Messiah would come. They took it for granted. You can tell by the early chapters of each of the gospels that people were looking for a Messiah, for the Anointed One that the Lord had promised would come. The Lord had said through Moses that He would "raise up a prophet" (see Deut. 18:15-19). But when this prophet came, He took everyone by surprise, because He—Jesus—presented Himself not just as the fulfillment of the kingly prophecies of the Messiah (which they were all quite comfortable with) but as a suffering one, as one who came to be rejected and to suffer in the place of His people. He brought together the prophecies about the Messiah as King with other prophecies about the Messiah as the One who would suffer in the stead of His people. He brought those two strands of prophecy together.

In fact, both the Old and the New Testaments teach us that this kingly, suffering Messiah is our only hope. Jesus solves the riddle of

Exodus 34. He shows how God can forgive our wickedness while at the same time punishing the guilty.

At the heart of understanding Jesus Christ is understanding what He came to do. He came as the one by whom you and I can have a restored relationship with God. The one for whom God's people had been waiting had come. Where Adam and Israel had failed and had been unfaithful, Jesus survived temptations without sin. Here is the prophet promised by Moses, the king prefigured by David, and even the divine "son of man" of Daniel 7. These all had come in Jesus of Nazareth. He was the Word of God made flesh. He was our prefigured substitute. He was the Lamb of God, slain for the sins of His people.

Jesus Christ was the faithful fulfillment of God's promise. Our creating God and our holy God is also an amazingly faithful God.

THE GOD OF THE BIBLE IS A LOVING GOD

Closely tied to the idea of God's faithfulness is the fact that He is a God of love, who has a special love for His covenant people. God has made us to reflect His image. He has made us to be in covenant with Him. So how could the Lord "forgive wickedness" and yet "not leave the guilty unpunished"? The answer, of course, is to be found in Jesus. He is the one who, though not guilty Himself, took on our guilt and was punished for it. This is what Jesus taught His disciples in Luke 24:

> Beginning with Moses and all the Prophets, he explained to them what was said in all the Scriptures concerning himself. . . . . Then he opened their minds so they could understand the Scriptures. He told them, "This is what is written: The Christ will suffer and rise from the dead on the third day, and repentance and forgiveness of sins will be preached in his name to all nations, beginning in Jerusalem" (vv. 27, 45-47).

"This is what is written"; this is what the Lord had prophesied—that He would show His love to His people in this very particular way. Remember the famous prophecies from Isaiah 53:

Surely he took up our infirmities and carried our sorrows, yet we considered him stricken by God, smitten by him, and afflicted. But he was pierced for our transgressions, he was crushed for our iniquities; the punishment that brought us peace was upon him, and by his wounds we are healed. We all, like sheep, have gone astray, each of us has turned to his own way; and the LORD has laid on him the iniquity of us all (Isa. 53:4-6).

This is what Christ did in His love! As He taught His disciples, "The Son of Man did not come to be served, but to serve, and to give his life as a ransom for many" (Mark 10:45).

Paul, too, described Christ Jesus as the one

"who, being in very nature God, did not consider equality with God something to be grasped, but made himself nothing, taking the very nature of a servant, being made in human likeness. And being found in appearance as a man, he humbled himself and became obedient to death—even death on a cross!" (Phil. 2:6-8)

On the third day He rose again. And His disciples, filled with the Holy Spirit, began to preach. In the first Christian sermon, Peter says,

"Men of Israel, listen to this: Jesus of Nazareth was a man accredited by God to you by miracles, wonders and signs, which God did among you through him, as you yourselves know. This man was handed over to you by God's set purpose and foreknowledge; and you, with the help of wicked men, put him to death by nailing him to the cross. But God raised him from the dead, freeing him from the agony of death, because it was impossible for death to keep its hold on him" (Acts 2:22-24).

In the New Testament we find, then, that God keeps all of His promises because of His covenant love for His people. And if we are Christians today, it is because God continues to do that. He continues to keep those promises.

What does it mean to become a part of God's covenant people, to be a Christian? What happens when someone becomes a Christian? Is it simply a matter of making a decision? Is it simply a matter of praying a prayer? What about repentance? Do we need to repent? Do we need to believe? If we do repent and believe, how is it that we're able to do that—if we're as bad as Scripture says we are? If we are dead in our sins and transgressions, how do we all of a sudden repent and believe?

Ultimately, it must have something to do not so much with us but with God. The reality of our salvation must show us something very important about God. As John wrote, "This is love: not that we loved God, but that he loved us and sent his Son as an atoning sacrifice for our sins. . . . We love because he first loved us" (1 John 4:10, 19).

The God of the Bible is a God of amazing love!

THE GOD OF THE BIBLE IS A SOVEREIGN GOD

Finally, we find that God is a sovereign God and that, in His sovereignty, even all of creation itself is to be involved in His renewing love.

Christians often pray the Lord's Prayer: "Your kingdom come, your will be done on earth as it is in heaven" (Matt. 6:10). Have you ever wondered what that means?

Some people limit their hopes very deliberately to today, to things that they can promise and that they can fulfill in their own power, their own strength—things that they know they can be certain of. They don't want to put their hearts on anything else. They want to be very careful and guarded with their hearts. They've been burned too many times. They're not going to once again let their trust run out after some promise whose fulfillment they cannot guarantee.

But Christianity has never been like that. We Christians have always had a hope that extends beyond ourselves and that exceeds what we could ever do in our own power. Peter wrote, "We are looking forward to a new heaven and a new earth, the home of righteousness" (2 Pet. 3:13). This points to the fulfillment of that final and that first hope of the Bible—the hope of the whole world being put right, as God's sovereign plan extends from Christ to His covenant people to creation itself.

We find this hope at the very end of the Bible. The book of Revelation picks up the prophetic tradition of the Old Testament, but with some changes. Revelation is presented as the consummation of God's plans to have a people in right relationship to Him. As the church militant becomes the church triumphant, the heavens and the earth are re-created (see Rev. 21:1-4; 21:22–22:5). We see the climax of the fulfillment of all of God's promises to His people. The holiness of God's people is finally complete. Finally God's people are truly holy and with Him. The Garden of Eden is restored. The presence of God is once again with His people. The Holy City (21:2) is in the shape of a cube, like the Holy of Holies in the Old Testament where God's presence was—only now it includes all of His people, from all times and places. The whole world becomes the Holy of Holies.

This is the great news that we as Christians have to offer. This is our vision of the future—not because we thought it up; not because a committee somewhere wrote it; not because it's simply a response to what we would wish to be the case, like my friend Bill—but because this is what God has revealed.

In our waiting time, it is very appropriate that the New Testament closes with this book. The book of Revelation was not written by someone who was on top of the world, who could see God's kingdom coming because his ship had come in and so he was sure everyone's fortunes were on the way. No, the book of Revelation was written by an old man whose life was just about over. He was in exile, utterly desperate and dependent, and yet full of hope in a sovereign God because he knew that whoever sat on the throne in Rome did not finally decide what would happen in the world. He knew that there was a God who sat in heaven who would bring all of His promises to fulfillment. John could sit there on Patmos full of hope, because he knew what this God was like.

This kind of biblical theology is practical. It makes a difference. The promises God made about all the earth being filled with the knowledge of its Creator would be kept in His new creation. The God of the Bible makes promises, and the God of the Bible sovereignly keeps them.

Do you see the importance of this? God completes His purposes. He fulfills His promises. As Christians, we need to know that God will continue to care for us, and that His continuing care is based not on our faithfulness but on His. It may be more exciting for a little while to try to run around and pretend that the world is some great laser-tag contest, spiritually, between the forces of darkness and the forces of light. And certainly there are very real evil forces that we as Christians come up against in the world and in our own hearts. But the outcome does not hang in the balance. Our God is a sovereign God. John the Revelator had hope, not because he knew what *he* would do but because he knew what *God* would do.

These questions are not simply matters for bookish theologians or young seminary students. They are important to each one of us as Christians. How you think about God impacts the way you live and what you want your church to be like. You must have a biblical understanding of God.

Those of us who are pastors especially need to know these things. If we change our thoughts about any one of these attributes of God, we would change the way we do our job. We would shepherd differently. Faithfulness to Scripture demands that we speak about these issues with clarity and authority. We will understand nothing about the Bible if we do not understand the God whom it is about. God Himself is the framework. What He reveals about Himself is how we understand everything else.

Our understanding of what the Bible teaches about God is crucial. We have seen that the biblical God is creating, holy, faithful, loving, and sovereign. This last item, His sovereignty, is for some reason often denied, even within the church. But we must be very careful here. For confessing Christians to resist the idea of God's sovereignty in creation or salvation is really to flirt with pious paganism. Many Christians will have honest questions about God's sovereignty. But a sustained, tenacious denial of God's sovereignty should concern us.

To baptize a person who is so antagonistic to God's sovereignty may be to baptize someone who in his heart still isn't really quite willing to trust God. That, after all, is the issue when it comes to God's sovereignty. Are we willing to trust Him? Are we willing to acknowledge, finally, that we are not God? That we are not the Judge? That we are not the ones to say what is fair and unfair? Are we willing to put our whole lives in God's hands and to truly trust Him? That is what's really at issue in this discussion about the sovereignty of God.

As dangerous as such resistance is for the spiritual life of any Christian, it is even more dangerous in the leader of a congregation. To appoint a person as a leader who doubts God's sovereignty or who seriously misunderstands the Bible's teaching on it, is to set up as an example a person who in his own heart may well be deeply unwilling to trust God. That is bound to hinder the church as it tries to trust the Lord together.

We must understand God by His revelation of Himself, not by our own hunches, not by our own wishes, not by the way we like to think of God. Too often today we speak as if evangelism were advertising and explain the Spirit's work in terms of marketing. Some even talk of God Himself as if He were made in the image of man, rather than the other way around.

If we are to be a healthy church in such times, we must be especially careful to pray for leaders in the church to have a biblical grasp of and an experiential trust in the sovereignty of God. Sound doctrine, in its full, biblical glory, marks a healthy church.

Disappointments have their purpose. The ruins of our own cherished plans are often the steps to finding the true God and the good that He has for us. The Bible is full of stories like this. Israel's hopes for the Messiah again and again drove her to the point of needing to trust God fully. Paul's "thorn in the flesh" drove him to be used by God and to trust Him and rely on Him and so to find God reliable in a way he never would have without that thorn.

And it is the same for us. We are at our most dangerous point spiritually when we think everything is fine. We need to know that God is entirely right to condemn us forever. And we need to know that God in Christ has offered us another way, if we rely not on our own righteousness and our own goodness and merit but on Christ and on Christ alone. That is when we find the way to peace with God.

If we're honest, we know that such trust is not our natural tendency. We cling with all our might to what we have in this world, as if it were going to last forever. But nothing that we physically possess in our lives right now will last forever in the state that it is in.

And yet, if we are God's children, we know that He has something even better prepared for us. As good as the best things may be in our lives right now, God has something even better prepared for us.

In the last paragraph of the last book of the Chronicles of Narnia, C. S. Lewis writes,

> And as [Aslan] spoke, He no longer looked to them like a lion; but the things that began to happen after that were so great and beautiful that I cannot write them. And for us this is the end of all the stories, and we can most truly say that they all lived happily ever after. But for them it was only the beginning of the real story. All their life in this world and all their adventures in Narnia had only been the cover and the title page: now at last they were beginning Chapter One of the Great Story, which no one on earth has read: which goes on forever: in which every chapter is better than the one before.[2]

If you are God's child, the conclusion He has in mind for you is unimaginably good. As John wrote, "Dear friends, now we are children of God, and what we will be has not yet been made known. But we know that when he appears, we shall be like him, for we shall see him as he is" (1 John 3:2). The apostle Paul, thinking about the same things, just dissolved into doxology: "Oh, the depth of the riches of the wisdom and knowledge of God! How unsearchable his judgments, and his paths beyond tracing out!" (Rom. 11:33).

This is the God of the Bible—the creating, holy, faithful, loving, sovereign God of the Bible. The Bible, in fact, is all about this God.

It is about promises made by God and promises kept by God. And in the Bible God calls out for us to respond to Him by trusting in Him and His Word.

In the Bible we see God giving us His Word—His promises— and we respond to Him by trusting Him—just as Adam and Eve did *not* do in the Garden of Eden; just as Jesus *did* throughout His life and especially in the Garden of Gethsemane. And as we hear and believe God's Word, we begin again to have that relationship with Him that He made us for. This is the God whom we can trust and should trust, because His Word will not disappoint. This is what the Bible is all about.

Will you believe Him? Will you trust Him?

WHAT'S COMING UP . . .

MARK THREE:
THE GOSPEL

The Good News Is Not Simply That We Are Okay

The Good News Is Not Simply That God Is Love

The Good News Is Not Simply That Jesus Wants to Be Our Friend

The Good News Is Not Simply That We Should Live Right

Repentance

Belief

THE GOSPEL

News is big business today. Sociologists have dubbed the emerging power elite in America as the "information class" because information is apparently the commodity they most value. And this commodity is more pervasive now than ever before. News is offered in America by the television networks—broadcast and cable, twenty-four hours a day—through scores of periodicals devoted to news, and through nearly 12,000 newspapers, not to mention the Internet, which these days allows millions of Americans to know about a "story" before leading newspapers or networks ever "break" it.

News seems vital, not only to those who earn their living from the news but to those of us who spend our lives consuming it as well. In the news we learn about everything from presidential elections to plant closures, from recent disasters to important trends. So addicted are some people to news that one wonders if they could exist without it. How many of those who decried all the recent scandals in Washington would have left their televisions or radios on all day at work if they could have done so?

We often have this sense of needing to keep up with the latest news. Recently on a plane, I was sitting behind someone who is in the news a lot. He was devouring the newspaper, reading a story about himself! He's got to know what's going on, which is understandable. Careers rise and fall on the speed with which information is learned and disseminated. For some people, keeping abreast of the news may seem as essential as eating. So they devour the *Post* and the *Times* and maybe even the other *Times* and the *Journal*, along with whatever regional papers they may be interested in. Being, for them, involves knowing. As Os Guinness has observed, the very "pursuit of relevance becomes a prime source of superficiality, anxiety, and burn-out. ('Hell,' it has been said, 'will be full of newspapers with a fresh edition every thirty seconds, so that no one will ever feel caught up.')"[1]

But what can you do when "all the news that's fit to print" (an obsolete saying if ever there was one!) keeps coming at you with such ever-increasing volume and frequency?

Accuracy is, of course, the only attribute of the news that trumps speed in importance. So it must have been with unreserved horror that the editor of an English newspaper a little more than a hundred years ago opened his printed and distributed paper to find in it a most embarrassing unintentional typographical conflation of two stories: one story being about a patent pig-killing and sausage-making machine and the other about a local clergyman, the Rev. Dr. Mudge, who was being presented with a gold-headed cane. A portion of the famously-mangled story reads as follows:

> Several of Rev. Dr. Mudge's friends called upon him yesterday, and after a conversation the unsuspecting pig was seized by the hind leg, and slid along a beam until he reached the hot-water tank. . . . Thereupon he came forward and said that there were times when the feelings overpowered one, and for that reason he would not attempt to do more than thank those around him for the manner in which such a huge animal was cut into fragments was simply astonishing. The doctor concluded his remarks, when the machine seized him and, in less time than it takes to write it, the pig was cut into fragments and worked up into a delicious sausage. The occasion will be long remembered by the doctor's friends as one of the most delightful of their lives. The best pieces can be procured for tenpence a

pound, and we are sure that those who have sat so long under his ministry will rejoice that he has been treated so handsomely.

Perhaps you think that, when you go to church on Sunday morning rather than staying at home and watching the talk shows, you've decided to deal with religion rather than with the news; but Christianity is all about news. It's the Good News—the best news the world has ever heard. And yet that news—far more important than any story about the Rev. Dr. Mudge and a patent pig-killing machine—is often every bit as scrambled and confused. Too often it becomes a thin veneer spread lightly over our culture's values, being shaped and formed to the contours of our culture rather than to the truth about God.

This idea of the Good News, you realize, wasn't some later Christian packaging of Christianity. Jesus Himself talks about the Good News. And in talking in these terms Jesus is reaching back to the language of Isaiah from hundreds of years earlier (Isa. 52:7; 61:1). Whatever Jesus may have said in Aramaic, the way the Christians and even His own disciples remembered it in Greek was with this word *evangel*—literally, Good News.

What exactly is this Good News? In this study, we want to try to set the story straight; we want to get the news right. If you are going to agree with just one chapter in this book, this is probably a good one to agree with—the Good News of the Bible. If you look at the table of contents, you'll find that these next three chapters have to do with salvation, but each comes at it from a slightly different angle. In the next chapter we will look at the very moment of salvation—conversion. In chapter 5 ("MARK FIVE") we will look at how we are to tell others about this great message that has changed us. In this chapter, we want to look at the message itself. What is the message of Christ, the Good News that we as Christians proclaim?

What is the Good News? Is it that "I'm okay"? Or that God is love? Is it that Jesus is my friend? Or that I should straighten up and start living right?

What is the Good News of Jesus Christ?

THE GOOD NEWS IS NOT SIMPLY THAT WE ARE OKAY

You know the often-quoted book title of over thirty years ago, *I'm O.K., You're O.K.* Some people seem to think that Christianity is fundamentally a religious therapy session, where we sit around trying to help each other feel better about ourselves. The pews are couches, the preacher asks questions, and the text to be expounded is your own inner self. And yet, when we have finished plumbing our own depths, why do we so often still feel empty? Or even dirty? Is there something about us and our lives that is incomplete or even wrong?

I remember hearing Loretta Lynn say, weeping, in an interview on CNN (April 7, 1998) just after her close friend Tammy Wynette had died, "Why does everyone I love die?"

Yes, why indeed? That's a good question. The Bible utterly rejects the idea that we are okay, that the human condition is just fine, that everyone is really in need of simply accepting their current condition, their finitude, their limitedness, their imperfections, or that we simply need to look on the bright side of things.

The Bible teaches that in our first parents, Adam and Eve, we have all been seduced into disobeying God. We are therefore neither righteous nor on good terms with God. In fact, according to Jesus, our sin is so serious that we need a whole new life (John 3); and according to Paul, we need to be created again (1 Cor. 15), because we are dead in our sins and transgressions (Eph. 2). "Transgression" is simply another word for sin, describing it as going across a boundary. In our day and age, Michel Foucault would live, like the Marquis de Sade before him, in order to transgress boundaries. Some have claimed that Foucault, having contracted the AIDS virus, deliberately sought to infect others. The bathhouses of San Francisco became the place where Foucault transgressed the boundaries not only of respect for sexuality but also of respect for life itself.[2]

Our individual transgressions may not seem so blatant or offensive, but they are surely no less deadly for our relationship with God. James reminds us that,

> Whoever keeps the whole law and yet stumbles at just one point is guilty of breaking all of it. For he who said, "Do not commit adultery," also said, "Do not murder." If you do not commit adultery but you do commit murder, you have become a lawbreaker (James 2:10-11).

Paul says that "the wages of sin is death" (Rom. 6:23), and in James 2 we can get a little better understanding of why this is so. We can see something more of the seriousness of each sin. James's point is that the laws of God are not simply external statutes, published and passed by some congress in heaven; rather, the laws of God reflect His very character. They are an expression of God Himself. So to break any of God's laws is to live against God. It is to live contrary to Him.

Let me explain with an example from marriage. Let's suppose that my wife asks me to go to the store and buy some things, but I deliberately buy a number of other things instead. It is not a mistake on my part; rather, I deliberately fail to get as much of this as I should get, and I get another brand of this than I should have gotten, and I omit some other things from the list altogether. What would be going on in such a case? I suggest that what would really be going on has little to do with any individual items that I didn't buy. My actions would be saying something about the larger, deeper issue of my relationship with my wife.

So it is with us and God. We can't just say, "Oh well, I only broke seventeen of God's laws this week—that's not so bad." No, the issue is, what does it say about our relationship with God Himself if we knowingly disregard His law? What's going on between us and God?

The Bible presents God not simply as our passive Creator but as our jealous Lover. He wants *all* of us. For us to think that we can disregard Him sometimes, set Him and His ways aside when it suits us, is to show that we have not understood at all the nature of our relationship with God. We cannot claim to be believers and yet knowingly, repeatedly, and happily break His law.

But this is in fact the state we find ourselves in. We have crossed over the bounds that God has rightly set for our lives. We have contradicted both the letter and the spirit of His law. We not only feel guilt, we *are* guilty before Him. We not only feel conflicted in ourselves, we actually *are* in conflict with God. We break God's laws again and again because, as Paul reminds us, we are dead in our sins and transgressions (Eph. 2). The New Testament book of Romans begins with an argument all about this dilemma. In chapter 1, Paul lays out very clearly how the Gentiles have sinned. All of the people of the nations have sinned and broken God's laws, says Paul. But then, lest his Jewish readers begin to feel righteous, in chapter 2 he makes it clear that the Jews also have sinned. In fact, in the middle of chapter 2, he makes it clear that, really, anyone who claims to know right from wrong should know themselves well enough to know that they have sinned. In chapter 3, therefore, Paul draws the obvious conclusion:

> What shall we conclude then? Are we any better? Not at all!
> We have already made the charge that Jews and Gentiles alike
> are all under sin. As it is written:

> "There is no one righteous, not even one;
>   there is no one who understands,
>   no one who seeks God.
> All have turned away,
>   they have together become worthless;
>   there is no one who does good, not even one."
> "Their throats are open graves;
>   their tongues practice deceit."
> "The poison of vipers is on their lips."
> "Their mouths are full of cursing and bitterness."
> "Their feet are swift to shed blood;
>   ruin and misery mark their ways,

and the way of peace they do not know."
"There is no fear of God before their eyes."

Now we know that whatever the law says, it says to those
who are under the law, so that every mouth may be silenced
and the whole world held accountable to God. Therefore no
one will be declared righteous in his sight by observing the
law; rather, through the law we become conscious of sin
(Rom. 3:9-20).

Now all of this may be seeming much too grim to have anything
to do with something called the "Good News." But there is no doubt
that an accurate understanding of where we are now is essential to
getting to where we need to be. One of the early stages of becoming
a Christian involves beginning to realize that your problems fundamentally are not that you have messed up your own life or that you
have failed to realize your own potential, but that you have sinned,
not primarily against yourself or even against someone else, but
against God. And now, because of that, it begins to dawn on you that
you are yourself rightly the object of God's wrath, of His judgment—
that you deserve death, separation from God, spiritual alienation
from Him now and forever.

This is what the theologians have called depravity. It is the death
which deserves death. And yet, do you see why all of these wrongs
are so tragic? These are sins committed against a perfect, holy, loving
God. These are sins committed by creatures made in His image.

True Christianity is realistic about the dark side of our world, our
life, our nature, our heart. But true Christianity is not finally pes-
simistic or morally indifferent, encouraging us merely to just settle
in and accept the truth about our fallen state. No, the news that we
as Christians have to bring is not just that our depravity is so pervasive but also that God's plans for us are so wonderful—because He
knows what He made us for.

When you begin to realize that, you become thankful for the fact
that Christianity is not finally about anesthetizing you to life's pain,

or even about waking you up to it and teaching you to live with it. The message of Jesus Christ is about teaching us to live with a transforming longing, with a growing faith, with a sure and certain hope of what's to come. The Gospel is not simply that we're okay.

THE GOOD NEWS IS NOT SIMPLY THAT GOD IS LOVE

Other times, we may simply hear the Gospel represented as the message that "God is love." This is sort of like the headline in the Stillwater, Oklahoma, *News-Press:* "Cold weather causes temperatures to drop." Well, that may be news in Oklahoma, but upon reading such a statement one wonders if something has been left out. The Bible does say that "God is love" (1 John 4:8), but is that the whole story?

If you are a parent, you may have had the experience of telling your child not to do something only to have them respond, "If you loved me, you would let me do it." As adults, of course, we know that love doesn't always let. Indeed, sometimes love prevents and sometimes love even punishes. So if we say that "God is love," what are we thinking that such divine love must look like?

Furthermore, is love *all* that the Bible says God is? Doesn't the Bible say that God is a Spirit? How does a Spirit love? Doesn't the Bible say that God is holy? How does a Holy Spirit love? Doesn't the Bible say that God is unique, that there is none other like Him? How does the only perfect Holy Spirit in the universe . . . love? How can you know the answer to such questions if God doesn't tell you?

In the last chapter we saw how God presents Himself in the Bible as loving but also as creative and holy and faithful and sovereign. Consider this passage from the Westminster Confession, as it gathered together the biblical teachings about God:

> There is but one only living and true God, who is infinite in being and perfection, a most pure spirit, invisible, without body, parts, or passions, immutable, immense, eternal, incomprehensible, almighty, most wise, most holy, most free,

most absolute, working all things according to the counsel of his own immutable and most righteous will, for his own glory; most loving, most gracious, merciful, long-suffering, abundant in goodness and truth, forgiving iniquity, transgression, and sin; the rewarder of them that diligently seek him; and withal most just and terrible in his judgements; hating all sin, and who will by no means clear the guilty.

God hath all life, glory, goodness, blessedness, in and of himself; and is alone in and unto himself all-sufficient, not standing in need of any creatures which he hath made, not deriving any glory from them, but only manifesting his own glory, in, by, unto, and upon them: he is the alone fountain of all being, of whom, through whom, and to whom, are all things; and hath most sovereign dominion over them, to do by them, for them, or upon them, whatsoever himself pleaseth. In his sight all things are open and manifest; his knowledge is infinite, infallible, and independent upon the creature, so as nothing is to him contingent or uncertain. He is most holy in all his counsels, in all his works, and in all his commands. To him is due from angels and men, and every other creature, whatsoever worship, service, or obedience, he is pleased to require of them.

In the unity of the Godhead there be three persons, of one substance, power, and eternity; God the Father, God the Son, and God the Holy Ghost. The Father is of none, neither begotten nor proceeding; the Son is eternally begotten of the Father; the Holy Ghost eternally proceeding from the Father and the Son.[3]

This is the God who reveals Himself in the Bible. This confessional statement speaks of many things other than His love. It tells us, for instance, that God requires holiness of all who would be in a loving relationship with Him. As the Bible says, "Without holiness no one will see the Lord" (Heb. 12:14).

It is only in the context of thus understanding something of God's character, of His righteousness and perfection, that we begin to understand the depth of meaning in a statement such as "God is love." It is only as we thus contemplate the greatness of God that we begin to realize that His love has a depth, a texture, a fullness, and a beauty that we in our present state can only wonder at.

The Gospel is not simply that God is love.

THE GOOD NEWS IS NOT SIMPLY THAT JESUS WANTS TO BE OUR FRIEND

Other times, the Gospel is represented rather simply as, "Jesus wants to be our friend," or that He wants to be our example.

But the Christian Gospel is not a matter merely of cultivating a relationship or following an example. You and I have a real past to be dealt with—real sins that we have committed, real guilt that we have incurred. So what is to be done? What will our holy God do? If He wants us to come to know Him, how can He make that happen without sacrificing His own holiness?

Would He simply let us know that our sin against Him is no big deal? That He's big so He's just going to forgive and forget? It is interesting to discover, as we study the gospels, that Jesus taught, above everything else, that He came to earth specifically to die. How unusual this seems, and yet it is what Jesus presented as the center of His ministry—not teaching, or being an example, but, "The Son of Man did not come to be served, but to serve, and to give his life as a ransom for many" (Mark 10:45). Jesus taught that His choice to glorify the Father by His death on the Cross was central to His ministry. It is not surprising, then, that the Cross is the center and focus of all four gospels.

But what does that mean? And why would something so horrifying be at the center of something called the Good News? Well, very simply, because the Cross is God's way to bring us back to Himself.

Jesus begins to explain this event even before it happened. In Mark 8:27-38, He weaves together two strands of Old Testament prophecy that, to my knowledge, had not been brought together before—as He presents Himself as the son of man spoken of in Daniel 7 but also as the suffering servant from Isaiah 53:

> Jesus and his disciples went on to the villages around Caesarea Philippi. On the way he asked them, "Who do people say I am?"
>
> They replied, "Some say John the Baptist; others say Elijah; and still others, one of the prophets."
>
> "But what about you?" he asked. "Who do you say I am?"
>
> Peter answered, "You are the Christ."
>
> Jesus warned them not to tell anyone about him.
>
> He then began to teach them that the Son of Man must suffer many things and be rejected by the elders, chief priests and teachers of the law, and that he must be killed and after three days rise again. He spoke plainly about this, and Peter took him aside and began to rebuke him.
>
> But when Jesus turned and looked at his disciples, he rebuked Peter. "Get behind me, Satan!" he said. "You do not have in mind the things of God, but the things of men."
>
> Then he called the crowd to him along with his disciples and said, "If anyone would come after me, he must deny himself and take up his cross and follow me. For whoever wants to save his life will lose it, but whoever loses his life for me and for the gospel will save it. What good is it for a man to gain the whole world, yet forfeit his soul? Or what can a man give in exchange for his soul? If anyone is ashamed of me and my words in this adulterous and sinful generation, the Son of Man will be ashamed of him when he comes in his Father's glory with the holy angels."

Jesus' death is often presented as a sacrifice, involving His blood. So, for example, we read, "Now in Christ Jesus you who once were far away have been brought near through the blood of Christ" (Eph. 2:13; cf. Rom. 5:9; Col. 1:19-20). Jesus chose to die at Passover, to make it clear that He was dying as an atoning sacrifice.

What does all this have to do with our being enslaved to sin? We find out about this in the "economic" language used about Christ's death. When the Bible says that we are redeemed, it is saying we have been bought out of slavery. Just as God bought and brought Israel out of slavery, so we as Christians have been bought and brought out of slavery to sin. Christ's death was the price paid for our freedom from sin. Christ's death is how God has redeemed us from our slavery to sin. This is what much of Paul's letter to the Galatians is about.

Along with such *economic* terms, the Bible also uses *relational* language to describe Christ's death. Through Christ's death God has reconciled Himself to us—His rebellious creatures who were made in His image but have had a falling out with Him and so have destroyed the relationship. Through Christ's death, fellowship with God is restored as *sin*—the root cause of the hostility that exists between God and sinners—is dealt with.

The New Testament also uses *legal* language in relation to Christ's death, showing how His death deals with the reality of our guilt before God and the punishment we deserve. It uses terms such as justification—a declaration of "not guilty"—describing the events of Christ's death in terms of our penalty being transferred to Him.

And there is *military* language as well, as we see the world portrayed as a spiritual battlefield. We are told, concerning Christ's death on the Cross, that He "disarmed the powers and authorities" (Col. 2:15; cf. Mark 3:22-27; John 16:33; 19:30; Rom. 8:39; 1 Cor. 15:54-57; Rev. 5:5; see also all the stories in the gospels of deliverance from demon possession).

So, the work of Christ is described as redemption—a purchase by which the liberty of certain oppressed people is secured. The work of Christ is described as reconciliation—where the enmity is resolved between two people. The work of Christ is described as a propitiation—an assuaging of God's just wrath against people for their sins. God's wrath is assuaged so that He can deal justly with sinners in terms of His love rather than in terms of His wrath.

In the New Testament none of this language refers to something that is merely potential or that is merely a possibility or an option; rather, it refers to God actually having accomplished His end and His purpose through Christ's death. The point of all these images is that the benefit has not merely been made available; it has been secured by Christ's death on the Cross and His resurrection to life.

There's no getting around the fact that the center of Christ's ministry was His death on the Cross, and that at the heart of that death was God's certainty that He was effectively dealing with the claims both of His love and of His justice. You see, Christ isn't just our friend. To call Him that as His supreme title is to offer Him "faint praise." Christ is our friend, but He is so much more. By His death on the Cross, Christ has become the Lamb that was slain for us, our Redeemer, the One who has made peace between us and God, who has taken our guilt on Himself, who has conquered our most deadly enemy and has assuaged the well-deserved wrath of God.

So much of this imagery comes together in the magnificence of John's final vision on Patmos:

> Then one of the elders said to me, "Do not weep! See, the Lion of the tribe of Judah, the Root of David, has triumphed. He is able to open the scroll and its seven seals."
>
> Then I saw a Lamb, looking as if it had been slain, standing in the center of the throne, encircled by the four living creatures and the elders. . . . He came and took the scroll from the right hand of him who sat on the throne. And when he had taken it, the four living creatures and the twenty-four elders fell down before the Lamb. Each one had a harp and they were holding golden bowls full of incense, which are the prayers of the saints. And they sang a new song:
>
> "You are worthy to take the scroll
>   and to open its seals,
> because you were slain,
>   and with your blood you purchased men for God
>   from every tribe and language and people
>   and nation" (Rev. 5:5-9).

The Gospel is not simply that Jesus is your friend.

THE GOOD NEWS IS NOT SIMPLY THAT
WE SHOULD LIVE RIGHT

One more common error is the idea that the Bible's "Good News" is simply that we should start living right. It is sometimes presented that Christianity is all about virtues public and private. Christians, it is thought, are busy doing religious things and good works: baptism and communion, going to church, obeying the Ten Commandments and the Golden Rule, reading our Bibles and praying; or good works such as building up the community, giving to others, contributing to soup kitchens, and not tearing down historical buildings to make room for parking lots.

But as startling as it may be to this kind of thinking, the biblical Gospel is not fundamentally about such things. To be a Christian is not merely to live in love, follow the Golden Rule, or practice "possibility thinking"—or indeed to do anything that we can do ourselves.

The Gospel calls for a more radical response than any of these things allow for. The Gospel isn't merely an "additive" that can make our already good lives better. No, the Gospel is a message of wonderful Good News for those who know and realize their desperation before God.

So what response does the Gospel call for? What should you do when your own sense of need, your understanding of who God is and of who Jesus is and what He has done . . . when these things all begin to come together, what should be your response? According to the Bible, your response should be to repent and believe. God calls us to repent of our sins, and to rely on Christ alone. Let's consider both of these briefly.

Repentance

We often find repentance and belief mentioned together in the New Testament. As Paul was meeting with the leaders of the church in Ephesus, he summarized the message he had preached in this way:

"I have declared to both Jews and Greeks that they must turn to God in repentance and have faith in our Lord Jesus" (Acts 20:21). This is the message you see very clearly throughout the New Testament. Once you have heard the truth about your sin and God's holiness, about His love in sending Christ, and about Christ's death and resurrection for our justification, then you are called to respond.

And what is the prescribed response? Is it to walk down an aisle? Is it to fill out a card, or to lift up a hand? Is it to make an appointment with a preacher, or to decide to be baptized and join the church? While any of those things may be involved, none of them necessarily is. The response to the Good News—the message that Paul preached and other Christians preached throughout the New Testament—is to repent and believe. Once we've heard the truth about our own sin and God's holiness, about His love in sending Christ, and about Christ's death and resurrection for our justification, then, as instructed by the first words of Jesus recorded in Mark's gospel, our response is to "Repent and believe the good news!" (1:15).

Belief

Along with repentance comes belief. First, we must honestly think that what the Gospel says is true. We must believe it in that sense. But there is much more to it than that. You can believe, for example, that the Angel Falls of Venezuela are nearly twenty times higher than Niagara Falls, or you can believe that a spider's web will help clot your blood if you have a bad wound. You can believe those things and they may in fact be true. Did you know that inhabitants of Iceland read more books per person per year than the inhabitants of any other country? Or that Sir Christopher Wren only had six months of training as an architect? But none of these kinds of believing are the believing that Jesus means here.

The belief that Jesus enjoins is not a mere mental assent; it is believing in and fully relying on the Good News of salvation. We must come to grips with the fact that we are unable to satisfy God's demands on us no matter how morally we live. We shouldn't end up trusting a little in ourselves and a little in God; we should come to realize that we must rely on God fully, to trust in Christ alone for our salvation.

Such a true believing and relying on makes a difference, and so this belief demands not only faith but also repentance; it demands that our lives actually change. Repentance and faith are actually the two sides of the same coin. It is not as though you can have the basic model (belief) and then, if you really want to get holy at some later time, start adding some repentance to it. No, that's not what's talked about here at all. "Repent" is what you do when you begin thinking rightly about God and yourself—belief without this kind of change is counterfeit. J. C. Ryle put it well when he said, "There is a common worldly kind of Christianity in this day, which many have, and think they have enough—a cheap Christianity which offends nobody, and requires no sacrifice—which costs nothing, and is worth nothing."[4]

The repentance that Jesus calls for here is connected, of course, with believing this news, because if it is a new message, it is no surprise that you change your mind when you hear it. The word for "repent" is *metanoia* and means literally "to change your mind." And because your mind changes, your life changes, too.

So, you see, real Christianity is never simply an addition, it is not merely a cultivation of something that has always been there. Rather, it is in some radical sense an about-face, a turning around. It is a turning around that all Christians make as we come to rely on Christ's finished work on the Cross. To say that you trust, without living as though you do, is not to trust in any biblical sense of the word. We change the way we act, but only because we change what we believe. Such change is the work of God's Spirit. We'll think about that in our next chapter.

I hope that all this has helped you understand that the Good News of Christianity has a specific, cognitive content. It is not simply a religious enthusiasm. It is not simply a deep personal intuition. It is news—news that says something about ourselves, about God, about Jesus. It is either right or wrong. Either we are sinful (as the

Bible claims) or we are not sinful. Either God does or does not exist. Either He is or He is not who the Bible says He is. Either Jesus did die on the Cross and rise from the dead or He did not.

In our own local church, I always ask prospective members to tell me the Gospel in one minute or less (unlike what I've done in this chapter!). I do that because I want it to be clear. I want people to know the Gospel, to understand what they're saying. Have you stopped and thought recently about what you claim to believe if you are a Christian? B. B. Warfield described it this way:

> A dozen ignorant peasants proclaiming a crucified Jew as the founder of a new faith; bearing as the symbol of their worship an instrument which was the sign of ignominy, slavery and crime; preaching what must have seemed an absurd doctrine of humility, patient suffering and love to enemies— graces undreamed of before; demanding what must have seemed an absurd worship for one who had died like a malefactor and a slave, and making what must have seemed an absurd promise of everlasting life through one who had himself died, and that between two thieves.[5]

As extraordinary as this message is, it is true. It really happened this way. This is what God has done. These other messages—"I'm O.K., you're O.K.," "Whatever you think of as love is God," "Jesus is your friend," "You should live right"—these messages are messages other than the Good News of Christianity. They are half true at best, and they are dangerously *untrue* when they are relied on as the Christian Gospel. But this Good News of Christ's death on the Cross as an atoning sacrifice for the sins of all those who would ever turn and trust in Him—this good news is not make-believe. This is for real!

So, what do you say about all this? Over the years, I've quoted many skeptical responses to the claims of Christianity, or indeed to any claims to truth.

"I don't believe in truth. I believe in style," said English actor Hugh Grant.[6]

"Whatever is, is right," maintained the Marquis de Sade.

We must not imagine that such responses are non-responses. Or that such responses have no consequences. As Dostoyevsky said, "If God didn't exist, everything would be possible"[7]

I fear for our nation. There's a popular suspicion abroad that the Christian Gospel, as expressed by evangelicals, is a threat to our freedoms. Go and study the history of Germany and note what kind of Christianity reigned for a century before Nazism. It was not a Christianity of absolute truths from an absolute God. It was a compromising, moralizing, relativizing kind of Christianity offering a gospel that could be shaped by human hands and human thoughts. What we should really fear, as a nation but primarily as individuals, are the consequences of ignoring the Gospel. For the day will come for each one of us when our time for responding is over, when our time for evaluating the claims of God is done, when *His* time of evaluating *us* finally comes.

John Wesley once mused on earthly greatness:

> I was in the robe-chamber, adjoining to the House of Lords, when the King put on his robes. His brow was much furrowed with age, and quite clouded with care. And is this all the world can give even to a King? All the grandeur it can afford? A blanket of ermine around his shoulders, so heavy and cumbersome he can scarce move under it! A huge heap of borrowed hair, with a few plates of gold and glittering stones upon his head! Alas, what a bauble is human greatness! And even this will not endure.[8]

As one T-shirt says, "He who dies with the most toys still dies."

Who dies? The guy with the toys, and the guy with the T-shirt. The king and John Wesley. Dostoyevsky and de Sade. The architect and the actor. You and me. At this point, the mortality rate shows no sign of dropping: One out of one still dies.

Have we heard the Gospel? Have we believed it with our lives or are we still playing at religion? Do we attend church occasionally when our curiosity is up or our guilt is aroused, while regularly and with great satisfaction serving first of all ourselves?

To really hear the Gospel is to be shaken to your core. To really hear the Gospel is to change. Have you heard the Gospel—not a soothing word about your goodness, or about God's acceptance, or about Jesus' inoffensive willingness to befriend all and sundry, or even some convicting word about getting rid of some sin in your life—but have you heard the Bible's great message about God and us? Does it sound like the best news you've ever heard? Old sins forgiven! New life begun! A personal relationship with your God, your Creator, now and forever!

What better news could you hear?

WHAT'S COMING UP . . .

A BIBLICAL UNDERSTANDING
OF CONVERSION

"I'm not the man I used to be. Can you ever forgive me?"

That was what one man said to a woman thirteen years after being charged with raping her. Had you known that man or had you heard of the case against him, would you have believed his claim that he had changed? I suspect most people would be somewhat skeptical, not just toward that one repentant man but toward anyone who claims to have changed in any deep and lasting way. People today are skeptical that anyone can really change. Politicians, lawyers, preachers, professors, reporters, lobbyists—all have their predetermined vices, don't they?

For many today, wisdom is seen as learning to accept your internal circumstances, to adjust to them, to adapt to them—not to try to fundamentally change them. The die is cast, the lot is fixed, our personality is assigned, and except for some terrible trauma, the assumption is that the leopard does not change his spots, the anxious person his personality, or the insecure person his psyche. "That's the way it is!" Maturity comes from facing up to the truth about yourself and resigning yourself to it.

Any suggestion that you can change *deeply* is regarded with serious suspicion. Any such suggestion is taken to be a potentially sinister tool of manipulation in the hands of those who would coerce you into conformity to their standards by cultivating in you self-hatred, a loathing of some characteristic of your self, whether it be your sexual desires, your vocational ambitions, your ethical standards, or your religious beliefs. We are who we are, so they say, and we should be proud of it!

But for all of this uncertainty and suspicion about the possibility of change, people do have a deep longing for change. There's a restlessness about the slings and arrows of outrageous fortune and, if the truth were known, a dissatisfaction with ourselves that is as widespread as it is deep-seated. We are not content, so we rearrange the furniture, paint the hallway, or buy new clothes. If things then just get worse, we wonder about changing where we live. We ask for flexible hours at our job, or even to change jobs. Sometimes we might even long for changing our spouse. Today even those more traditionally fixed boundaries of sexuality and of life itself are transgressed in a vain attempt to find satisfaction. And yet, as work conditions and jobs, marriages and families, and even gender and death become subject to our own choices, we seem to find ourselves defeated, trapped, and hopeless.

So are the cynics right? Is any real change impossible?

What does the Bible say about deep, real, personal change? In the context of this book, of course, we are talking about the change—you could call it "the great change"—that takes place in conversion. A biblical understanding of conversion is one characteristic of a healthy church, and as we consider what conversion is all about—as we seek a biblical understanding of conversion—we will do so by asking five questions.

IS CHANGE NEEDED?

First we must ask, is change needed?

Many will immediately answer no to such a question. Many will choose complacency about our human condition. When confronted with the idea that they might need some great alteration in their life, many will simply say, "Why change? You shouldn't impose your ideas on others, you know. Besides, you're surely not suggesting that *your* way of living, *your* way of looking at the world, is any better than mine? If you are suggesting that, you must be some kind of self-righteous hypocrite! I'll kindly thank you to manage your own neuroses and leave me to mine!"

Be that as it may, the Bible clearly teaches that change is needed, that we are not "just fine." In fact, the Bible teaches that we're in trouble.

A reporter a couple of years ago asked Sam Perkins (at the time with the Seattle SuperSonics), "How will you rebound from your thirty-five-point loss?"

Perkins replied: "We just have to maintain our consistency."

Of course, consistency in losing won't do.

We considered in our last study something of the depth of our moral desperation before God. Jesus said, "Light has come into the world, but men loved darkness instead of light because their deeds were evil. Everyone who does evil hates the light, and will not come into the light for fear that his deeds will be exposed" (John 3:19-20).

Paul reminded the Ephesian Christians that before they were converted they were dead in their sins and transgressions (Eph. 2:1). And he taught clearly that this spiritual death was shared by all humanity. You'll recall from the last chapter how Paul quotes the Old Testament in a sweeping denunciation of any claim we might make to being righteous in and of ourselves:

What shall we conclude then? Are we any better? Not at all! We have already made the charge that Jews and Gentiles alike are all under sin. As it is written:

"There is no one righteous, not even one;
    there is no one who understands,
    no one who seeks God.
All have turned away,
    they have together become worthless;
    there is no one who does good, not even one."

"Their throats are open graves;
  their tongues practice deceit."
"The poison of vipers is on their lips."
"Their mouths are full of cursing and bitterness."
"Their feet are swift to shed blood;
  ruin and misery mark their ways,
and the way of peace they do not know."
"There is no fear of God before their eyes."

Now we know that whatever the law says, it says to those who are under the law, so that every mouth may be silenced and the whole world held accountable to God. Therefore no one will be declared righteous in his sight by observing the law; rather, through the law we become conscious of sin (Rom. 3:9-20).

Now consider these twin truths: We are in desperate need of God's grace; and yet God owes His grace to no one. That's the very nature of grace—it is not something owed. What God owes us is justice for our sins.

And when God's Spirit begins powerfully to call us to turn from our sins, there is a great sense of conviction. We begin to sense something of the seriousness of sin.

It is not that you become spiritually paranoid and begin to imagine that you have committed more sins than you had previously realized (though in a sense you do begin to do this). What really happens, as God's Spirit begins to convict you in this way, is that, as He brings a particular sin to your attention, that particular sin seems more serious than it did before. You begin to realize the seriousness of sin, particularly the seriousness of its deadly character as an act of revolt against God Himself. You begin to feel like the psalmist who prayed, "Against you, you only have I sinned and done what is evil in your sight, so that you are proved right when you speak, and justified when you judge" (Psalm 51:4).

When you read through the Bible and look at the images God

uses about the state of our human nature, these images are quite radical—images of being in debt, in slavery, bankrupt, even dead. This is what the Bible presents as our condition, our situation. We are in a disastrous situation, and we had best get out of it. Clearly, a change is needed.

IS CHANGE REALLY POSSIBLE?

But then comes this second question: We agree that a change is needed; but is such a change really possible?

Here, as we have seen, many are skeptical. We are the way we are, it is thought, and maturity comes in simply accepting this idea. Maybe we need to do a little work on reintegrating our personalities, but it is manifestly unhelpful, really, to get up hopes that any kind of fundamental change will occur. Any idea that you can deeply change is only a deception. Our secular mindset does not allow for any such hope of change. Our resources are limited to the narrow scope of this world, and within this world and in our own power we find no evidence that self-transformation is even possible. And if you say that you're looking for help from beyond this world, well, people are going to wonder if you're talking about UFOs. There will be the kind of bemused acceptance that you'd find upon introducing your invisible friend "Bert" at a dinner party.

Is fundamental change just a fantasy? Not according to the Bible. The Bible says not only that we need change, but that change is possible. God has made us all, each and every one, with a capacity to know, love, and serve Him; and the Bible teaches that we should admit that we are on a course away from God, and that we should change that course in order to return to Him. And this, we're taught, can really be done.

How many of us have marveled as we've thought about the Gospel as the possibility of really having a new start? We're amazed that God can actually give us a fresh start, a new life, once we have spent this one. But that's what we find in the New Testament. That's the great news. As amazing as it may seem to us, from John 3 to Acts

9 to Ephesians 2 to 1 Peter 1 and on and on and on, we find this amazing message.

According to the Bible, this is a crucial part of the Good News: Change is possible.

WHAT CHANGE IS NEEDED?

A third, more specific question is, What change is needed?

Many who concede that they need to change say that they really just need to be more uninhibited about serving themselves, perhaps—to learn better how to marshal their resources to meet their goals. Gandhi, when he spoke of conversion, said that the crying need of our times is the conversion of self-purification and self-realization. Many would say that our problems come only from this—our confused inability to do what we want to do—and any change, any conversion must simply be one that helps us to fulfill our own potential. Any change must simply reinforce ourselves; it should never fundamentally alter ourselves or convict us of wrong.

Robert Jenson has reflected on our tolerant society's strange intolerance to Christian conversion:

> Imagine yourself at a dinner party in Manhattan or in a college town in Minnesota and relate two conversions, one to Christianity and the other away from it, and see what will happen; one will be received as a tale of horrid narrow-mindedness and the other as an example of an open society's marvelous possibilities.[1]

But the Bible says that the change we need is not merely to "discover" ourselves, but to *turn*. The word *repent* in the Old and New Testaments literally means to turn. It means to turn *from* our sin and *to* the one true God. We need to resign our claim to be the final judges and governors of our own lives, and acknowledge that that role belongs to God alone. Our past sins need to be forgiven. Our present lives need to be reoriented. Our future destiny needs to be changed from the hell of God's righteous judgment to the heaven of God's gracious forgiveness in Christ.

This is the great change that we need. It is not just adjusting our lives to ourselves and our own desires. It is adjusting our lives to God and His ways with us. It is acknowledging His claims upon us. As someone has said, the first step toward the one true God is to acknowledge that we are not that God.

It is in this great change that we are saved. We understand our state apart from this change to be dire, and so we call this change conversion, or salvation. We call it being born again.

The real change that we need is this conversion from worshiping ourselves to worshiping God, from being guilty in ourselves before God to being forgiven in Christ. This is the change we need.

WHAT WILL THIS CHANGE INVOLVE?

This brings us to the fourth question we should consider about conversion: What will this change involve?

Mental Acceptance?

Many say that conversion is merely a mental acceptance. We simply need to make a decision, walk down an aisle, fill out a card, pray a prayer. The change, as they conceive of it, may be fairly slight. It may involve beginning to cherish some moral sentiments, joining the church, enlisting yourself in programs and activities, volunteering to help the needy. It's sort of a large version of a New Year's resolution.

But the Bible says the great change that we need involves much more: It involves a turning from our sins and a turning to God. It involves repenting of our sins and following God. Conversion includes both the change of the heart toward God that is repentance, and the belief and trust in Christ and His Word that is faith. As a pastor, this is where I fear many go wrong today; and they go wrong in one of two different ways.

First, there is the problem of people who don't think that

they're converted when they really are. Yes, there are such people. They know that the Scriptures teach that Christians will not be given over to sin, and so whenever they sin they feel the accusation of the devil and they tend to agree with him that perhaps they are not truly Christians. But my poor, doubting friend, if this is you, if you are quick to agree with the charges of the devil whenever you sin, let me urge you not to leave off so quickly recognizing God's goodness to you, the good work that He has done in your heart, the work that perhaps even your friends have seen God doing in you. We can join with Joan of Arc in her prayer, as she was asked a tricky, entrapping question by some judges: "Asked if she knew that she was in God's grace, she replied: 'If I am not, may it please God to put me in it; if I am, may it please God to keep me there.'" That would be a good prayer for each of us. The truly changed, truly converted, truly Christian heart can say with John Newton, "I am not what I ought to be. I am not what I wish to be. I am not what I hope to be. Yet I can truly say, I am not what I once was. By the grace of God, I am what I am."

The other problem, I have to confess, worries me even more: the problem of people who think they are converted when really they are not. Every pastor knows this problem as well. You have perhaps heard the story of Spurgeon, the great pastor in nineteenth-century London, who was walking down the street one day when a man who was drunken and leaning on the lamppost yelled out to him, "Hey, Mr. Spurgeon, do you remember me?" And Spurgeon replied, "No, why should I?" The man said, "Because I'm one of your converts." To which Spurgeon responded, "Well, you must be one of mine; you're certainly not one of the Lord's."

As a pastor, Spurgeon was well acquainted with this problem, particularly among people who had gone to church enough to learn to talk differently—to talk the Bible and talk Christianity—but whose hearts hadn't changed so that they lived differently. In one sermon he characterized these people who were sure that they had been converted and were happy to talk about it, even though their lives didn't seem to reflect it:

They say they are saved, and they stick to it they are, and think it wicked to doubt it; but yet they have no reason to warrant their confidence. There are those who are ready to be fully assured; there are others to whom it will be death to talk of it. There is a great difference between presumption and full assurance. Full assurance is reasonable: it is based on solid ground. Presumption takes for granted, and with brazen face pronounces that to be its own which it has no right to whatsoever. Beware, I pray thee, of presuming that thou art saved. If with thy heart thou dost trust in Jesus, then thou art saved; but if thou merely sayest, "I trust in Jesus," it doth not save thee. If thy heart be renewed, if thou shalt hate the things that thou didst once love, and love the things that thou didst once hate; if thou hast really repented; if there be a thorough change of mind in thee; if thou be born again, then hast thou reason to rejoice: but if there be no vital change, no inward godliness; if there be no love to God, no prayer, no work of the Holy Spirit, then thy saying, "I am saved," is but thine own assertion, and it may delude, but it will not deliver thee. Our prayer ought to be, "Oh that thou wouldst bless me indeed, with real faith, with real salvation, with the trust in Jesus that is the essential of faith; not with the conceit that begets credulity. God preserve us from imaginary blessings!"[2]

We must realize that it is possible to be an active member of a local church and yet not truly be a member of the people of God.

Moral Resolve?

Others believe that conversion is all about living a good life. It is an effort to be more moral—a collection and codification of my moral resolutions. It is taking responsibility to craft my own morality, my own goodness, my own righteousness. It means I've got to simply start resolving my moral dilemmas, cleaning up my act, making myself more acceptable in God's sight. It means no more messing around.

Mere relying on Christ

According to the Bible, however, the real change of Christian conversion involves relying on Christ alone. We are not simply to try to justify ourselves before God, to improve our life a little bit here and a little bit there, and think that somehow such changes will hide our sins from God or will make our hearts appear righteous before Him. Instead of this, in true conversion we begin to rest in Christ, to trust in Him and in His merits before God. This great change is all about realizing that we can never go to church enough, we can never teach enough Sunday school classes, we can never give enough money, we can never be kind enough or beautiful enough or happy and contented with our religious lives enough to merit God's good will toward us.

We must realize that, because of our sin, we are truly desperate before God. Regardless of how prosperous our outward situation may seem to be, we are truly desperate before God. Our only hope comes in understanding that God has taken on flesh in Christ, that Christ lived a perfect life and died on the Cross in the place of all those who would ever turn and trust in Him, and that He rose in victory over our sins and now offers to pour out His Holy Spirit into our hearts. Beginning to have this reliance, this trust in God alone, is the nature of the great change that takes place in conversion.

We must repent of our sins and trust in Christ.

HOW DOES THIS GREAT CHANGE HAPPEN?

All this brings us to the final question: How does this great change of conversion happen?

We Do Nothing?

Some say that, to be converted, we need do nothing. If we do not save ourselves, they reason, then it is a simple fact that God has saved us. The story is told that, when the famous theologian Karl Barth met with Billy Graham during a series of evangelistic meetings in Switzerland, Barth told Graham that he liked Graham's message except for one thing: Barth urged Graham to tell people, not that they must be saved, but that they were already saved in Christ!

But the Bible teaches, as we have seen, that in the process of conversion we must do something. Jesus didn't exhort His followers simply to stop striving and to realize that they were in a right relation with God by His grace. Jesus didn't tell His followers to begin a course of self-examination to see if they could discern any signs of God's grace in their lives. No, Jesus told everyone that they must turn from their sins and turn to God. From the very beginning of His ministry, Jesus told people that the great conversion that they need is to turn away from their sins and to God.

So, is conversion simply a matter of exercising our will?

We Do Everything?

Do we simply need to make a decision? And if that's the case, then must we be *able* to make this decision? According to the Bible, it is clear that we should make this decision ourselves, and that we should encourage everyone we know to make this decision for themselves. So shouldn't we persuade them and urge them to make this decision? Shouldn't we perhaps even pressure them? To put it bluntly, shouldn't we manipulate them? If we can actually get people to make a decision that will change their eternity, then shouldn't we? If we can manipulate them into forsaking their sins and embracing God and trusting in Him, then shouldn't we?

Ironically, even we evangelicals often imagine the great change of conversion to be a kind of religious self-help. But if we read our Bibles, we know that Christianity does not preach self-salvation.

God Works This Saving Faith in Us

Perhaps every other religion on the planet preaches self-salvation, but Christianity does not. And here's the great puzzle for many: The Bible says that this change is really a matter of our character, of our heart changing. That's the change we need. That's the change that must be effected. But the Bible also teaches that we will not begin making these right choices if God does not first change our heart. We have the ability to love and to obey God. We were made with it, having it as part of being made in His image. The problem, though, is in our hearts. We do not choose to do what we are formally able to do. And so we need God to give us new hearts.

And we find in the Bible that that is exactly what God has promised to do: "I will give them an undivided heart and put a new spirit in them; I will remove from them their heart of stone and give them a heart of flesh" (Ezek. 11:19). We find this idea throughout the Bible. This kind of heart-transplanting is God's work. And He must work this change in us if we are to accept the spiritual truths of the Bible (see 1 Cor. 2:14). As Jesus said, "No one can come to me unless the Father who sent me draws him" (John 6:44).

Christians sometimes talk about being "born again." Did you ever think about that language? We get that language from Jesus Himself. It wasn't a marketing ploy of the Southern Baptist Convention back in the 1970s. No, it comes right from Jesus, in John chapter 3. He's the one who comes up with the image. In John 3 we read of a very religious leader named Nicodemus who came to speak to Jesus. This leader wanted to know what he must do to see the kingdom of God, and Jesus didn't say that he should simply keep up the good work, keep living a good, moral, religious life, or keep teaching. No, Jesus said, in fact, that this leader needed a whole new life. Nicodemus asked Jesus how anyone could get such a new life, and Jesus said that only God could give it, and so Nicodemus must simply believe in Jesus and live by the truth.

Jesus taught clearly that we must act, but He also taught that we can act only if God's actions are behind our own. In so teaching, Jesus reflected the Old Testament. For example, look at the book of Joel. Joel was a prophet through whom the Lord prophesied great judgment. But Joel also offered words of hope: "Everyone who calls on the name of the LORD will be saved" (Joel 2:32). Paul quotes that verse in Romans 10, and if you have ever shared the Gospel with anyone you may very well have quoted that verse yourself: "Everyone who calls on the name of the LORD will be saved." Now, Joel had just been writing for two chapters about the judgment that was coming upon the Israelites for their unbelief. But why would such unbelievers call on the Lord in this saving way? We find the answer in the rest of verse 32: "Everyone who calls on the name of the LORD will be saved; for on Mount Zion and in Jerusalem there will be deliverance, as the LORD has said, among the survivors whom the LORD calls." Who calls on the name of the Lord? Those whom the Lord calls!

In 1 Corinthians 1:18-24, we again find that it is God's call that makes the crucial difference. Most Jews and most Gentiles, says Paul, consider the Gospel foolish. But "those whom God has called, both Jews and Greeks" consider the Gospel to be "the wisdom of God."

More than a hundred years ago, a group of men and women who lived on Capitol Hill in Washington, D.C., began meeting together for prayer. They committed themselves to begin the church where I am presently a pastor. At that meeting they set out clearly what they believed the Bible taught, including what they believed it taught about this great change that they had known in their own lives and that they wanted to see happen in the lives of the people around them. They expressed their belief about conversion in the words of the New Hampshire Confession of Faith, Article VIII:

> We believe that Repentance and Faith are sacred duties, and also inseparable graces, wrought in our souls by the regenerating Spirit of God; whereby being deeply convinced of our guilt, danger and helplessness, and of the way of salvation by Christ, we *turn* to God with unfeigned contrition, confession, and supplication for mercy; at the same time heartily receiving the Lord Jesus Christ as our Prophet,

Priest and King, and *relying* on Him alone as the only and all sufficient Saviour.[3]

Notice what this statement says about conversion. We turn because we are "deeply convinced of our guilt, danger and helplessness, and of the way of salvation by Christ." And how does that turning happen? It is "wrought in our souls by the regenerating Spirit of God." The statement then cited two Scriptures to support this idea. It cited Acts 11:18, where the apostles are reflecting on the conversion of Cornelius the Gentile: "When they heard this, they had no further objections and praised God, saying, 'So then, God has granted even the Gentiles repentance unto life.'" And it cited Ephesians 2:8: "It is by grace you have been saved, through faith—and this not from yourselves, it is the gift of God."

Ephesians 2 is a particularly important passage about conversion. According to the Bible, repentance is a gift of God and faith is a gift of God, given not because of our merit but because of Christ's merit. If you would have the gifts of repentance and faith, simply turn from your sins and turn to God in Christ.

One of the main things the Bible says about this great change, this conversion, is that it normally comes through studying God's Word. We recall what the psalmist says in Psalm 19:7:

The law of the LORD is perfect, reviving the soul.
The statutes of the LORD are trustworthy,
    making wise the simple.

Again and again we find in the Bible that conversions come through the preaching of and lively listening to the Word of God. He has promised that it will be this way:

"As the rain and the snow come down from heaven,
and do not return to it without watering the earth
and making it bud and flourish,
    so that it yields seed for the sower and bread for the eater,

so is my word that goes out of my mouth:
It will not return to me empty,
but will accomplish what I desire
and achieve the purpose for which I sent it" (Isa. 55:10-11).

Consider this carefully: God would not promise this, if He were
not the one ultimately responsible for bearing the fruit, for our conversion, for our response to Him. That's why we read in the book of
Acts that, as a result of the Gospel being proclaimed in Antioch, "All
who were appointed for eternal life believed" (Acts 13:48). Neither
we who are converted nor those who brought the Gospel to us can
take any credit. If any have come to know God under the sound of
my preaching of the Word of God, I cannot go back and put a notch
on my belt, because I know that the One who converts is not the
preacher. The one who converts ultimately is God Himself.

We are called to tell people that they must turn to God. But we
must understand that in doing this God is calling us to talk to a bunch
of corpses! That is how the Bible describes our natural state: We are
spiritually dead, as we saw in Ephesians 2. So how can those who are
spiritually dead ever turn to God in faith? They can do so only if God
gives them life. And how does God give them life? We find throughout both the Old and the New Testaments that God has chosen to
give life to the spiritually dead through our proclaiming His Word to
them. We have seen this in Ezekiel 37, the vision of the valley of dry
bones. There God gives Ezekiel a vision of going and preaching to a
valley full of corpses. But through that very preaching of His Word,
His spirit goes out and He brings life.

One of the most amazing New Testament examples of this is in
Acts 10, where we see God desiring to bring the Gentile centurion
Cornelius to Himself. You would think that would be a pretty
straightforward matter for the sovereign God of the universe. God
could just directly, immediately "zap" Cornelius. But for some reason God didn't do that. For some reason God decided to work as He
had worked throughout the whole Bible. God would not convert
Cornelius without someone who knows God's Word himself com-

ing and telling Cornelius the Good News. So God gave Cornelius a vision. Cornelius had to send some of his men to another city to find Peter. God then sent another vision to Peter, to convince him that it was okay to talk to a Gentile about Jesus. He then got Peter to accompany the angel back to Cornelius.

Now, that's doing things the long way around! Why God does it this way I don't know; but you will find in your Bible again and again that God does things this way. When God would bring life, He does it through His Word. He does it through the Good News of Jesus Christ, through you and me telling people around us the truth about the great change we can have in Christ. This is how God does it. This is how it has always been. God could have simply saved Cornelius directly, but He chose to do it as He has always done, through His Word and through human agents. He went to quite some trouble to do this, involving angels and visions and people traveling great distances to proclaim God's Word. As Peter himself would later observe, "You have been born again, not of perishable seed, but of imperishable, through the living and enduring word of God" (1 Pet. 1:23).

God has always done it this way, from Noah, to Abraham, to Moses, to the nation of Israel, to Jesus calling His disciples. As Jesus explained to His disciples, "You did not choose me, but I chose you . . . to go and bear fruit" (John 15:16). This is how God has always worked.

We are reminded also of Peter's words at Pentecost: "The promise is for you and your children and for all who are far off—for all whom the Lord our God will call" (Acts 2:39).

Later in Acts, Paul spoke to a gathering of women in Philippi, among whom was the merchant Lydia. Lydia heard the Gospel, but in order to find salvation she would need to respond. And of course she did, but how did it happen? We are told that, "The Lord opened her heart to respond to Paul's message" (Acts 16:14).

And speaking of Paul, didn't Paul himself know something about God's initiative in salvation? He was knocked off his horse while on his way to persecute Christians! God in His love took the initiative to reveal Himself to Paul.

We could continue finding examples of this from the Bible, but the point is clear. Again and again God has shown the truth of what John wrote: "This is love: not that we loved God, but that he loved us and sent his Son as an atoning sacrifice for our sins" (1 John 4:10).

We show that we understand God's initiative in salvation whenever we pray that He will save a particular person, that He will "bring them to Himself." We know that it is God who saves, so we pray that God in His great love will pour out His Spirit that the Gospel will be faithfully preached, and that He will save people.

Do you see why understanding this is important for your own spiritual health, and for the spiritual health of any church you would be involved with? If our conversion, our turning, is basically understood to be something we do ourselves instead of being something God does in us, then we misunderstand it. Conversion certainly includes our own actions. We must make a sincere commitment. We must make a self-conscious decision. Even so, conversion—real conversion—is more than that. Scripture is clear in teaching that we are not all journeying toward God—some having found Him, others still seeking. Instead, Scripture presents us as needing to have our hearts replaced, our minds transformed, our spirits given life. We can do none of this for ourselves. The change each human needs, regardless of how we may outwardly appear, is so radical, so near our roots, that only God can bring it about. We need God to convert us.

I fear that one of the results of misunderstanding the Bible's teaching on conversion may well be that evangelical churches are full of people who have made sincere commitments at some point in their lives but who have not experienced the radical change that the Bible calls conversion. According to one recent study by the Southern Baptist Sunday School Board, Southern Baptists have a divorce rate equal to or even slightly above the national average in America. Another more recent national study suggests that the "Bible Belt" states are among the highest in the nation in divorce rates. Why is this the case? Whence comes this "reverse witness"? Could it have come about in part because the pastors in our churches have not preached the truth about conversion—perhaps out of a concern simply to have larger churches? Or perhaps they simply haven't understood what a real, radical change is required, what conversion truly is. And so, our churches have come to resemble Elks Clubs and Moose Lodges more than churches of the truly regenerated. The cause of such a negative witness among reputed followers of Christ must be at least in part the unbiblical preaching about conversion by many pastors—with blame to be shared by the church congregations that have allowed them to do that.

According to the Bible, our repentance and faith are gifts of God to us; our conversion, our great change, occurs only by God's grace.

We see that change is both needed and possible. And the change that we need is a change from living guilt-incurring lives of sin, to living forgiven lives of trust in Christ. To do this we must repent of our sins and trust in Christ. And this can happen only by God's grace through the preaching of His Word.

Now, as I have cited various examples from the Bible of how Christian conversion occurs, you may have begun to wonder whether such change has ever happened outside of the Bible. The good news for you is that it has. Down through the ages, men and women have continued to experience this great change. For an African man named Augustine, it came when he heard a child's voice in the next yard saying, "Take up and read, take up and read." Augustine, who had been living a very dissolute life, happened to have a copy of the New Testament beside him as he heard those words. So he looked down, and his eyes fell upon a verse in the book of Romans that read,

> The hour has come for you to wake up from your slumber, because our salvation is nearer now than when we first believed. The night is nearly over; the day is almost here. So let us put aside the deeds of darkness and put on the

armor of light. Let us behave decently, as in the daytime, not in orgies and drunkenness, not in sexual immorality and debauchery, not in dissension and jealousy. Rather, clothe yourselves with the Lord Jesus Christ, and do not think about how to gratify the desires of the sinful nature (Rom. 13:11-14).

Having read these words, Augustine arose a changed man.

Martin Luther was a monk who, in his study of the Psalms and of Paul's letters to the Romans and the Galatians, began to see that the righteousness God requires of us is not our own righteousness but is God's own righteousness and is God's gift to all who trust in Christ. When Luther came to realize this, he said, "It was as if the gates of paradise themselves swung open."

William Perkins, a young man in Cambridge, was walking through the streets when he heard a distressed mother say to her young, disobedient son, "Mind yourself, or you'll turn out to be like drunken Perkins there!" God used the comment of that woman to smite his heart, to convict him of the dissolute and drunken way he had lived his undergraduate life in Cambridge, to the point that his name had even become a byword. God convicted him of his sin and caused him to turn to Christ.

Not far away, in Bedford, a young tinker (a pot-fixer) named John Bunyan overheard two old washer-women talking about God as if they really knew Him. He couldn't get their conversation out of his mind, and God used that to strike his heart. Bunyan asked himself if there was something he had missed. He began to wonder, "Can you really know God?" And God used this to bring Bunyan, who would later write *Pilgrim's Progress,* to faith in Christ.

For the hard-hearted John Newton, a slave trader, it was the prospect of drowning in a violent storm at sea that God used to change his heart.

For young C. H. Spurgeon it was a snowstorm, which led to an old Primitive Methodist deacon filling in for the preacher at the church Spurgeon attended. As Spurgeon later described, the church was almost empty, Spurgeon was sitting in the back, almost by himself, and the old deacon got up there, looked straight at Spurgeon, and in broken sentences repeated just one phrase again and again: "Look unto Christ! That's all you gotta do, just look unto Christ!" He just kept saying it, "Look unto Christ! Look unto Christ!" And God used that to open Spurgeon's eyes to the truth.

For C. S. Lewis it was the recurring idea of the redeemer-god in mythology that began to suggest to him that something might be going on.

For a friend of mine it was hearing an open-air preacher at the University of Maryland; hearing him come again and again, year after year, and preach the Gospel.

For me it was coming to believe that Jesus Christ had indeed risen bodily from the dead.

For many people in my church, it was the faithful teaching of their parents or of a Sunday school teacher.

God has used many ways to get His Word out. But however He does it, He does it to this end—to give us the gifts of repentance and faith. He does it so that we will turn from our sins and turn to Him, and so experience this great conversion, this great change that we all so desperately need.

So much for the idea that we humans are unchangeable. God has, down through the ages, changed people. I don't know if the person referred to at the beginning of this chapter really became a changed man. But I know that by God's grace, many, many people have. Indeed, so far is such change from being impossible (as many secular cynics think), it would seem rather in some ways to be the order of the day. In our pursuit to keep our options open, a protean, ever-changing, undefined self seems to be the idol of our popular culture. All we do is change.

Reflecting on it as a Christian, I have to agree that our present life really is one of great flux and change. As Tozer expressed it, "Human nature, as we know it, is in a formative state. It is being changed into the image of the thing it loves."[4] Heraclitus's proverbial stream would seem stable compared to some people today! The only problem is that most of the changes are not for the good.

Your life, you see, is like one of those old Polaroid snapshots. It is slowly but surely developing into a picture of the God you worship. Before your very eyes you see in yourself the image of your god, the picture of the person or the thing you worship, coming into focus as its character is replicated in your life.

Some of us have heard this call, this desperate need that we have for a change, for what the Bible calls *conversion*.

And by God's grace, some of us have experienced that.

If you haven't, you need to turn from your sin and turn to God.

To change as you need to change may seem beyond you. But the good news is, it's not beyond God. You need only to heed the words of Jesus: "Repent, and believe the good news."

WHAT'S COMING UP . . .

MARK FIVE:
A Biblical Understanding of Evangelism

Who Should Evangelize?

How Should We Evangelize?

1. Tell people with honesty that if they repent and believe they will be saved—but it will be costly.

2. Tell people with urgency that if they repent and believe they will be saved—but they must decide now.

3. Tell people with joy that if they repent and believe the Good News they will be saved. However difficult it may be, it is all worth it!

4. Use the Bible.

5. Realize that the lives of individual Christians and of the church as a whole are a central part of evangelism.

6. Remember to pray.

What Is Evangelism?

1. It Is Not Imposition.

2. It Is Not Personal Testimony.

3. It Is Not Social Action or Political Involvement.

4. It Is Not Apologetics.

5. It Is Not the Results of Evangelism.

Why Should We Evangelize?

A Desire to Be Obedient to the Great Commission

A Love for the Lost

A Love for God

A BIBLICAL UNDERSTANDING
OF EVANGELISM

†

What do you think of when you hear the word *evangelist?* Do you
think of Billy Graham? Or the character called Evangelist in *Pilgrim's
Progress?* Do you think perhaps of a television preacher of question-
able repute? A KFC bucket being passed down the row for the offering? A fund-raising letter complete with business reply envelope?

When you hear the word *evangelist,* which comes more quickly to
mind—a charlatan or a saint?

Evangelism is undoubtedly a tangled topic today. Sinclair Lewis's
scandalous fictitious evangelist Elmer Gantry pales in comparison to
the lurid reality of recent scandals involving famous evangelists.

And when we get beyond the personalities of evangelists and
think about the process of evangelism itself, is Christian evangelism
as practiced today any different from the excesses of the Crusades in
the eleventh to the thirteenth centuries?

When the subject of evangelism comes up, even among
Christians, many questions arise and feelings can range from guilt to
genuine perplexity:

"Shouldn't evangelism be left to the professionals?" some may
ask. "Shouldn't it be done by those who really know how to do it? I
mean, it is so often done so badly. I wouldn't want to add to that! I
don't know enough."

Others may say, "I'm really not sure what evangelism means. I guess we're supposed to convince other people that they're wrong and we're right? Is that what evangelism is?"

Skeptics may wonder, "Isn't it really just an ego trip, to be so filled with self-importance that you try to cause someone else to accept your Gospel? It isn't really kosher, is it, in these pluralistic times, to try to get other people to change their beliefs and accept yours? I mean, religious faith is so personal and all."

Christians often leave evangelism to "the professionals" out of a sense of inadequacy, apathy, ignorance, fear, or simply feeling that it is inappropriate for them to do it. Perhaps they're not sure of what evangelism entails and how it should be done. And this situation is tragic. I'm convinced that one of the distinguishing marks of a healthy church is a biblical understanding and practice of evangelism. And that is our topic in this chapter. This is a fifth mark of a healthy church.

You may recall my mentioning that chapters 3, 4, and 5 of this book are all tied very closely to salvation, with each of these chapters viewing it from a slightly different angle. In chapter 4 we looked at the very moment of salvation—conversion, the great change—and we considered what the Bible teaches about this. In chapter 3 we considered the content of the Gospel message itself. In this chapter we want to consider how we are to tell others that great message that has changed us. How are we to "gospelize," to evangelize? What is evangelism and why should we do it?

To help us understand and practice evangelism, I want us to consider four simple questions:

1. Who should evangelize?
2. How should we evangelize?
3. What is evangelism?
4. Why should we evangelize?

Actually, these are not four entirely different questions. Our answers will weave in and out and influence each other. But each of these questions will provide a distinct viewpoint from which to see and understand this great biblical topic of evangelism. We can't answer all possible questions about evangelism, of course, but after considering these four questions I hope we will at least find that we can be more understanding and more obedient ourselves and have a healthier church culture when it comes to our great calling to evangelize.

Before proceeding, permit me to recommend four other books for you to read on this important topic:

Will Metzger's book *Tell the Truth*[1] is probably the best single book I know of on evangelism. It offers lots of practical helps and presents a particularly good theological understanding of the Gospel and of the process of evangelism.

Mack Stiles's book *Speaking of Jesus*[2] is a pleasure to read and is full of good stories of how you can actually, practically, talk to your friends about Jesus. He gives entertaining and informative examples of turning conversations to the Gospel, and some encouraging accounts of real-life conversions.

Iain Murray's book *Revival and Revivalism*[3] is a bit of a heavier read than the first two, but well worth it. In this historical work, Murray looks at how the practice of evangelism in America changed from 1750 to 1850 and how those changes continue to affect us today. If you're one of the more serious-minded types and you like history or edifying stories, this would be a great book to read.

One more book I would commend is J. I. Packer's *Evangelism and the Sovereignty of God*.[4] This book is as good as it is short! It has only four chapters and less than a hundred pages, but people consistently find it helpful in answering basic questions on what biblical evangelism is.

So much for the book reviews; on with the chapter.

WHO SHOULD EVANGELIZE?

Whatever discomfort one might feel about the topic of evangelism, it is hard to avoid it when you read your Bible. Evangelism is found throughout the New Testament. Passages about spreading the Good News are there from start to finish. For example, Paul wrote to the Romans, "I am obligated both to Greeks and non-Greeks, both to the wise and the foolish. That is why I am so eager to preach the gospel also to you who are at Rome" (Rom. 1:14-15). Is this simply Paul's description of his particular call as an evangelist? Do his words apply only to himself and the other apostles? Or do they apply to us as well?

Reading through the New Testament, we don't find the call to evangelism being limited to Paul or even to the apostles. At the end of His earthly ministry, Jesus said,

> "All authority in heaven and on earth has been given to me. Therefore go and make disciples of all nations, baptizing them in the name of the Father and of the Son and of the Holy Spirit, and teaching them to obey everything I have commanded you. And surely I will be with you always, to the very end of the age" (Matt. 28:18-20).

This statement, commonly called the Great Commission, seems to be a commission for *all* of Jesus' disciples.

It is clear as you read the New Testament that these early disciples took to heart this Great Commission from their Lord. Read through the letters they wrote, or read through the book of Acts, and again and again you see these disciples out evangelizing. They evangelized constantly (e.g., Acts 5:42; 8:25; 13:32; 14:7, 15, 21; 15:35; 16:10; 17:18). Some today are asking, "Who is supposed to evangelize?" Is it only preachers? Is the one time a week that most churches evangelize the time when the guy they pay full-time to sit around and read the Bible stands up and gives the Gospel? Is that how your church evangelizes? Is the Great Commission only for professional, religious types? Or does it have something to do with you, if you are a Christian?

The Bible would seem to indicate that all believers have received this commission. Looking more closely at the book of Acts, we get glimpses of this universal obedience to the call to evangelize. We don't just read of the *apostles* spreading the Gospel. Look at Acts 8:1:

> On that day a great persecution broke out against the church at Jerusalem, and all except the apostles were scattered throughout Judea and Samaria. Godly men buried Stephen and mourned deeply for him. But Saul began to destroy the church. Going from house to house, he dragged off men and women and put them in prison. Those who had been scattered preached the word wherever they went (Acts 8:1-4).

It wasn't just the apostles who were described as evangelizing in these verses. In fact, these verses focus on the evangelistic activities of "those who had been scattered" (v. 4), which included "all except the apostles" (v. 1)! Well, you could say maybe it was just the elders, because they were particularly gifted to teach. But the rest of Acts 8 is the story of Philip, who was not even an elder. Philip was "only" a deacon, and yet he was evangelizing (8:5-12, 26-40).

Going on to Acts 11:19-21, you see this story of "lay evangelism" continuing:

> Now those who had been scattered by the persecution in connection with Stephen traveled as far as Phoenicia, Cyprus and Antioch, telling the message only to Jews. Some of them, however, men from Cyprus and Cyrene, went to Antioch and began to speak to Greeks also, telling the Good News about the Lord Jesus. The Lord's hand was with them, and a great number of people believed and turned to the Lord.

So there again you have "ordinary" Christians going out to spread the Good News.

We should recall as well the admonition of Peter: "Always be prepared to give an answer to everyone who asks you to give the reason for the hope that you have" (1 Pet. 3:15). Peter wrote this to the whole church, not just to its leaders.

All Christians, not just the professional clergy, are to spread the Good News. Part of our evangelistic activity has to do with the way we relate to each other as believers. Jesus said, "By this all men will know that you are my disciples, if you love one another" (John 13:34-35). If you are not expressing proper Christian love to every member of your church, you are in disobedience to God and you are hindering the evangelistic work of your church.

Sometimes, though, if we're honest, the main reason we want to shift the responsibility for evangelism to others is that we're not exactly sure how to do it.

HOW SHOULD WE EVANGELIZE?

How should we evangelize? The most obvious answer to this question would be, by preaching the Word, by spreading the message, by telling the Good News. Biblically, that's how you evangelize.

But exactly how should that be done? This is a more important question than some people have realized. More than thirty years ago, Joseph Bayly entertainingly rebuked (if you can use those two words together!) Christians with his book *The Gospel Blimp*. As he tells the story:

> The idea really began that night several years ago when we were all sitting around in George and Ethel Griscom's backyard.
>
> We'd just finished eating an outdoor picnic supper (a real spread), and there wasn't much to do except swat mosquitoes and watch the fireflies. Every so often an airplane flew over, high in the sky. You could see the twinkling red and white lights.
>
> I guess that's what got us started on the Gospel Blimp. Or maybe it was George and Ethel's next-door neighbors, who were playing cards and drinking beer on the porch.
>
> Anyway we began talking about how to reach people with the gospel. Herm's active in the local businessmen's group

(he and Marge were there that night, their first time out after the baby was born). So when we started talking about reaching people, Herm says, "Let's take those folks next door to you, George, for example. You can tell they're not Christians. Now if we wanted to give them the gospel, how'd we—"

"Herm, for goodness' sake, keep your voice down," Marge interrupted. "D'you want them to hear you?"

"Herm's right, they're not Christians," George agreed. "Go to church—a liberal one—Christmas and Easter. But drink and play cards most other Sundays. Except the summer. In a few weeks they'll start going to the shore each weekend until Labor Day."

"OK now. Any suggestions?" Herm is a good discussion leader.

"Hey, look at that plane, it's really low. You can almost see the lights in the windows."

"Portholes. More potato chips, anyone?"

"Like I was saying, here's a test. How do we go about giving the gospel to those people over there?" And Herm motioned to the house next door.

"Too bad that plane didn't carry a sign. They looked up from their card playing long enough to have read it if it had carried one."

"Hey, you know you may have something there. Any of you seen those blimps with signs trailing on behind? You know, Drink Pepsi Cola, or Chevrolet Is First?" . . .

"What I mean is this. Why not have a blimp with a Bible verse trailing—something like 'Believe on the Lord Jesus Christ and thou shalt be saved.'" . . .

"Sounds like a terrific idea. Really terrific! Why, everybody would get the gospel at the same time."[5]

As the story progresses, these Christian friends buy a blimp, put a Gospel message on it, and drop tracts from the blimp to make sure everyone gets the Gospel. And what happens? You'll have to get the book yourself!

But what they were doing with the Gospel Blimp was spreading the Word, wasn't it? How do you think everyone can get the Word? We could say that they should all come to church. But they're not all going to do that. So what do we do? How do we spread the Word? How do we get the message to people? Is a blimp the answer?

Well, we certainly can spread the Word publicly through media, through public meetings; and we can spread it privately, too, through personal conversation. But whatever the context, whether through print or preaching, through conversation or evangelistic Bible study, how should we do it? Here are six biblical guidelines about how to evangelize:

1. Tell people with honesty that if they repent and believe they will be saved—but it will be costly.

We must be accurate in what we say, not holding back any important parts of the message out of a fear that those parts are too awkward or difficult to explain. Many people don't like having anything negative in a presentation of the Good News. Talking about sin and guilt and repentance and sacrifice is thought to be too negative for our age of self-esteem. We don't want the Gospel presented that way. Here's what one of America's most popular television preachers said not long ago:

> I don't think that anything has been done in the name of Christ and under the banner of Christianity that has proven more destructive to human personality, and hence counter-productive to the evangelistic enterprise, than the unchristian, uncouth strategy of attempting to make people aware of their lost and sinful condition.[6]

In case you're wondering, that was Robert Schuller. And Robert Schuller is not the only one who feels that way. But according to the Bible, making people aware of their lost and sinful condition is part and parcel of sharing the Good News of Jesus Christ. If you read the summaries of Peter's sermons in the early chapters of the book of

Acts, you'll find again and again that Peter is breathtakingly honest about the sinfulness of those to whom he is talking.

We can't pretend that everyone is engaged in an honest search for truth. The Bible teaches that people are by nature estranged from God, at enmity with Him. We must be honest about that. It may not be polite to say, but it is true and therefore it is faithful.

Holding back important and unpalatable parts of the truth is manipulative. It amounts to selling a false bill of goods.

2. Tell people with urgency that if they repent and believe they will be saved—but they must decide now.

We must make clear the urgency of the message, and that our listeners certainly should not wait until a "better deal" comes along.

Are you the kind of person who waits to subscribe to a magazine until you've gotten two or three different offers through the mail? You know, you save them, then you sit down and compare them and use the one that's the best deal? What about long-distance phone service? You could use up a good proportion of your life trying to find the best long-distance deal!

But when it comes to the Gospel, there's no point in waiting for a better deal. According to the New Testament, Jesus is the only way to God (see John 14:6; Acts 4:12; Rom. 10). How else would you suggest that sinners and the holy God be reconciled? There is no other way than Christ, and if Christ is the only way, then what are we waiting for? As the Bible warns, "Today, if you hear his voice, do not harden your hearts" (Heb. 4:7; quoting Ps. 95:7-8).

Jesus was urgent in His teaching. Consider, for instance, this parable recorded in Luke:

> "A man had a fig tree, planted in his vineyard, and he went to look for fruit on it, but did not find any. So he said to the man who took care of the vineyard, 'For three years now I've been coming to look for fruit on this fig tree and haven't found any. Cut it down! Why should it use up the soil?'

"'Sir,' the man replied, 'leave it alone for one more year, and I'll dig around it and fertilize it. If it bears fruit next year, fine! If not, then cut it down'"(Luke 13:6-9).

It is not manipulative or insensitive to bring up urgent warnings such as this. It is simply the truth. None of us has an unlimited amount of time in which to decide whether or not to follow Christ.

As Christians, we have come to realize that history is not cyclical, always repeating itself in an endless rotation of events, but that God will one day bring history to a close in judgment. We know that He has given us this life, and that He will require it back. The time that we have is limited, the amount is uncertain, and how we use it is up to us. So Paul tells the Ephesians to make the most of every opportunity (Eph. 5:16).

Like a collector buying up every known specimen of some cherished item, we should desire to capture each fleeting hour and turn it into a trophy for God, using it for Him. We shouldn't be content with thinking, "I'll live another couple of years in selfishness and then, when all of my desires are taken care of, I'll turn and follow Christ." No, we shouldn't be content with that! We should know, as Paul knew, that, "The time is short. From now on . . . those who use the things of the world [should use them] as if not engrossed in them. For this world in its present form is passing away" (1 Cor. 7:29, 31).

What situations are you in right now that you won't always be in? How are you using those situations in obedience to God? Trust the Lord to use you in those situations instead of always seeking for new situations. Trust the Lord to use you in this moment, instead of waiting until the next one, since you don't even know if the next one will come. Don't let the passing permanence of great buildings and established institutions, or the lulling tedium of long hours and minutes, make a fool of you! "The days are evil," says Paul in Ephesians 5:16, meaning that they are dangerous, they are a fleeting opportunity, and so we must redeem the time, we must make the most of every opportunity. So we say with Paul that, in view of certain judgment, Christ's love compels us to proclaim the Good News (cf. 2 Cor. 5:10-14).

3. Tell people with joy that if they repent and believe the Good News they will be saved. However difficult it may be, it is all worth it!

Hebrews 11 recounts the stories of those who suffered hard things for the faith and yet endured. In Hebrews 12 we read that Jesus Himself endured the Cross for the joy set before Him.

You may have read that famous statement of Jim Elliot, "He is no fool who gives what he cannot keep to gain what he cannot lose."

What do we gain in coming to Christ? We gain a relationship with God Himself. We gain forgiveness, meaning, purpose, freedom, community, certainty, and hope. Being honest about the difficulties when we're sharing the Gospel doesn't mean we have to mask the blessings. Nor, of course, does it mean that we have to pretend that the Christian life is difficult simply so that people will think we're being credible and honest. No, we need to be fully honest; that means telling people that we have great news in Jesus Christ. For all of the difficulties there are, it is infinitely more than worth it to make the decision to die to self and to follow Christ.

4. Use the Bible.

It is not only in public preaching that the Bible should be used. Learn the Bible for yourself and share it with others. By doing that you show those you speak with that your message isn't just your own thoughts or your own ideas. In Acts 8 we see Philip going to share the message with the Ethiopian official. Philip started with the Old Testament and used it to tell him about Jesus.

When we use the Bible in sharing the Gospel, we help people to realize that we're not just talking about our own ideas but about the very words of God.

5. Realize that the lives of individual Christians and of the church as a whole are a central part of evangelism.

Our lives, individually and as church congregations, should give credibility to the Gospel we proclaim. This is one of the reasons why church membership is so important. We as a church bear a corporate responsibility to present to the world what it means to be a Christian. We should understand clearly what church membership means and should help our fellow believers understand it as well. God is glorified not just by our speaking the message but by our actually living consistently with it—not that any of us can live perfectly, but we can at least try to live in a way that commends the Gospel. Remember Jesus' words in the Sermon on the Mount: "Let your light shine before men, that they may see your good deeds and praise your Father in heaven" (Matt. 5:16; cf. 1 Pet. 2:12). That's talking about your life. Your life can be lived in such a way that it brings glory to God as others who see it begin to believe the Gospel.

And remember, this involves more than just your individual life; it involves how believers live together as well. Again, remember the words of Jesus: "A new command I give you: Love one another. As I have loved you, so you must love one another. By this all men will know that you are my disciples, if you love one another" (John 13:34-35).

Live a life of committed love to the other members of your local church, as a fundamental part of your own sanctification and of your evangelistic ministry. Our individual lives alone are not a sufficient witness. Our lives together as church communities are the confirming echo of our witness.

6. Remember to pray.

Remember the importance of prayer in all of this—because, of course, salvation is the work of God.

WHAT IS EVANGELISM?

Sometimes we share the Gospel wrongly because we misunderstand what evangelism is. That brings us to our third question: What is evangelism? There are a number of things that people take to be evangelism that are not evangelism. Let me mention five:

1. Probably the most common objection to evangelism these days is, "Isn't it wrong to impose our beliefs on others?" Some people

think evangelism is an *imposition*. And the way evangelism is often done, I can understand the confusion. But when you understand what the Bible presents as evangelism, you understand that it's really not a matter of imposing your beliefs.

First, you must understand that the things you believe in as a Christian are facts. They are not mere beliefs or opinions; they are facts.

Second, these facts are not *yours* in the sense that they uniquely pertain to you or your perspective or experience, or in the sense that you made them up on your own. When you evangelize, you are presenting the facts of the Christian Gospel.

And, of course, in biblical evangelism we don't *impose* anything. In fact we really can't. According to the Bible, evangelism is simply telling the Good News; it does not include making sure that the other person responds to it correctly. I wish we could make people respond to the Gospel, but we cannot. According to the Bible, the fruit of evangelism comes from God, not from our clever techniques or our personal passion for what we are doing. As Paul wrote to the Corinthians,

> What, after all, is Apollos? And what is Paul? Only servants, through whom you came to believe—as the Lord has assigned to each his task. I planted the seed, Apollos watered it, but God made it grow. So neither he who plants nor he who waters is anything, but only God, who makes things grow (1 Cor. 3:5-7; cf. 2 Cor. 3:5-6).

This is an important point for us to get ahold of, especially in a world that is so hostile to evangelism. One time at Cambridge I was talking with a Lebanese Muslim friend of mine about a mutual friend who was a fairly secular Muslim. My friend wanted him to embrace a more faithful Muslim lifestyle, and I wanted him to become a Christian. So, in a strange way, he and I had something in common. We were both concerned about this friend, though we had very different solutions for his problem. We commiserated on the difficulty of living in a secular British culture. Then my friend remarked on the corruption of this Christian country. I responded that Great Britain is not a Christian country, that in fact there is no such thing as a Christian country. That, my friend said, quickly seizing the opportunity, is the problem with Christianity compared to Islam. Christianity does not provide answers and guidelines for all of the complexities of real life, he maintained. It has no overarching sociopolitical pattern to offer people for the real questions they come up against.

I responded that that is because of Christianity's realistic portrayal of the human condition. He asked me what I meant. I said that, to speak frankly, Islam is shallow in thinking that the human problem is simply a matter of behavior. According to Islam, it is merely a question of the will. But Christianity, I said, teaches that there is a much deeper problem, and this is a more accurate understanding of the human situation. Christianity includes a frank admission of human sinfulness not merely as an aggregate, a collection, of bad actions, but as an expression of a bad heart, a heart in rebellion against God. Christianity recognizes our problem as a matter of character, of human nature. Christianity has nothing that could be recognized as a comprehensive political program because we don't think that the real human problem can ultimately be dealt with by political power.

To make it clear, I said to my friend, "Look, I could put a sword to a person's throat and make him at least a sufficiently good Muslim."

He agreed that that was true.

"But," I continued, "I cannot put a sword to a person's throat and make him a Christian. Becoming a Christian is not merely a matter of your doing this and not doing that, or of your following that law and not doing that thing. To be a Christian is to have your life transformed by God. The Bible presents the human problem as something that could never be solved by coercive force or human imposition. All I can do is to present the Good News accurately to you, live a life of love toward you, and pray that God will convict you of your sins. I can pray for God to show you your need of a Savior, and to give you the gifts of repentance and faith. But I can't make you a Christian."

Christian evangelism by its very nature involves no coercion, only proclamation and love. We are to present the Gospel freely to all; we cannot manipulate anyone to truly accept it. Truly biblical evangelism is never an imposition.

2. Some think of a *personal testimony* as evangelism. Certainly a testimony of what God has done in our lives may include the Good News, but it also may not include it. In telling other people how much Jesus means to you, you may not have told them the Gospel at all. Have you explained what Christ did by dying on the Cross? It is good to share your own testimony of what God has done in your life, but in your testimony, you may not actually make clear what Christ's claims are on other people.

Testimony is, of course, very popular in our postmodern, "that's-good-for-you" age. Who would object to your thinking you've gotten something good from Christ? But wait and see what happens when you try to move the conversation from what Jesus has done for you to the facts of the life, death, and resurrection of Christ and how that all applies to your nonbelieving friend. That's when you discover that testimony is not necessarily evangelism.

3. Some people mistake *social action or political involvement* for evangelism. When our eyes fall from God to humanity, it's not surprising that social ills replace sin in our concerns. Today, horizontal problems—problems between people—often obscure the fundamental vertical problem between us and God. Too often, what passes for evangelism may really be crusades for public virtues or for programs of compassion or for other social changes. But as Donald McGavran, well-known missionary to India in the mid-twentieth century, said,

> Evangelism is not proclaiming the desirability of a liquorless world and persuading people to vote for prohibition.

Evangelism is not proclaiming the desirability of sharing the wealth and persuading people to take political action to achieve it."[7]

Evangelism is not declaring God's political plan for the nations. It is not recruiting for the church. Evangelism is a declaration of the Gospel to individual men and women. Societies are challenged and changed when, through this Gospel, the Lord brings individual men and women together in churches, to display His character in the interactions of those whom He has saved.

4. Other people may mistake *apologetics* for evangelism. The term *apologetics* refers to the process of answering questions and objections people may have about our Christian beliefs. As with sharing your testimony, such question-answering and defending may often be a part of your conversations with others about Christ, and may include evangelism. But it is not the same thing as evangelism. Defending the virgin birth of Christ or the historicity of the Resurrection is very important, but it is not evangelism. Apologetics is defending the faith, answering the questions others have about Christianity. It is responding to the agenda that others set. Evangelism, however, is following Christ's agenda, giving out the news about Him. Evangelism is the positive act of telling the Good News about Jesus Christ and the way of salvation through Him.

5. Finally, one of the most common and dangerous mistakes is to confuse *the results of evangelism* with evangelism itself. This may be the most subtle of the misunderstandings. Evangelism must not be confused with the fruit of evangelism. If you combine this misunderstanding—thinking evangelism is the fruit of evangelism—with a different understanding than we have set forth in the previous chapters about the Gospel and about conversion, then it is very possible to end up thinking not only that evangelism is simply seeing others converted, but thinking also that it is within your own power

to convert others. This kind of thinking may lead you to be very manipulative.

According to the Bible, evangelism may not be defined in terms of results or methods, but only in terms of faithfulness to the message preached. In the book of Acts you will read of occasions when Paul preached the Gospel and few if any responded. At the great Lausanne gathering in 1974, John Stott said that "To 'evangelize' . . . does not mean to win converts . . . but simply to announce the good news, irrespective of the results."[8] At that gathering, evangelism was defined as follows:

> To evangelize is to spread the good news that Jesus Christ died for our sins and was raised from the dead according to the Scriptures, and that as the reigning Lord he now offers the forgiveness of sins and the liberating gift of the Spirit to all who repent and believe.[9]

Look with me at 2 Corinthians 2:15-16, a very interesting couple of verses to meditate on: "For we are to God the aroma of Christ among those who are being saved and those who are perishing. To the one we are the smell of death; to the other, the fragrance of life."

Paul is not saying that he gave out two different messages, or that he could look out onto a crowd and say, "Okay, I can see who the elect are. To you I'm going to preach one message. Now, to all of those who are not becoming Christians, let me preach another message." No. Paul preached the same Gospel to everyone, and yet, in evangelizing the same way toward everyone, he was to some an aroma of life and to others the smell of death. The same ministry had two different effects.

Jesus taught this in His parable of the soils (Matt. 13:1-23). In this parable, the sower went out and scattered the same seed on several different kinds of soil. The parable says nothing about the methods of the sower. Presumably he used the same method each time. The message of the parable is that some people will respond to the Gospel and some will not, even though all hear the same message. We cannot finally judge the correctness of what we do in evangelism by the immediate response that we see. It is important to understand this truth, because a failure to understand it can distract well-meaning churches into pragmatic, results-oriented endeavors and it can transform pastors into neurotic people-manipulators. We make a terrible mistake when we misunderstand evangelism so badly that we think we can tell from the immediate results whether we are evangelizing properly. As Christians we should know that, even if we are faithful in telling the Gospel, people still may not respond. Their lack of acceptance of the Gospel does not necessarily mean that we have been wrong in how we have presented the Gospel.

Misunderstanding this point can cripple individual Christians with a deep sense of personal failure and, ironically, can cause an aversion to evangelism itself. Imagine the guilt some Christians feel because they've shared the Gospel for thirty years with a particular person who hasn't come to know Christ. They may feel that it must somehow be their fault. But the biblical teaching is that conversions do not come merely by our evangelistic proficiencies, just as resistance to the Gospel is not merely a reflection of our evangelistic failures. Evangelism is not fundamentally a matter of our methods but of our faithfulness in proclamation.

Some of us who are Christians today became Christians through presentations of the Gospel that may have been terrible in a number of ways. The person may have been scared, stuttering, forgetful, intimidating, pushy, even obnoxious. But somehow the truth was there amid all their errors, and God's Holy Spirit used it to bring us to repentance and faith.

Of course, on our side, we as evangelists must work to try to present the Gospel as well as we can. That's our responsibility. But on the other side, we exult in the fact that God is a big God. He can use our mistakes; in His grace He overlooks all of our faults and works everything for His glory.

One writer put it this way:

Evangelism is not a making of proselytes; it is not persuading people to make a decision; it is not proving that God exists, or making a good case for the truth of Christianity; it is not inviting someone to a meeting; it is not exposing the contemporary dilemma, or arousing interest in Christianity; it is not wearing a badge saying "Jesus Saves"! Some of these things are right and good in their place, but none of them should be confused with evangelism. To evangelize is to declare on the authority of God what he has done to save sinners, to warn men of their lost condition, to direct them to repent, and to believe on the Lord Jesus Christ.[10]

Who can deny that much modern evangelism has become emotionally manipulative, seeking simply to cause a momentary decision of the sinner's will yet neglecting the biblical idea that conversion is the result of the supernatural, gracious act of God toward the sinner?

The Christian call to evangelism is a call not simply to persuade people to make decisions but rather to proclaim to them the Good News of salvation in Christ, to call them to repentance, and to give God the glory for regeneration and conversion. We don't fail in our evangelism if we faithfully present the Gospel and yet the person is not converted; we fail only if we don't faithfully present the Gospel at all.

When you understand that evangelism isn't converting people, but that it is telling them the wonderful truth about God, the great news about Jesus Christ, then obedience to the call to evangelize can become certain and joyful. Understanding this increases evangelism, as it moves away from being a guilt-driven burden to being a joyful privilege.

WHY SHOULD WE EVANGELIZE?

A final question—and this may seem a strange question to ask: What is the motivation for our evangelism?

To ask such a question may sound as silly as asking, "What is my motivation in loving my wife?" or, "What is my motivation in caring for my kids?" Does it really matter? If it is really a good thing to do, why worry about the motive?

Is there really a problem with having a wrong motivation for evangelism? I actually think there can be a problem. There can be such a thing as a selfish motive for evangelism. Do some churches perhaps have no concern for the salvation of the people around them while at the same time having a great concern that their church not have to close its doors? And what's true of churches can be true of us as individuals. As grotesque as it may seem, you could evangelize out of wanting to be right, or wanting to win an argument with a friend, or wanting some kind of psychological reinforcement for your own beliefs, or wanting to look spiritual in front of your Christian friends or before God Himself, or to have a reputation as a successful evangelist. I could go on, but you get the idea.

What is the *right* reason to tell the Good News? According to the Bible, good motives for evangelism are:

- a desire to be obedient to the Great Commission (see Matt. 28:18-20; 1 Cor. 9:16-17);
- a love for the lost (e. g., Matt. 9:36; John 3:16; Rom. 10:1); and finally and preeminently,
- a love for God.

In the final analysis, love for God must be our motive if we are to evangelize as God would have us to:

Love for God is the only sufficient motive for evangelism. Self-love will give way to self-centeredness; love for the lost will fail with those whom we cannot love, and when difficulties seem insurmountable. Only a deep love for God will keep us following his way, declaring his gospel, when human resources fail. Only our love for God—and, more important, his love for us—will keep us from the dangers which beset us. When the desire for popularity with men, or for success in human terms, tempts us to water down the gospel, to make it palatable, then only if we love God will we stand fast by his truth and his ways.[11]

Ultimately, this love for God leads to a desire to see Him glorified. Throughout the Bible, God makes Himself known to His creation. We share the Gospel to glorify God as the truth about Him is made known to His creation. The call to evangelism is a call to turn our lives outwards—from focusing on ourselves and our needs to focusing on God and the world that He has made. And that includes loving people who are made in God's image and yet are at enmity with Him, alienated from Him and in need of salvation from sin and guilt. We bring God glory when we tell the great thing He has done in Christ for these creatures made in His image. This is not the only way that we can bring glory to God, but it is one of the chief ways He has given us as Christians, as those who know Him through His grace in Christ, to glorify Him. Remember Peter's exhortation to the Christians in the first century to live for the glory of God: "Live such good lives among the pagans that, though they accuse you of doing wrong, they may see your good deeds and glorify God on the day he visits us" (1 Pet. 2:12).

We should all evangelize. We should all tell the Good News about Jesus. We should do so with honesty, urgency, and joy, living a life that backs up our message—and doing it all for the glory of God.

I have a book in my study by C. S. Lovett, titled *Soul-Winning Made Easy*. In this little book, Lovett laid out a "Soul-Winning Plan" based on sales techniques of the time when he wrote, in 1959. "You are in command," Lovett said, talking to Christians as salespeople:

> The trained soul-winner can bring his prospect to a decision for Christ. There is no middle ground as he moves with surety and deftness right up to the point of salvation. It is his conversation control that makes this possible. He knows exactly what he is going to say each step of the way and can

even anticipate his prospects' responses. He is able to keep the conversation focused on the main issue and prevent unrelated materials from being introduced. The controlled conversation technique is something new in evangelism and represents a real break-through in soul-winning.[12]

Lovett then instructed the earnest Christian about various tools needed, and gave some "helpful hints," such as, "Get your prospect alone." At one point he taught how to "press for the decision," even illustrating his point with photographs. When you have finished presenting the Gospel, he explained,

> Lay your hand firmly on the subject's shoulder (or arm) and with a semi-commanding tone of voice, say to him: "Bow your head with me." Note: Do not look at him when you say this, but bow your head first. Out of the corner of your eye you will see him hesitate at first. Then, as his resistance crumbles, his head will come down. Your hand on his shoulder will feel the relaxation and you will know when his heart yields. Bowing your head first, causes terrific psychological pressure.[13]

How many churches today are full of people who have been psychologically pressured in such a manner but not truly converted by the Spirit of God? And what about Christians who have done this kind of evangelism? Have we filled our churches full of people who responded when they were eight years old because they sincerely wanted to please Mom and Dad? Who bowed their heads, closed their eyes, and even came down to the front, but who have not truly repented and believed? What have we done to the Gospel in America by the way we have evangelized?

C. S. Lovett may well have been a more faithful evangelist than most of us are. He may have been very faithful in caring for people and sharing the Gospel with them. And we have already observed that God can use worse presentations than this to bring people to Himself.

May God give each one of us the heart and the faithfulness that would care about evangelism so much that we would write a book about it; but may God also prevent our misunderstanding evangelism in such a way that fills our churches with people who don't know the Lord.

A few years ago, after a Sunday morning service, a visitor came up to me, took me by the hand, pulled me close to himself and said, "Dr. Dever, I just want you to know that was one of the best sales presentations I've ever heard in my life. But there was only one problem: You didn't close the sale!"

I didn't really know how to respond to him. I didn't say much of anything. But what I thought was, "Friend, I know what kind of sales I can close, and I know what kind I can't close, and the redemption of an eternal soul is one sale that I, in my own strength, cannot accomplish."

I need to know that, not so that I won't preach the Gospel, but so that I won't allow my presentation of the Gospel to be molded by what I think will finally get a response and close a sale. Instead of using all my powers to convict and change the sinner, while God stands back as a gentleman quietly waiting for the spiritual corpse, His declared spiritual enemy, to invite Him into his heart, I'm going to preach the Gospel like a gentleman, trying to persuade but knowing that I can't convert, and then stand back while God uses all of *His* powers to convict and convert and change the sinner. Then we'll see clearly just who can really call the dead to life.

God can use *anybody* for His glory. He likes using "anybodies." He chose to use Moses the stutterer; and He used Paul the Jewish nationalist to reach the Gentiles. By using such unlikely people, God gets the glory.

Charles Spurgeon tells how George Whitefield,

the great eighteenth-century evangelist, was hounded by a group of detractors who called themselves the "Hell-fire Club." When Whitefield would stand outside preaching this little group of guys would stand off on the side and mimic him. They didn't believe a word of it. The ring leader was called Thorpe. One day Thorpe was mimicking Whitefield to his cronies, delivering his sermon with brilliant accuracy, perfectly imitating his tone and facial expressions, when he himself was so pierced that he sat down and was converted on the spot.[14]

The Gospel, in and of itself, is powerful.

May we as individuals and as churches be involved in the ministry of evangelism. And may God help us not to do it in a wrong way but in a way that presents the Gospel clearly.

And when we do, we'll begin to see some good fruit. Church membership will begin to regain its meaning (more on this in the next chapter). And the Gospel will begin to become visible to the world around, and even to the world that is in the church!

Sometimes the charge is leveled, "If you believe in election, you won't evangelize." But I have to tell you that many of the greatest evangelists in the history of the Christian church have believed that salvation is by God's election; that hasn't dulled the evangelistic zeal of a Whitefield or an Edwards, of a Carey or a Judson, of a Spurgeon or a Lloyd-Jones, of a Francis Schaeffer or a D. James Kennedy, of a Tim Keller or a John Piper. In fact, as someone who wants to see more evangelism, my concern is just the opposite: I am concerned that if you *don't* believe what we've considered in these last few studies—that the Gospel is the Good News of God's action, the Father electing, the Son dying, the Spirit drawing; and that conversion is only our response to God's giving us the grace-gifts of repentance and faith; and that evangelism is our simple, faithful, prayerful telling of this Good News—if you don't believe these things, then I'm concerned that you will actually damage the evangelistic mission of the church by making false converts, filling churches with people who don't really know Jesus. You will tell them stories in such a way that they will cry, their hearts will be tugged, and they will make a sincere decision, but they will not be confronted by the reality of their sins, by their need to repent, and by the Holy Ghost. Such a method will not give them new life. And yet they'll be baptized, made members of the church, and enlisted in church activities.

We need to understand how radical the Gospel is, and how radically bad the human situation is, because if we do not understand this we will obscure the Gospel. Evangelism isn't all about our ability to hawk our religious wares. I know that the discouragement can be painfully sharp sometimes as we do our best to share the Good News and it is received as either unimportant or incredible. But that's where we must remember that it is our part simply to give out the message; God will bring the increase.

Once when Paul was discouraged, the Lord said something to encourage him to continue proclaiming the Gospel, and what the Lord said could actually be considered a statement of the doctrine of election: "One night the Lord spoke to Paul in a vision: 'Do not be afraid; keep on speaking, do not be silent. For I am with you, and no one is going to attack and harm you, because I have many people in this place'" (Acts 18:9-11).

God used the doctrine of election as an encouragement to Paul in evangelism.

We need to see an end to a wrong, shallow view of evangelism as simply getting people to say yes to a question, or to make a one-time decision. We need to see an end to the bad fruit of false evangelism. We need to see an end to worldly people having assurance that they're saved just because they once took a stand, shook a hand, or repeated a prayer. We need to see real revival not being lost amid our own manufactured and scheduled meetings that we euphemistically call "revivals," as if we could determine when the wind of God's Spirit would actually blow. We need to see an end to church memberships markedly larger than the number of those involved with the church, and an end to inaction in our own lives as we ignore the evangelistic mandate—the call to share the Good News. We need to see the end of this debilitating, deadly coldness to the glorious call to tell the Good News.

And we need to see a renewed commitment to, and joy in, the great privilege we have of sharing the Good News of Christ with the lost and dying world around us. It was because someone else was faithful with this commission that you are a Christian today. Let us pray that because of our own faithfulness now, when we get to this season next year there will be others who have come to be reconciled to God in Christ.

And if God in His mysterious sovereignty deigns it not to be so, may it not be because we have failed in our commission to make Him and His grace in Christ known to every creature made in His image.

We must recognize the importance of this Good News of Jesus Christ. Until we do, we can learn nothing helpful about evangelism. Evangelism will be no more for us than an unpleasant duty or an occasional impulse. But when the message of the Cross captures our hearts and captivates our imaginations, our tongues, stammering, halting, insulting, awkward, sarcastic, imperfect as they may be, won't be far behind. As Jesus said, "Out of the overflow of the heart the mouth speaks" (Matt. 12:34).

What is your heart full of? What do you spend your words on?

WHAT'S COMING UP . . .

MARK SIX:
A BIBLICAL UNDERSTANDING OF CHURCH MEMBERSHIP

What Is a Church?

Why Join a Church?

    1. To Assure Ourselves

    2. To Evangelize the World

    3. To Expose False Gospels

    4. To Edify the Church

    5. To Glorify God

What Does Church Membership Entail?

    In Action Initially by Baptism

    In Writing by Signing a Statement of Faith and Church Covenant

(Special Responsibilities of Membership at Capitol Hill Baptist)

    1. Attend Services Regularly

    2. Attend Communion Particularly

    3. Attend Members' Meetings Consistently

    4. Pray Regularly

    5. Give Regularly

A Biblical Understanding
of Church Membership

All the statistics seem to point to our age being an age of "commit-ment-phobia." Commitment-phobia is the fear that in promising to do something good we will miss out on getting something even better. And so, although we see many good things we could be doing, we would rather just "keep our options open."

Surely that is the wisdom of our age. One writer has observed:

> Public-opinion research points to a deepening paradox in society: the combination of commitment to religion with a deepening moral relativism. For example, while 91 percent of the American people consider religion very important in their lives, 63 percent reject the concept of absolutes.[1]

George Barna called this rather bizarre poll result one of his top five statistics for the end of 1998: Only 43 percent of adults who say they are Christian are "absolutely committed to the Christian faith"!

Can you be a commitment-phobe and be a Christian, too? I'm not asking if a Christian can be uncertain about things or have doubts. Most of us who are Christians have doubts. But can you be a commitment-phobe and a Christian at the same time? What could be more "options-closing" than following Jesus, who told His disciples that anyone who would follow Him must "take up his cross" (Matt. 16:24)?

Add to this the problem of lone-rangerism: Why depend on someone else if you can do it yourself? We are concerned today with ease and simplicity. Why entangle yourself with others? You may be a burden to them; they certainly may be a burden to you.

Put these tendencies together and you get a culture that is fairly hostile to New Testament Christianity, and certainly not very comfortable with church membership.

Besides, isn't the whole idea of church membership really counterproductive? Isn't it unfriendly, and maybe even elitist, to say that we're in and you're out? Can we go so far as to say that it is unbiblical, and maybe even un-Christian? The end of Acts 2 simply says that, "the Lord added to their number" those who were being saved. Isn't that all there is to it? Isn't the church simply a reality created by our salvation? For example, in Acts 8, when the Ethiopian official responded to the Gospel and was baptized, wasn't he automatically a member of the church?

I'm convinced that getting this concept of membership right is a key step in revitalizing our churches, evangelizing our nation, furthering the cause of Christ around the world, and so bringing glory to God. Remember that this chapter is part of a book called *Nine Marks of a Healthy Church*. As I said in the introduction, this book is not meant to include everything that there is to say about a healthy church, but in these nine chapters I am trying to call attention to some important aspects of church life that have been overlooked or even forgotten in modern American Christian life.

My own fellowship of churches is a prime example. According to one recent Southern Baptist Convention study, the typical Southern Baptist church has 233 members, only 70 of whom are present at the typical Sunday morning worship service. So where are the other 163 members? Are they all at home sick, in a rest home, at college or on vacation, or in the military? Maybe some are, but all 163 of them? What do such churches convey about Christianity to the world around us? What do we understand this to mean about the importance of Christianity in our lives? And what is the spiritual state of those people if they haven't attended church for months or even longer? Is their nonattendance really any of our business?

In this chapter, we will consider three questions:

1. What is a church?
2. Why join a church?
3. What is entailed in church membership?

WHAT IS A CHURCH?

The word *church* does not simply refer to an organizational unit of any particular religion. You won't hear anyone speak of Buddhist "churches" or Jewish "churches." In that sense, *church* is a thoroughly Christian word. By "church" we don't fundamentally mean a building; only in a secondary sense is it that. The building is simply where the church meets—thus the New England Puritan name for the church building: "meeting house." The earliest New England churches looked like large houses from the outside—they were the houses where the church met.

According to the New Testament, the church is primarily a body of people who profess and give evidence that they have been saved by God's grace alone, for His glory alone, through faith alone, in Christ alone. This is what a New Testament church is; it is not a building. The early Christians didn't have buildings for almost 300 years after the church began. The collection of people committed to Christ in a local area constitute a church.

A few passages in the New Testament seem to refer to the church in the abstract, or universally, but the overwhelming majority of references to the church are to a local, living, and loving collection of people who are committed to Christ and committed to each other. That's what the word means again and again in the New Testament. It is a body from which you can be excluded and in which, therefore, you can clearly be included. Consider this: If there is no way for you to be excluded from the local church you are currently attending, perhaps that's because you have not *included* yourself in it as the Bible intends.

One interesting side note for historians: The idea of the church being a covenanted community of believers—and not just for everyone who lives in a particular locality—is an important contribution that Baptists particularly have made to our nation's religious liberty. The church is not finally something that's for you and every member of your family by physical, natural descent, or that is yours as a citizen of this nation. No, the New Testament teaches that the church is for believers, for those to whom God's Holy Spirit has given the new birth and who join together in a covenanted community. America today has laws that allow such churches to operate in liberty. Some nonbelievers fear that Christians are seeking some kind of official or "established" church in America. But Christians who have inherited this Baptist understanding of the church are actually the firmest foes of such an "established" church. Our very understanding of the church will not allow that. Rather, we desire the evangelization of our nation through churches that are allowed to freely cooperate as believers in Christ.

If you read the story of the early churches recorded in the book of Acts, there is no evidence that any of them meant to have anyone other than believers as members. When you read the letters of Paul, it seems clear that Paul too wrote as if the churches were composed entirely of believers; thus he addressed them as saints—those whom God has specially chosen. The church is the body of Christ, the local collection of Christians committed to Christ and to each other.

WHY JOIN A CHURCH?

The second question is, Why join a church?

Any church growth specialist would tell me that inviting people to join a church is exactly the wrong thing to do today. They would warn me, "Mark, you might just cause them to be disaffected. Why don't you just not mention this topic?" But I think that this topic is a must for our churches, and for us as Christians today. Church membership is a crucial topic for understanding what Christ is calling you to as His disciple. Joining a church will not save you any more than your good works, your education, your culture, your friendships, your financial contributions, or your baptism will save you. Non-Christians should not seek to join a church, but to learn more about what it means to be a Christian.

But for those of you who are confessing Christians, let me ask you what it means to live the Christian life. Do we live the Christian life alone? Is it merely a matter of our individual, isolated virtues, or spiritual disciplines that we work on—the fact that we're honest at work, that we don't cheat on our spouse, that we believe certain things to be true?

Or maybe that's not describing you. Maybe you know that the Christian life is to include others. But who are these others? Are they simply the other people at work or the other women in your women's Bible study or your friends from back in school days or your fellowship group at college? Which Christians are we called to relate to? The church is for everyone who is a Christian. The church is not a homogeneous group, centered around one sub-task such as evangelizing college students or publishing a magazine. The church is for everyone.

Let me give you just five good reasons (you can probably think of more) to join a church that preaches the Gospel and models Christian living.

1. To Assure Ourselves

You should not join the church simply in order to be saved, but you may want to join the church to help you in making certain that you are saved. Remember the words of Jesus:

> "Whoever has my commands and obeys them, he is the one who loves me. He who loves me will be loved by my Father, and I too will love him and show myself to him. . . . If you obey my commands, you will remain in my love, just as I have obeyed my Father's commands and remain in His

love. . . . You are my friends if you do what I command. . . .
Now that you know these things, you will be blessed if you
do them" (John 14:21; 15:10, 14; 13:17).

I could go on and on reading you words from Jesus that teach us
how we are to follow Him, and that we must be careful about delud-
ing ourselves. In joining the church, we put ourselves in a position
where we ask our brothers and sisters to hold us accountable to live
according to what we speak with our mouths. We ask the brothers and
sisters around us to encourage us, sometimes by reminding us of
ways that we have seen God work in our lives and other times by
challenging us when we may be moving away from obeying Him.
(For more on this topic, see Jonathan Edwards's little book,
*Distinguishing Marks of a Work of the Spirit of God.*²)

Membership in a local church is not an antiquated, outdated,
unnecessary add-on to true membership in the universal body of
Christ; membership in a local church is intended as a testimony to
our membership in the universal church. Church membership does
not save, but it is a reflection of salvation. And if there is no reflection of our salvation, how can we be sure that we are truly saved? As
John explains, "If anyone says, 'I love God,' yet hates his brother, he
is a liar. For anyone who does not love his brother, whom he has seen,
cannot love God, whom he has not seen" (1 John 4:20).

In becoming a member of the church, we are grasping hands
with each other to know and be known by each other. We are agree-
ing to help and encourage each other when we need to be reminded
of God's work in our lives or when we need to be challenged about
major discrepancies between our talk and our walk.

We need to give up trying to live the Christian life on our own.
We need individually to covenant together with others to follow
Christ. Christians must stop being selfish in their understanding of
the Christian life. The Christian life is not just about you and those
you are personally trying to reach with the Gospel. God also intends
you to be a committed part of helping to make disciples out of the
flock of sheep He has already saved.

2. To Evangelize the World

Another reason you should join a local church is for the sake of evangelizing the world. Together we can better spread the Gospel at home and abroad. We can do this by our words, as we share the Good News with others, and by helping others to do that. A local church is, by nature, a missionary organization. And we back up this missionary outreach with our actions as we show God's love by meeting the physical needs of orphans and those otherwise disadvantaged.

We promote the Gospel by cooperating to take it to those who have not yet heard it, and by making the Gospel visible to the world by the lives that we live. Those not yet saved may see us, and may see something of the Gospel. Even as imperfect as we are, if God's Spirit is genuinely at work in us He will use our lives to help demonstrate to others the truth of His Gospel. This is a special role we have now that we won't have in heaven—to be part of God's plan, to take His Gospel to the world. If you are reading this but haven't yet joined in that great task, do so today.

3. To Expose False Gospels

As we interact with other Christians, we show the world what Christianity really is; we expose the false notion that Christians are nauseatingly self-righteous people who are worried that someone somewhere might be having fun, and who believe, above all else, in their own goodness. This is how many non-Christians think of Christianity. We can combat that false image by having a church that is not marked by such an attitude.

Some years ago I went to see a relative whom I hadn't seen since childhood. When I told her I was planning to be a Baptist preacher, it didn't go over very well. She paused, looked down at her coffee, and said, "I've given up on organized religion. I think I've decided that churches are just pits of vipers."

"Really?" I replied.

She said, "Yep."

I said, "Do you really think the world outside is so much better?"

She thought for a second and said, "Well, I guess not. They're vipers too. But at least they *know* they're vipers."

I said, "You might be surprised how much I agree with you. I know the world outside is a pit of vipers. And I know the church is a pit of vipers, too. But the difference is, I don't really think the world outside knows that they are. And I think Christians know that we are, and that's why we come to church—because we know we need help. Because we know that we're dependent on God, that we're saved by His grace alone."

All we can bring to our salvation is our sins. It must be God's love in Christ that saves us. He came and lived a perfect life for us and died on the Cross in the place of all those who would ever turn and trust in Him, and rose in victory over death and over sin. Our faith in Him alone is the instrument by which we are saved.

So, join a church that believes in *that* Gospel. Join with other Christians in covenanting to make the truth known.

4. To Edify the Church

A fourth reason you should join the church is to help in the edification or building up of other believers. Joining a church will help counter our wrong individualism and will help us to realize the corporate nature of Christianity.

Beware, though: It is easy to fool ourselves into thinking we're Christians simply because at one time we made a tearful decision and then joined a church. Perhaps we've gone along through the life of the church for years, supporting its organizations, making friendships based around activities, liking some of the hymns, complaining about others, but never really knowing Christ. Do you have a vital relationship with Christ that changes your life and the lives of those around you?

How can you tell if you do? One of the ways you can discover the truth about your own life is to ask this question: Do you understand your following Christ fundamentally to involve how you treat other people, especially other people who are members of your church? Have you covenanted together to love them and do you give yourself to that?

Or, have you claimed that you know a love from God in Christ and yet live in a way that gives the lie to that claim? Do you claim that you know this kind of love that knows no bounds, and yet in your loving others you have set bounds, saying in effect, "I'll go this far but no farther"?

Such a claim to love, without a life backing it up, is a bad sign. And yet, if you just hang out by yourself and refuse to join a church, other Christians can't help you. You're sailing your own little ship your own little way. You'll come to church when you like the sermons, you'll come when you like the music or when you like something else that the church does, then you'll sail on out to wherever else you may go when you want something else.

If you commit yourself to a church, you commit yourself to a local body of people who will try to help you work through such problems. So, for example, if it is found that you have a problem with gossip, your brothers and sisters will try to talk with you about that. If you're getting discouraged and falling away, your brothers and sisters will try to encourage you.

The New Testament shows clearly that our following Jesus is supposed to involve care and concern for each other. That is part of what it means to be a Christian. And though we do it imperfectly, we should be committed to doing it.

I once had a friend who worked for a campus Christian ministry while attending a church where I was a member. He would always slip in right after the hymns, sit there for the sermon, and then leave. I asked him one day why he didn't come for the whole service.

"Well," he said, "I don't get anything out of the rest of it."

"Have you ever thought about joining the church?" I responded.

He thought that was just an absurd comment. He said, "Why would I join the church? If I join them, I think they would just slow me down spiritually."

I asked, "Have you ever considered that maybe God wants you to link arms with those other people, and that perhaps even though they might slow you down a little, you might help to speed them up—and that that's part of God's plan for how we're supposed to live as Christians together?"

Of course you don't join a church because you're perfect and you're only going to bring benefits to the church. Whenever you join a church, you will bring problems into that church! But don't let that stop you—they've got problems already! That's why they're in a church. I've got problems; you've got problems. But we know that Jesus is Lord, and that His Spirit in us has already begun to work on those problems. Let's say, for example, that you're paranoid—that you don't really trust anyone. In Christ, God will begin to work on that. He can begin to show you that He is trustworthy and that other people can be trustworthy too. Problem after problem, you can see God working in your life. Slowly, imperceptibly sometimes, but deliberately He will work on your problems, and most likely He will do that through His church.

It simply will not do for Christians to be self-centered, even in the name of Christ. God is not only concerned about the length and regularity of your quiet time each morning; He is also concerned about how you treat others—and that includes how you treat others with whom you have nothing in common except for Jesus Christ. That's why you need to invest your life in others and allow others to invest their lives in you. Being a member of a church should inculcate in you a committed concern for others. Growing as a Christian is not merely an individual matter; rather, it is a matter for the whole church.

Hebrews 10:19-25 has been called the "lettuce patch" of the New Testament. The writer keeps saying "let us . . . let us" throughout the passage. These are good verses to meditate on in our individualistic age:

> Therefore, brothers, since we have confidence to enter the Most Holy Place by the blood of Jesus, by a new and living way opened for us through the curtain, that is, his body, and since we have a great priest over the house of God, let us draw near to God with a sincere heart in full assurance of faith,

having our hearts sprinkled to cleanse us from a guilty conscience and having our bodies washed with pure water. Let us hold unswervingly to the hope we profess, for he who promised is faithful. And let us consider how we may spur one another on toward love and good deeds. Let us not give up meeting together, as some are in the habit of doing, but let us encourage one another—and all the more as you see the Day approaching.

Church membership is our opportunity to grasp hold of each other in responsibility and love. By identifying ourselves with a particular church, we let the pastors and other members of that local church know that we intend to be committed in attendance, giving, prayer, and service. We allow fellow believers to have greater expectations of us in these areas, and we make it known that we are the responsibility of this local church. We assure the church of our commitment to Christ in serving with them, and we call for their commitment to serve and encourage us as well.

We see this concept of church life reflected, among other places, in Paul's use of body imagery about the local church. We see it also in Scripture's "together" and "one another" passages.

Joining a church increases our sense of ownership of the work of the church, of its community, of its budget, of its goals. We move from being pampered consumers to becoming joyous proprietors. We stop arriving late and complaining that we don't get exactly what we want; instead, we arrive early and try to help others with what they need. We must begin to view membership less as a loose affiliation useful only on occasion and more as a regular responsibility involving us in one another's lives for the purposes of the Gospel.

Many Christians today seem to have forgotten church membership—or to have forgotten the church altogether. That's why you find Christian books that talk about growing as a Christian but completely ignore the role of the church.

In Paul's first letter to the Corinthians the purpose of spiritual gifts is to "build up the church" (1 Cor. 14:12). This is to be one of the main goals of your Christian life. If you're thinking there's nothing for you to do as a Christian, you must have missed this one. According to Paul, this applies to every Christian.

Incorporation into the church is both a glorious privilege and a practical help. Joining a church will help you to encourage and edify your fellow Christians and to be encouraged and edified by them. It will help both you and others as you struggle with temptation. In my own local church, we covenant together that,

> We will walk together in brotherly love, as becomes the members of a Christian church; exercise an affectionate care and watchfulness over each other and faithfully admonish and entreat one another as occasion may require.

What about you? Do you love the people of God? Do you not merely feel well-disposed toward them but actually, actively give to them? Do you use your hands for them? Your money? Your lips?

In the church, discipleship is both an individual project and a corporate activity as we follow Christ and help each other along the way. We can hold each other accountable in times of temptation. We can study God's Word together to prepare us for spiritual warfare. We can sing God's praises together and pray together. We can encourage each other's joy and share each other's burdens. As Jesus told us, "My command is this: Love each other as I have loved you. . . . This is my command: Love each other" (John 15:12, 17). John reinforced that when he wrote, "Dear children, let us not love with words or tongue but with actions and in truth" (1 John 3:18). Link arms with the other Christians around you, to build the church.

5. To Glorify God

Finally, if you are a Christian, you should join a church for the glory of God. Though it may be surprising to us, the way we live our lives can bring glory to God. As Peter wrote to some early Christians, "Live such good lives among the pagans that, though they accuse you of doing wrong, they may see *your* good deeds and glorify God on the day he visits us" (1 Pet. 2:12, emphasis added).

Amazing, isn't it? But then, you can tell that Peter had heard the teaching of His Master. Remember what Jesus had taught in the Sermon on the Mount: "Let your light shine before men, that they may see your good deeds and praise your Father in heaven" (Matt. 5:16).

Again, the surprising assumption seems to be that God will get the glory for our good deeds. If that is true of our lives individually, it shouldn't come as too much of a surprise to find that it is also true of our lives *together* as Christians. God intends that the way we love each other will identify us as followers of Christ. Recall Jesus' words in John 13:34-35: "A new command I give you: Love one another. As I have loved you, so you must love one another. By this all men will know that you are my disciples, if you love one another."

Our lives together are to mark us out as His and are to bring Him praise and glory.

Jesus said, "I will build my church" (Matt. 16:18). If Jesus is committed to the church, should we be any less committed to it?

If you are a Christian and you regularly attend a God-centered, Bible-preaching church, you may have been frustrated by one thing or another, but consider the obligations and opportunities of membership. Our basis as a congregational church family must always be found in *being* even more than in doing. If you join a church, you are not being included merely for a function you could perform (whether for your sake or the church's) but you are being adopted into a family. And the relationships to which you are committing yourself will bring glory to God.

This is why, if you are a Christian, you should join a church.

WHAT DOES CHURCH MEMBERSHIP ENTAIL?

Fundamentally, church membership entails a life of repentance and belief. The church is intended to be the community of those who have been born again. God's grace in our life, granting us repentance and faith, is signaled by two things:

In Action Initially by Baptism

This is what the Bible presents as the first step for the Christian, and the assumption in the New Testament is that all Christians have been baptized. In Romans 6, for instance, Paul is assuming that the Christians to whom he is writing have all been baptized. This universal practice was rooted in the command of Christ recorded in the Great Commission (Matt. 28:18-20) and is written about in the book of Acts and throughout the New Testament. One must wonder why some who say they are Christ's disciples refuse to do something that they know is clearly commanded. As one writer observed,

> The church has not been given authority to make commandments; it is the duty of the church to obey the commandments already made. It is not the prerogative nor the privilege of any church to modify, minimize or in any way obscure . . . any commandment, of Jesus Christ.[3]

Rejecting baptism or the Lord's Supper or any other clear biblical command is rejecting membership among Christ's disciples—among those who follow His commands.

Also, historically, in many Baptist and other evangelical churches, our commitment to God and each other has been expressed . . .

In Writing by Signing a Statement of Faith and Church Covenant

In my study I have a little booklet that our denomination has kept in print for more than sixty years. Its purpose is to encourage new church members. The first thing in the book is an example of a church covenant. At the bottom of the sample covenant is a place for the person to sign it. Such signing of a covenant is not a new practice; it simply fell into disuse in the middle decades of the twentieth century. But earlier in American history, such signing was the general practice. In our church, hanging in a prominent place, are the signatures of the founding members of the church, underneath the covenant to which they were subscribing in joining the church. Consider such signatures, and the seriousness of them. These men and women chose to covenant together in response to God's grace in their lives. Do we do any less today in joining a church?

At Capitol Hill Baptist Church we encourage the following *five responsibilities of membership:*

1. Attend Services Regularly

In Hebrews 10:25 we read that we should not forsake "the assembling of ourselves together" (KJV). That means we should regularly attend the weekly meetings of the church. At Capitol Hill, that means attending more than just the Sunday morning service.

2. Attend Communion Particularly

It was Capitol Hill's custom a hundred years ago to have Thursday evening "covenant meetings" where members would renew their covenant and check on the status of their relations with each other before taking communion together the following Sunday. And in many churches, to be absent from communion without a clear excuse was sufficient grounds for someone to be excluded from the membership of the church.

3. Attend Members' Meetings Consistently

As a congregational church, the members' meeting is an important time in our lives together. It is the meeting of the church for making decisions as a church.

4. Pray Regularly

Or, as Paul says, "without ceasing" (1 Thess. 5:17, KJV). If your church has a membership directory, consider using it as a prayer list.

5. Give Regularly

Scripture is full of instructions about giving. For example, Solomon taught that we should, "Honor the LORD with your wealth, with the firstfruits of all your crops" (Prov. 3:9).

Through the prophet Malachi, the Lord exhorted the Israelites to,

> "Bring the whole tithe into the storehouse, that there may be food in my house. Test me in this," says the LORD Almighty, "and see if I will not throw open the floodgates of heaven and pour out so much blessing that you will not have room enough for it" (Mal. 3:10).

Jesus taught His disciples,

> "Give, and it will be given to you. A good measure, pressed down, shaken together and running over, will be poured into your lap. For with the measure you use, it will be measured to you" (Luke 6:38).

Paul told the Corinthian Christians,

> Do what I told the Galatian churches to do. On the first day of every week, each one of you should set aside a sum of money in keeping with his income, saving it up, so that when I come no collections will have to be made" (1 Cor. 16:1b-2).

And he wrote back to them again that,

> Each man should give what he has decided in his heart to give, not reluctantly or under compulsion, for God loves a cheerful giver (2 Cor. 9:7).

This is some of what being a member of a church entails.

If the church is a building, then we must be bricks in it; if the church is a body, then we are its members; if the church is the household of faith, then we are part of that household. Sheep are in a flock, and branches on a vine. Biblically, if we are Christians we must be members of a church. This membership is not simply the record of a statement we once made or of affection toward a familiar place. It must be the reflection of a living commitment or it is worthless.

Worse than being worthless, it is dangerous. Uninvolved members confuse both real members and non-Christians about what it means to be a Christian. We "active" members do the voluntarily "inactive" members no service when we allow them to remain members of the church. Membership is the church's corporate endorsement of a person's salvation. Yet how can a congregation honestly testify that someone invisible to it is faithfully running the race? If members have left our company and have not gone to any other Bible-believing church, what evidence do we have that they were ever truly a part of us? We do not necessarily know that such uninvolved people are *not* Christians; we may simply be unable to affirm that they are. We don't have to tell them that we know they're going to hell, only that we can't tell them that we know for sure that they are going to heaven.

At Capitol Hill Baptist, I hope to see our membership directory become more meaningful, as all who are members in name become members in fact. In the years that I have been here our membership has roughly fallen in half, and yet our attendance and giving have, by the grace of God, about tripled. Many members have made a renewed commitment to the life of the church. New members are being instructed in the faith. As we have sought to become the healthy church we were historically, our number in attendance has once again exceeded the number of members.

Pray that church membership may come to mean something more than it currently does in your church, too, so that you as a church can better know those for whom you are responsible, so that you can pray for them, encourage them, and challenge them.

We should not allow people to keep their church membership for sentimental reasons. Considered biblically, such membership is no membership at all. In our church's covenant we also pledge that, "We will, when we move from this place, as soon as possible, unite with some other church where we can carry out the spirit of this covenant and the principles of God's Word." Such commitment is part of healthy discipleship, particularly in our transient age.

Church membership means being incorporated in practical ways into the body of Christ. It means traveling together as aliens and strangers in this world as we head to our heavenly home. Certainly another mark of a healthy church is a biblical understanding of church membership.

In the next-to-the-last scene in Thomas Bolt's play *A Man for All Seasons,* the doomed More's daughter Meg comes to his cell to convince him to say what he needs to say to free himself. As she expresses it, "Then say the words of the oath and in your heart, think otherwise." She continues to argue with him.

"Well, . . . finally," says More, "it isn't a matter of reason; finally it's a matter of love."[4]

Finally, joining a particular local church is an outward reflection of an inward love—for Christ and for His people. And, as we see so often in this life, the greatest love is rarely merely spontaneous; it is more often planned, premeditated, and characterized by commitment.

We read in Ephesians 5:25 that, "Christ loved the church and gave himself up for her." Acts 20:28 reminds us that He "bought His church with His own blood." If we are Christ's followers, we too will love the church that He gave Himself for.

So, do not merely attend a church (though you should attend), but join a church. Link arms with other Christians. Find a church you can join, and do it so that non-Christians will hear and see the Gospel, so that weak Christians will be cared for, so that strong Christians will channel their energies in a good way, so that church leaders will be encouraged and helped, so that God will be glorified.

Christians in our country used to know all this, but as the nineteenth century wore on, social action replaced church action. Christians shifted their energies away from keeping their own churches pure, to trying to purify their communities. By the time of the 1920s and '30s, evangelicals had learned something of the fickleness of our world through the celebrated Scopes trial and the repeal of Prohibition. The "fundamentalists" withdrew and attempted to preserve the Gospel. In all the social involvement of the previous decades, the Gospel had not been lost, but the church had very nearly been. This century has largely been a time of extreme individualism in American evangelicalism. Now we pray that we are on the verge of a recovery of the church as God's great tool for evangelism, discipleship, missions, and so much more. Through our love for one another, may God's love for the world again become visible.

WHAT'S COMING UP . . .

MARK SEVEN:
BIBLICAL CHURCH DISCIPLINE

Is All Discipline Negative?

What Is Church Discipline?

What Does the Bible Say About Church Discipline?

Hebrews 12:1-14

Matthew 18:15-17

1 Corinthians 5:1-11

Galatians 6:1

2 Thessalonians 3:6-15

1 Timothy 1:20

1 Timothy 5:19-20

Titus 3:9-11

How Have Christians in the Past Handled Church Discipline?

"Our Church Would Never Do This, Would We?"

Why Practice Church Discipline?

1. For the Good of the Person Disciplined

2. For the Good of the Other Christians, as They See the Danger of Sin

3. For the Health of the Church as a Whole

4. For the Corporate Witness of the Church

5. For the Glory of God, as We Reflect His Holiness

So What If We Don't Practice Church Discipline?

BIBLICAL CHURCH DISCIPLINE

Emily Sullivan Oakey was born, educated, and then taught in Albany, New York. As with many other women of the mid-nineteenth century, she spent a good bit of time writing down her thoughts—sometimes as part of a journal, other times as part of articles, very often in poetry. She published many of her articles and poems in daily newspapers and in magazines. As a young woman of twenty-one, perhaps inspired by having read Jesus' Parable of the Sower, she wrote a poem about sowing and harvesting. Some twenty-five years later, in 1875, the poem was set to music by Philip Bliss and appeared in print for the first time under the title "What Shall the Harvest Be?"[1] The little group of Christians who formed what would become Capitol Hill Baptist Church selected that very song as the first song to be sung in their meetings together, in February of 1878:

> Sowing the seed by the daylight fair,
> Sowing the seed by the noonday glare,
> Sowing the seed by the fading light,
> Sowing the seed in the solemn night.
> O, what shall the harvest be?
> O, what shall the harvest be?

Very appropriate words to ring off the bare walls and bare floorboards of the building they met in. Those thirty people were planning to covenant to form a church: "What would the harvest be?"

In that same church, now more than a century later, we are still helping to determine what will be the harvest of their efforts. We are determining this by what we think and how we live, by whom we plan to see and what we plan to do, by what we feel and what we care about, what we give ourselves for and what we pray about.

What has the harvest been, and what shall the harvest be?

That gets to the very heart of our question in this chapter: Are we to live as Christians on our own? Or do we have some obligation to each other? Do our obligations to each other involve merely encouraging each other positively? Or do they possibly include a responsibility to speak honestly to each other of faults, shortcomings, departures from Scripture, or specific sin? Could our responsibilities before God also include sometimes making such matters public?

One vital aspect of a healthy church is church discipline. As we approach this subject, let's ask ourselves seven questions:

1. Is all discipline negative?
2. What is usually meant by "church discipline"? What does it involve?
3. Where does the Bible talk about church discipline? What does it say?
4. How have Christians in the past handled church discipline?
5. "Our local church would never do this, would we?"
6. Why practice church discipline?
7. What if we don't?

IS ALL DISCIPLINE NEGATIVE?

Church discipline sounds like a pretty negative topic, I admit. There isn't going to be much about this in "The Positive Bible," is there? When we hear of discipline, we tend to think of correction or of a spanking; we think of our parents when we were little. If we're particularly literate we have visions of Hester Prynne wearing her scarlet *A* around a nightmarish Puritan New England town of Nathaniel Hawthorne's misdirected imagination.

We should all, without hesitation, admit our need for discipline, our need for shaping. None of us are perfect, finished projects. We may need to be inspired, nurtured, or healed; we may need to be corrected, challenged, even broken. Whatever the particular method of cure, let's at least admit the need for discipline. Let's not pretend or presume that you or I are just as we should be, as if God had finished His work with us.

Once we have come to that admission, however, notice that much of discipline is *positive* discipline, or as it is traditionally called, "formative discipline." It is the stake that helps the tree grow in the right direction, the braces on the teeth, the extra set of wheels on the bicycle. It is the repeated comments on keeping your mouth closed when you're eating, or the regular exhortations to be careful about your words. It is the things that are simply shaping the person as he or she grows emotionally, physically, mentally, and spiritually. These are all examples of the basic shaping that takes place in our relationships, in our families, and also in our churches. We are taught by books at school, and by sermons and services and classes at church. All of this is part of discipline. It is positive, shaping, formative discipline. Every truth that you have ever heard someone talk about is part of formative discipline. This chapter right now is part of discipline in the broadest sense of teaching.

So discipline is not only a negative matter.

WHAT IS CHURCH DISCIPLINE?

When we hear the term *church discipline,* we tend to think only of the negative aspects of discipline, such as correction. We may even become defensive and say something like, "Didn't Jesus say 'Judge not, lest you be judged'?"

Certainly, in Matthew 7:1, Jesus did forbid judging in one sense, and we'll consider that later in the chapter. But for now, note that if you read through that same gospel of Matthew, you'll find that Jesus also clearly called us to rebuke others for sin, even rebuking them publicly if need be (Matt. 18:15-17; cf. Luke 17:3). Whatever Jesus meant by not judging in Matthew 7, He didn't mean to rule out the kind of judging He mandated in Matthew 18.

Remember that God Himself is a Judge, and, in a lesser sense, God intends others to judge as well. He has given the state the responsibility to judge (Rom. 13:1-7). In various places we are told to judge ourselves (1 Cor. 11:28; 2 Cor. 13:5; Heb. 4; 2 Pet. 1:5-10). We are also specifically told to judge one another within the church (though not in the final way that God judges); Jesus' words in Matthew 18, Paul's in 1 Corinthians 5–6, and other passages (which we'll turn to in just a moment) clearly show that the church is to exercise judgment within itself.

If you think about it, it is not really surprising that we as a church should be instructed to judge. After all, if we cannot say how a Christian *should not* live, how can we say how a Christian *should* live?

A couple of years ago I was asked to lead a special seminar because our church had been growing numerically and other churches wanted to know how and why that was happening. In preparing for the seminar, I reviewed some of the church growth material coming from our denominational headquarters. One publication said that, in order to get our churches growing again, we should "open the front doors and close the back doors." The writer was saying that we need to open the front doors in the sense of trying to make our churches more accessible by helping people to understand what we're doing. Then, the writer said, we need to close the back door, that is, make it more difficult for people just to flow through our churches, uncared-for and undiscipled.

These are valid criticisms of many of our churches, no doubt. But I have to say that, as I thought about it, I didn't think either of those were really the critical problems we face. What we actually need to do is to close the front door and open the back door! If we really want to see our churches grow, we need to make it harder to join and we need to be better about excluding people. We need to be able to show that there is a distinction between the church and the world—that it means something to be a Christian. If someone who claims to be a Christian refuses to live as a Christian should live, we need to follow what Paul said and, for the glory of God and for that person's own good, we need to exclude him or her from membership in the church.

The first place to reflect this kind of discipline should be in the way we take in new members. In 1 Corinthians 5, while dealing with a difficult situation in the church at Corinth, Paul made an assumption that we need to consider. In verses 9-10, he says,

> I have written you in my letter not to associate with sexually immoral people—not at all meaning the people of this world who are immoral, or the greedy and swindlers, or idolaters. In that case you would have to leave this world.

Notice that Paul has a very clear distinction in his mind between the church and the world. Do we as Christians today make the same distinction? Do we assume that the church is different than the world? Not that the church is full of perfect people and the world is full of sinners, but do we assume that there is to be some kind of difference between the lives of those in the church and those in the world? Paul draws a sharp contrast. Membership in a local church is to be reflective (as best we can tell) of true membership in the body of Christ.

So, when we're taking in new members, we have to consider whether those who are under consideration are known to be living Christ-honoring lives. Do we understand the seriousness of the commitment we are making to them when they join the church, and have we communicated to them the seriousness of the commitment that they are making to us? If we are more careful about how we recognize and receive new members, we will have less occasion to practice corrective church discipline later.

Let me suggest some books that may be helpful to you on this matter. Since this is a topic that hasn't been talked about in about a hundred years, you might like to know something beyond the bounds of this one chapter.

In *The Compromised Church*, edited by John Armstrong, there is an excellent article by R. Albert Mohler, Jr., president of the Southern Baptist Theological Seminary. It is called "Church Discipline: The Missing Mark,"[2] and is a great brief argument for the importance of church discipline.

On the practical side, there is a little booklet called *Biblical Church Discipline,* by Daniel Wray, a pastor.[3]

For historical background, you could look at Greg Wills's book, *Democratic Religion.*[4] He studied the practice of church discipline among Baptist churches in the South, particularly in Georgia, in the nineteenth century. The book includes some good stories and some very shrewd observations.

If you want a traditional manual of church order that talks about how you actually practice church discipline, look at John L. Dagg, *Manual of Church Polity.*[5] This manual discusses what the Bible says about how churches are to be ordered and how to practically carry out our business.

Then there is a book that I edited, *Polity: How Christians Should Live Together in a Church,* a compendium of eighteenth- and nineteenth-century works on church discipline and polity, published by the Center for Church Reform. It includes introductions by Greg Wills and by me, and also includes the Mohler article mentioned above.[6]

If you want something more modern, the best guide that I've found is the *Handbook of Church Discipline,* by Jay Adams.[7]

Finally, if you would like to see what should happen between Christians, portrayed in a series of good meditations, read Dietrich Bonhoeffer's little book, *Life Together.*[8]

Now on to question 3.

WHAT DOES THE BIBLE SAY ABOUT CHURCH DISCIPLINE?

There are many Bible passages we could look at concerning discipline; let me draw your attention to eight of them:

Hebrews 12:1-14

The place to begin is in Hebrews 12, where we see that discipline is fundamentally a positive thing and that God Himself disciplines us:

> Therefore, since we are surrounded by such a great cloud of witnesses, let us throw off everything that hinders and the sin that so easily entangles, and let us run with perseverance the race marked out for us. Let us fix our eyes on Jesus, the author and perfecter of our faith, who for the joy set before him endured the cross, scorning its shame, and sat down at the right hand of the throne of God. Consider him who endured such opposition from sinful men, so that you will not grow weary and lose heart.
>
> In your struggle against sin, you have not yet resisted to the point of shedding your blood. And you have forgotten that word of encouragement that addresses you as sons:
>
> > "My son, do not make light of the Lord's discipline,
> >   and do not lose heart when he rebukes you,
> > because the Lord disciplines those he loves,
> >   and he punishes everyone he accepts as a son."
>
> Endure hardship as discipline; God is treating you as sons. For what son is not disciplined by his father? If you are not disciplined (and everyone undergoes discipline), then you are illegitimate children and not true sons. Moreover, we have all had human fathers who disciplined us and we respected them for it. How much more should we submit to the Father of our spirits and live! Our fathers disciplined us for a little while as they thought best; but God disciplines us for our good, that we may share in his holiness. No discipline seems pleasant at the time, but painful. Later on, however, it produces a harvest of righteousness and peace for those who have been trained by it.

> Therefore, strengthen your feeble arms and weak knees. "Make level paths for your feet," so that the lame may not be disabled, but rather healed.
>
> Make every effort to live in peace with all men and to be holy; without holiness no one will see the Lord.

God Himself disciplines us and, as we will see, He commands us to do the same for each other. The local church congregation has a special responsibility and a special competence in this regard.

Matthew 18:15-17

In Matthew 18, we have one of the two passages (along with 1 Corinthians 5) most often cited in discussions of church discipline. How do you respond when someone sins against you? Do you sound off at them once and then refuse to talk to them anymore? Do you just build up resentment in your heart? Here's what the Lord Jesus taught His disciples to do in such situations:

> "If your brother sins against you, go and show him his fault, just between the two of you. If he listens to you, you have won your brother over. But if he will not listen, take one or two others along, so that 'every matter may be established by the testimony of two or three witnesses.' If he refuses to listen to them, tell it to the church; and if he refuses to listen even to the church, treat him as you would a pagan or a tax collector."

That, according to Jesus, is how we are to deal with disagreements and difficulties with fellow-believers. And that's exactly what the early Christians did, as we see in Paul's letters.

1 Corinthians 5:1-11

This is the longest and best-known passage in this regard. There was apparently someone in the Corinthian church who was living an immoral lifestyle. Paul says:

It is actually reported that there is sexual immorality among you, and of a kind that does not occur even among pagans: A man has his father's wife. And you are proud! Shouldn't you rather have been filled with grief and have put out of your fellowship the man who did this? Even though I am not physically present, I am with you in spirit. And I have already passed judgment on the one who did this, just as if I were present. When you are assembled in the name of our Lord Jesus and I am with you in spirit, and the power of our Lord Jesus is present, hand this man over to Satan, so that the sinful nature may be destroyed and his spirit saved on the day of the Lord.

Your boasting is not good. Don't you know that a little yeast works through the whole batch of dough? Get rid of the old yeast that you may be a new batch without yeast—as you really are. For Christ, our Passover lamb, has been sacrificed. Therefore let us keep the Festival, not with the old yeast, the yeast of malice and wickedness, but with bread without yeast, the bread of sincerity and truth.

I have written you in my letter not to associate with sexually immoral people—not at all meaning the people of this world who are immoral, or the greedy and swindlers, or idolaters. In that case you would have to leave this world. But now I am writing you that you must not associate with anyone who calls himself a brother but is sexually immoral or greedy, an idolater or a slanderer, a drunkard or a swindler. With such a man do not even eat.

Why did Paul say all that? Because he had come to hate the man? No, but because that man was deeply deceived. He thought he could be a Christian while deliberately disobeying the Lord. Or perhaps he thought—and the church allowed him to think—that there was nothing wrong with his having his father's wife. Paul says that such a person is deluded, and that in order truly to serve such a deluded person and to glorify God, you need to show him the falsity of his profession of faith in light of the way he is living.

Elsewhere in his letters, Paul sheds more light on how such a process of loving confrontation should occur.

Galatians 6:1

This short verse is an important addition to our thinking on church discipline. Here Paul describes how Christians are to restore someone who has been caught in sin:

> Brothers, if someone is caught in a sin, you who are spiritual should restore him gently. But watch yourself, or you also may be tempted.

Paul was concerned not just with what was to be done in such a difficult situation but also with how it was to be done.

2 Thessalonians 3:6-15

In Thessalonica, it seems there were some people who were being lazy and not doing anything. To make matters worse, they were defending their inactivity, saying that it was God's will. Paul said it was not:

> In the name of the Lord Jesus Christ, we command you, brothers, to keep away from every brother who is idle and does not live according to the teaching you received from us. For you yourselves know how you ought to follow our example. We were not idle when we were with you, nor did we eat anyone's food without paying for it. On the contrary, we worked night and day, laboring and toiling so that we would not be a burden to any of you. We did this, not because we do not have the right to such help, but in order to make ourselves a model for you to follow. For even when we were with you, we gave you this rule: "If a man will not work, he shall not eat."
>
> We hear that some among you are idle. They are not busy; they are busybodies. Such people we command and urge in the Lord Jesus Christ to settle down and earn the bread they eat. And as for you, brothers, never tire of doing what is right.

If anyone does not obey our instruction in this letter, take special note of him. Do not associate with him, in order that he may feel ashamed. Yet do not regard him as an enemy, but warn him as a brother.

1 Timothy 1:20

Writing to Timothy, pastor of the church in Ephesus, Paul referred to some who had made "shipwreck" of their faith. Look at what he said should be done with such people:

Among them are Hymenaeus and Alexander, whom I have handed over to Satan to be taught not to blaspheme.

1 Timothy 5:19-20

As he continued his letter to Timothy, Paul wrote specifically about what to do with church leaders who are caught in sin:

Do not entertain an accusation against an elder unless it is brought by two or three witnesses. Those who sin are to be rebuked publicly, so that the others may take warning.

Titus 3:9-11

Apparently some people in the church where Titus pastored were causing divisions over issues that weren't that important. Paul wrote,

But avoid foolish controversies and genealogies and arguments and quarrels about the law, because these are unprofitable and useless. Warn a divisive person once, and then warn him a second time. After that, have nothing to do with him. You may be sure that such a man is warped and sinful; he is self-condemned.

Taking all of these passages together, we see that God cares about both our understanding of His truth and our living it out. He cares especially about how we live together as Christians. All kinds of situations mentioned in these passages are, according to the Bible, legitimate areas for our concern—areas in which we as a church should exercise discipline.

One more thing: Did you notice how serious were the consequences Paul mandated in these descriptions of church discipline? "Put out of your fellowship . . ." (1 Cor. 5:2); "hand this man over to Satan" (1 Cor. 5:5); ". . . not to associate with . . . do not even eat . . . with such a man" (1 Cor. 5:9, 11); "keep away from . . ." (2 Thess. 3:6); "take special note of him. Do not associate with him, in order that he may feel ashamed" (2 Thess. 3:14-15); ". . . handed over to Satan . . ." (1 Tim. 1:20); "rebuked publicly" (1 Tim. 5:20); "Have nothing to do with them" (2 Tim. 3:5); "have nothing to do with him" (Titus 3:10).

Is Paul just an unusually severe kind of man? What did Jesus Himself say about the person who refused to listen even to the church? "If he refuses to listen even to the church, treat him as you would a pagan or a tax collector" (Matt. 18:17).

This is what the Bible says about church discipline.

HOW HAVE CHRISTIANS IN THE PAST HANDLED CHURCH DISCIPLINE?

In times past, Christians have actually done quite a bit about church discipline. You may be surprised to learn that disciplinary actions were a substantial part of the business at members' meetings of Baptist churches in the eighteenth and nineteenth centuries.

Writing about fifty years ago, Greek scholar H. E. Dana observed that,

> The abuse of discipline is reprehensible and destructive, but not more than the abandonment of discipline. Two generations ago the churches were applying discipline in a vindictive and arbitrary fashion that justly brought it into disrepute; today the pendulum has swung to the other extreme—disci-

pline is almost wholly neglected. It is time for a new generation of pastors to restore this important function of the
church to its rightful significance and place in church life.[9]

Greg Wills, professor of church history at the Southern Baptist
Theological Seminary, has brought to light a crucial change in this
regard between the generations of our great-grandparents and our
grandparents; what he finds is the virtual disappearance of corrective
discipline from our churches. Wills's book *Democratic Religion* offers
a wealth of quotations reminding us that pastors of the early 1800s
clearly considered their most important tasks to be faithfully preaching the Word and faithfully administering godly discipline. In fact, a
great part of the historic Baptist commitment to religious liberty was
motivated by a desire that churches be free to exercise church discipline without the interference of the state.[10]

Wills shows that in pre-Civil War days, "Southern Baptists
excommunicated nearly 2 percent of their membership every year"![11]
Incredible as it may seem, while they were doing that their churches
grew! In fact, their churches grew at twice the rate of the population
growth! So the concern that a move to such biblical church discipline
might be "anti-evangelistic" seems unfounded, to say the least.

Jesus intended our lives to back up our words. If our lives don't
back up our words, the evangelistic task is injured, as we have seen so
terribly this last century in America. Undisciplined churches have
actually made it harder for people to hear the Good News of new life
in Jesus Christ.

If that's the case, what happened? Why did we stop practicing
church discipline? We don't really know, but Wills suggests that,
"This commitment to a holy corporate witness to the world declined
as other things gained the attention of the Christians late in the last
century and earlier in this one." Wills writes:

> In fact, the more the churches concerned themselves with
> social order, the less they exerted church discipline. From
> about 1850 to 1920, a period of expanding evangelical solici-

tude for the reformation of society, church discipline declined steadily. From temperance to Sabbatarian reform, evangelicals persuaded their communities to adopt the moral norms of the church for society at large. As Baptists learned to reform the larger society, they forgot how they had once reformed themselves. Church discipline presupposed a stark dichotomy between the norms of society and the kingdom of God. The more evangelicals purified the society, the less they felt the urgency of a discipline that separated the church from the world.[12]

As Wills explains,

> After the Civil War, . . . observers began to lament that church discipline was foundering, and it was. It declined partly because it became more burdensome in larger churches. Young Baptists refused in increasing numbers to submit to discipline for dancing, and the churches shrank from excluding them. Urban churches, pressed by the need for large buildings and the desire for refined music and preaching, subordinated church discipline to the task of keeping the church solvent. Many Baptists shared a new vision of the church, replacing the pursuit of purity with the quest for efficiency. They lost the resolve to purge their churches of straying members. No one publicly advocated the demise of discipline. No Baptist leader arose to call for an end to congregational censures. No theologians argued that discipline was unsound in principle or practice. . . . It simply faded away, as if Baptists had grown weary of holding one another accountable.[13]

As Baptist churches of the nineteenth century retreated from church discipline, the work of the pastor was also changing. It had subtly though certainly become more public. Previously, it had been thought that the work of a pastor was to see that souls were mended by repeated private conferences with families or individuals. But what came to happen more and more were protracted series of meetings and entertainments and impassioned calls to immediate decision, with the pastor being called upon now and then to deal with only the most serious cases of church discipline. The church, increasingly, didn't really have anything to do with such problems and, in fact, wasn't even aware of them. There was no longer a community that mutually covenanted together for accountability. Instead, the pastor alone was expected to deal with just a few cases—those that could cause the church the most public embarrassment.

In all of these changes, important boundaries were blurred. The pastor's role was confused. Even more fundamentally, the distinction between the church and the world began to be lost. And this loss was to the great detriment of the churches' evangelistic ministry—and to our own lives as Christians.

All evangelical Christians in the past tended to practice biblical church discipline. In fact, in 1561, Reformed Christians expressed their understanding of these matters in the words of the Belgic Confession:

> The marks by which the true Church is known are these: If the pure doctrine of the gospel is preached therein; if she maintains the pure administration of the sacraments as instituted by Christ; if church discipline is exercised in punishing of sin; in short, if all things are managed according to the pure Word of God, all things contrary thereto rejected, and Jesus Christ acknowledged as the only Head of the Church. Hereby the true Church may certainly be known, from which no man has a right to separate himself.[14]

It is clear that, in the past, churches intended to practice biblical discipline.

"OUR CHURCH WOULD NEVER DO THIS, WOULD WE?"

The local church I pastor in Washington has from its earliest days recognized the importance of church discipline. When the group of

Christians met together that first day and sang that hymn, they incorporated as a church. One of the first things they did that day, in February of 1878, was to adopt the following rules about the church censuring people either by admonition (warning) or by exclusion, which would happen after they had been warned. About admonishing a member, they said,

> When one member of the church trespasses against another member, if the offence is not of a public character, it is the duty of the offended to seek an opportunity to converse privately with the offender, with a view to the reconcilement of the difficulty, according to the rule laid down in Matthew 18:15.
>
> If the offender refuses to give satisfaction, it shall be the duty of the offended to select one or two members of the church, and with their aid to endeavor to reconcile the offender, according to the rule laid down in Matthew 18:16.
>
> If these efforts fail to secure a satisfactory adjustment of the difficulty, it shall be the duty of the offended to lay the matter before the church, as directed in Matthew 18:17, and if, after the offender shall have been admonished, in a spirit of meekness and forbearance, he or she shall continue obstinate and incorrigible, it shall be the duty of the church to investigate the case, and take such action as may be necessary.
>
> Charges to be preferred against a member shall be in writing, and shall not be presented to the church without the previous knowledge of the Pastor and Deacons, nor until a copy shall have been presented to the offender.

They also discussed what was to happen if the erring member did not repent. The next step was exclusion. They said that exclusion,

> . . . is a judicial act of the church, passed upon an offender by the authority of the Lord Jesus Christ, by which he or she is cut off from the membership and communion of the church, according to the rule . . . from Matthew 18:17.

No member shall be excluded until he or she shall have been notified to appear before the church, and has had the privilege of answering in person the charges which have been preferred, except in cases of notorious and flagrant immorality, when it shall be the duty of the church to vindicate the honor of its holy calling by proceeding to cut off such an offending member without delay.

What sin did they consider of sufficient seriousness to take such action? If you got upset at someone over picking the wrong hymn, or if someone dropped a hymnbook on your toe? Did they go to church discipline over this? What matters were so serious that they felt biblically required to respond with such strong measures? What matters are so serious that we today are called to these kinds of actions? What would warrant being so warned or even excluded from membership in the church? Here's what they said:

Members shall be liable to the discipline of the church for the following causes:

For any outward violations of the moral law.

For pursuing any course which may, in the judgement of the church, be disreputable to it as a body.

For absenting themselves habitually without good reasons, from the church at the seasons set apart for public worship.

For holding and advocating doctrines opposed to those set forth in [the statement of faith].

For neglecting or refusing to contribute toward defraying the expenses of the church according to their several abilities.

For treating the acts and doings of the church contemptuously, or pursuing such a course as is calculated to produce discord.

For divulging to persons not interested, what is done in the meetings of the church.

For pursuing any course of conduct unbecoming good citizens and professing Christians.

So, if you were in our church 120 years ago, would you be warned by the church about something? I regularly see the names of our founding members. Their signatures are on the original church covenant that hangs prominently on a wall in our church. There on that church covenant, among those first thirty-one people who subscribed to it 120 years ago, I also find the very names of some of those involved in the first recorded cases of church discipline. I find that two members were excluded (out of about eighty total members of the church) in 1880. Who were they and what happened? Well, we don't know much, but it seems that this difficult situation is what the church clerk referred to in an annual church letter; in his otherwise glowing report for 1879, we have this very brief note from Francis McLean, the church clerk:

> One thing I must whisper softly: the thrifty growth and the dense foliage do not quite conceal a few apparently dead limbs on the tree. Here lies a responsibility—a care—let us act wisely and well.

It seems that one of those "dead limbs" was actually one of the people who had signed as a founding member of the church. His name was Charles L. Patten. He had served as secretary of the Sunday school. And yet, in the minutes for a meeting of the church on December 17, 1879, we find this brief note:

> Pastor presented applications for letters of dismission from this Church to the First Baptist Church, this city, each dated Oct. 30, 1879, from Sister Alma C. Smith and Bro. Charles L. Patten. Pastor stated these letters had been withheld, in his discretion, and he now presented them for the action of the church. Bro. Williamson moved that Sister Smith be granted letters of dismission. Lost. On motion of Bro. Kingdon, a Committee was chosen, composed of the Pastor, Brethren C. W. Longan, and Ward Morgan, to consider this application of Bro. Patten, and that he be requested to appear before

that committee, to state the reasons why he had separated from his wife.

That was in the public meeting of the church. They did not want it thought that Christians leave their wives. About a month later, at a church meeting on January 21, 1880, we read,

> Pastor, on behalf of Committee to investigate case of Bro. Patten, reported that a letter had been written to him, to which he had responded in writing, but that further effort of Committee had failed to meet with any response. The Committee was considered as having reported progress and still retaining the matter in charge.

At the same meeting, a second disciplinary matter was raised in the case of yet another founding member of the congregation:

> Clerk presented the following motion, which was adopted, viz: That a Committee, composed of the Pastor and Deacons, be and is hereby requested to take into consideration such facts in the case of Sister Lucretia E. Douglas, as may explain the reasons, if any, of her nonattendance at the meetings of the church for over a year past, and to recommend at the next Quarterly Meeting what they shall deem to be the wisest and best course in the matter on the part of this church.

Nonattendance, as in the case of Sister Douglas, was considered one of the most sinister of sins, because it usually veiled all the other sins. When someone began to be in sin, you would expect them to stop attending.

So, not only *would* Capitol Hill Baptist Church practice church discipline—we can and have! This was the regular business of the church.

But, you may ask, why do something like this?

That's our sixth question.

WHY PRACTICE CHURCH DISCIPLINE?

For what purpose does your church exist? How do you know if it is fulfilling its purpose? How do you know that things are going well in your church?

The Bible says that "love covers over a multitude of sins." As pragmatic Americans, we sometimes seem to think that *size* covers over a multitude of sins. We often assume that if a church is large or at least is growing, then it must be a good church. Os Guinness writes about this mistake: "One Florida pastor with a seven-thousand member megachurch expressed the fallacy well: 'I must be doing right or things wouldn't be going so well.'"[15]

But imagine this church: It is huge and is still numerically growing. People like it. The music is good. Whole extended families can be found within its membership. The people are welcoming. There are many exciting programs, and people are quickly enlisted into their support. And yet, the church, in trying to look like the world in order to win the world, has done a better job than it may have intended. It does not display the distinctively holy characteristics taught in the New Testament. Imagine such an apparently vigorous church being truly spiritually sick, with no remaining immune system to check and guard against wrong teaching or wrong living. Imagine Christians, knee-deep in recovery groups and sermons on brokenness and grace, being comforted in their sin but never confronted. Imagine those people, made in the image of God, being lost to sin because no one corrects them. Can you imagine such a church?

Apart from the size, have I not described many of our American churches?

It won't be easy for us to be faithful in this matter of church discipline when so many churches are unfaithful in this regard. It is hard enough to try to reestablish a culture of meaningful membership in a church. Personally, I have often become the focus of someone's anger because they don't appreciate the importance of having membership taken so seriously. But I see no other way that we can be faithful to what Jesus taught. We must try, praying for God's Spirit to give us sufficient love and wisdom.

Let's be honest. The state of churches in America today is not good. Even if the membership numbers of some groups look okay, as soon as you ask what the membership numbers actually stand for, you start finding the trouble. Alan Redpath has said about the membership of the average American church that 5 percent don't exist, 10 percent can't be found, 25 percent don't attend, 50 percent show up on Sunday, 75 percent don't attend the prayer meeting, 90 percent have no family worship, and 95 percent have never shared the Gospel with others.

There are some reasons *not* to practice church discipline, of course. We certainly should not practice church discipline to be vindictive. Paul reminded the Roman Christians, "Do not take revenge, my friends, but leave room for God's wrath, for it is written: 'It is mine to avenge; I will repay,' says the Lord" (Rom. 12:19). Corrective church discipline is never to be done out of meanness of spirit but only out of a love for the offending party and the members of the church individually, and ultimately out of our love for God Himself.

Nor should corrective church discipline ever take place out of the mistaken notion that we have the final word from God on a person's eternal fate. Corrective church discipline is never meant to be the final statement about a person's eternal destiny. We don't know that. Such a pronouncement is not our role. It is beyond our competence.

We're to practice church discipline because, with humility and love, we want to see good come.

We considered earlier Jesus' words in Matthew 7:1: "Do not judge, or you too will be judged." He went on to say, "For in the same way you judge others, you will be judged, and with the measure you use, it will be measured to you" (v. 2). When any kind of church discipline or even merely criticism is mentioned today, many think of this verse. But it would seem that the essence of what Jesus forbids here is not simply being critical; rather, it is doing that which is not in our authority to do. Personal revenge is wrong (see Matt. 5:40), but final justice is right (see Matt. 19:28). It is wrong to ask people to measure up to your whims and wishes, but it is completely appropriate for God to require His creatures to reflect His holy character. We do not in ourselves have the right or the ability to condemn finally, but one day God will ask His followers to pronounce His judgments—awesome, wonderful, and terrible—upon His creation (see 1 Cor. 6:2).

Some churches ask their members to covenant together to promote not only their own holiness but also the holiness of their brothers and sisters in Christ. Could it be that, in our day, a misunderstanding of Matthew 7:1 has been a shield for sin and has worked to prevent the kind of congregational life that was known by churches of an earlier day and could be known by us again?

Certainly a "holier-than-thou," judgmental attitude indicates a heart ignorant of its debt to God's grace and mercy. But likewise, people who are unconcerned with sin in their own lives or in the lives of those they love are not exhibiting the kind of holy love that Jesus had and that He said would mark His disciples.

We do not exclude someone from fellowship in the church because we know their final state will be eternal separation from God. Rather, we exclude someone out of a concern that they are living in a way that displeases God. We do not discipline because we want to get back at someone. We discipline in humility and in love for God and for the person disciplined.

We should want to see discipline practiced in this way in our churches for other reasons as well, five of which we'll briefly consider:

1. For the Good of the Person Disciplined

The man in Corinth (1 Cor. 5:1-5) was lost in his sin, thinking God approved of his having an affair with his father's wife. The people in the churches in Galatia thought it was fine that they were trusting in their own works rather than in Christ alone (see Gal. 6:1). Alexander and Hymenaeus (1 Tim. 1:20) thought it was alright for them to blaspheme God. But none of these people were in good standing with God. Out of our love for such people, we want to see church discipline practiced. We don't want our church to encourage hypocrites who are hardened, confirmed, lulled in their sins. We don't want to live that kind of life individually, or as a church.

2. For the Good of the Other Christians, as They See the Danger of Sin
Paul told Timothy that if a leader sins he should be rebuked publicly (1 Tim. 5:20). That doesn't mean that anytime I, as the pastor, do anything wrong, members of my church should stand up in the public service and say, "Hey, Mark, that was wrong." It means when there is a serious sin (particularly one that's not repented of) it needs to be brought up in public so that others take warning by seeing the serious nature of sin.

3. For the Health of the Church as a Whole
Paul pleads with the believers at Corinth, saying that they shouldn't have boasted about having such toleration for sin in the church (1 Cor. 5:6-8). He asked rhetorically, "Don't you know that a little yeast works through the whole batch of dough?" Yeast, of course represents the unclean and spreading nature of sin. So, says Paul,

> Get rid of the old yeast that you may be a new batch without yeast—as you really are. For Christ, our Passover lamb, has been sacrificed. Therefore let us keep the Festival [the Passover supper] not with the old yeast, the yeast of malice and wickedness, but with bread without yeast, the bread of sincerity and truth.

For the Passover meal a lamb was slaughtered and unleavened bread was eaten. Paul tells the Corinthians that the lamb (Christ) had been slaughtered, and that they (the Corinthian church) were to be the unleavened bread. They were to have no leaven of sin in them. They, as a whole church, were to be an acceptable sacrifice.

Of course, none of this means that discipline is to be the focal point of the church. Discipline is no more the focal point of the church than medicine is the focal point of life. There may be some times when you are necessarily consumed with discipline, but generally it should be no more than something that allows you to get on with your main task. It is certainly not the main task itself.

4. For the Corporate Witness of the Church

(See Matthew 5:16; John 13:34-35; 1 Corinthians 5:1; 1 Peter 2:12.) Church discipline is a powerful tool in evangelism. People notice when our lives are different, especially when there's a whole community of people whose lives are different—not people whose lives are perfect, but whose lives are marked by genuinely trying to love God and love one another. When churches are seen as conforming to the world, it makes our evangelistic task all the more difficult. As Nigel Lee of English InterVarsity once said, we become so like the unbelievers they have no questions they want to ask us. May we so live that people are made constructively curious.

Finally, the most compelling reason to practice church discipline is,

5. For the Glory of God, as We Reflect His Holiness

(See Ephesians 5:25-27; Hebrews 12:10-14; 1 Peter 1:15-16; 2:9-12; 1 John 3:2-3.) That's why we're alive! We humans were made to bear God's image, to carry His character to His creation (Gen. 1:27). So it is no surprise that, throughout the Old Testament, as God fashioned a people to bear His image, He instructed them in holiness so that their character might better approximate His own (see Lev. 11:44a; 19:2). This was the basis for correction and even exclusion in Old Testament times, as God fashioned a people for Himself; and it was the basis for shaping the New Testament church as well (see 2 Cor. 6:14–7:1). Christians are supposed to be conspicuously holy, not for our own reputation but for God's. We are to be the light of the world, so that when people see our good deeds they will glorify God (Matt. 5:16). Peter says the same thing: "Live such good lives among the pagans that, though they accuse you of doing wrong, they may see your good deeds and glorify God on the day he visits us" (1 Pet. 2:12). This is why God has called us and saved us and set us apart (Col. 1:21-22).

What else should we look like, if we bear His name? Paul wrote to the church at Corinth,

> Do you not know that the wicked will not inherit the kingdom of God? Do not be deceived: Neither the sexually immoral nor idolaters nor adulterers nor male prostitutes nor homosexual offenders nor thieves nor the greedy nor drunkards nor slanderers nor swindlers will inherit the kingdom of God. And that is what some of your were. But you were washed, you were sanctified, you were justified in the name of the Lord Jesus Christ and by the Spirit of our God (1 Cor. 6:9-11).

From the very beginning, Jesus had instructed His disciples to teach people to obey all that He had taught (Matt. 28:19-20). God will have a holy people to reflect His character. The picture of the church at the end of the book of Revelation is of a glorious bride who reflects the character of Christ Himself, while, "Outside are the dogs, those who practice magic arts, the sexually immoral, the murderers, the idolaters and everyone who loves and practices falsehood" (Rev. 22:15).

Taking 1 Corinthians 5 as a model, churches have long recognized church discipline as one of the boundaries that makes church membership mean something. The assumption is that church members are people who can appropriately take communion without bringing disgrace on the church, condemnation on themselves, or dishonor to God and His Gospel (see 1 Cor. 11).

When we consider such passages, and the qualifications for leaders in the church, we see that we as Christians bear much more actively the responsibility to have a good name than do people in the world. In our secular courts we rightly maintain a very strict burden of proof on those who would charge others with guilt. We presume innocence until one is proved guilty. But in the church, our responsibility is slightly but importantly different. Our lives are the storefront display of God's character in His world. We cannot finally determine what others think of us, and we know that we are to expect such strong disapproval that we will even be persecuted for righteousness. But so far as it lies within us, we are to live lives that commend the Gospel to others. We actively bear a responsibility to live lives that will bring praise and glory to God, not ignominy and shame.

Our biblical theology may explain church discipline. Our teaching and preaching may instruct about it. Our church leaders may encourage it. But it is only the church that may and must finally enforce discipline.

Biblical church discipline is simple obedience to God and a simple confession that we need help. We cannot live the Christian life alone. Our purpose in church discipline is positive for the individual disciplined, for other Christians as they see the real danger of sin, for the health of the church as a whole, and for the corporate witness of the church to those outside. Most of all, our holiness is to reflect the holiness of God. It should mean something to be a member of the church, not for our pride's sake but for God's name's sake. Biblical church discipline is a mark of a healthy church.

SO WHAT IF WE DON'T PRACTICE CHURCH DISCIPLINE?

We have to wonder what it means to be a church if our church won't practice church discipline. You see, finally, this is a question about the nature of our churches.

Greg Wills has written that, to many Christians in the past, "A church without discipline would hardly have counted as a church."[16] John Dagg wrote that, "When discipline leaves a church, Christ goes with it."[17] If we can't say what something is not, we can't very well say what it is.

We need to live lives that back up our professions of faith. We need to love each other. We need to hold each other accountable because all of us will have times when our flesh wants to go in a way different than what God has revealed in Scripture. And part of the way we love each other is by being honest and establishing relationships with each other and speaking in love to each other. We need to love each other and we need to love those outside our church whom our witness affects; and we need to love God, who is holy, and who calls us not to bear His name in vain, but to be holy as He is holy. That's a tremendous privilege and a great responsibility.

If we would see our churches healthy, we must actively care for each other, even to the point of confronting. It all gets very practical, doesn't it, when you get right down to it—all this talk about a church, new life, covenant, committed relationships?

What shall the harvest be?

Sowing the seed by the wayside high,
Sowing the seed on the rocks to die,
Sowing the seed where the thorns will spoil,
Sowing the seed in the fertile soil:
Sowing the seed with an aching heart,
Sowing the seed while the teardrops start,
Sowing in hope till the reapers come
Gladly to gather the harvest home:
O, what shall the harvest be?

WHAT'S COMING UP . . .

MARK EIGHT:
A CONCERN FOR DISCIPLESHIP AND GROWTH

A Biblical Theology of Growth

A Biblical Practice of Growth

Expositional Preaching

Biblical Theology

A Biblical Understanding of the Gospel

A Biblical Understanding of Conversion

A Biblical Understanding of Evangelism

A Biblical Understanding of Church Membership

A Biblical Understanding of Church Discipline

A Biblical Understanding of Church Leadership

Hopes for Growth

Pastoral Visitation

Growth Together as a Church.

The Importance of Good Growth

What If We Don't Grow?

A CONCERN FOR DISCIPLESHIP
AND GROWTH

Rob prayed to receive Christ when he was seventeen. He had had a hard few months, and at the end of it he had simply felt done in. To say that he was at the end of his rope might be too dramatic, but that's basically how he felt. Rob had never been much for church, but he had nothing against it. He wasn't an atheist or anything. He simply had never seen much in it.

Then his friend Shawn invited Rob to go to a Christian meeting with him, and Rob was feeling so down that he thought, *Maybe this will help.* So Rob had gone to the meeting with Shawn, and there he talked with Shawn and with a nice young lady named Sarah—until almost midnight.

The conversation had started out light but had gotten fairly serious when Shawn and then Sarah had begun to share some things that they had gone through recently. Eventually it just got to Rob. He didn't break down and cry or anything; he just opened up and was more honest with these two people than he usually was even with himself. "My life feels out of control. Everything seems to be going wrong. And the things that aren't going wrong don't seem to matter to me."

And that's when he did it. In five minutes—or less—Sarah and Shawn had told him about the wonderful life he could have as a

Christian, and the free gift he could have right now of forgiveness from God for everything he had ever done wrong, and eternal life with God in heaven when he died. It seemed like the best thing Rob had been offered in a long time, and it also seemed kind of, well, sweet that these two people would sit there and listen to him and tell him these kinds of things.

So, when Rob asked how he could "sign up," Shawn and Sarah handed him a little booklet and pointed to a paragraph in bold letters, printed on the back cover. It was a prayer. "Repeat after me," said Shawn, and Rob did. Each time Shawn read a line and paused, Rob repeated the line. He was reading them to God. He was praying. And that was that. Shawn and Sarah told him, excitedly, that he had become a Christian, because God promised that if anyone confessed his sins, God would forgive him. Rob knew that he had done bad things. So he had prayed. And there it was. It was over and done with. He was saved.

In the years that followed, Rob lived a pretty upstanding life.

By the time Rob was forty, some people even thought of him as a pillar of the church.

He ended up getting involved in a church where the preaching was usually exciting. The sermons were short, to the point, filled with good stories and memorable anecdotes and moving illustrations. Rob really loved to listen, especially to the stories.

He would have had to confess, had anyone cornered him, that he didn't really know his Bible very well. Though he had taught Sunday school for several years, he couldn't really tell you where most of the books in the Bible were, or why the Exodus was important, or what the book of Revelation was about. Rob had his own thoughts about God and shared these with people, but he didn't really get them from the Bible. They were just the things he had heard and thought himself.

He imagined the Gospel to be a pretty straightforward offer from God—to forgive our sins if we would just own up to them ("Yeah, that one's mine"). He knew that Jesus and the Cross were important; he wasn't sure exactly how, but he knew they were important.

If the truth were known, Rob thought of conversion kind of like the decision to buy a new car or some other momentous decision in your life. It was big, and a little scary, but it was just something you had to do. Everyone, he thought, should get around to it sometime, and sooner would be better than later . . . because, you know, you never know . . .

Evangelism, to Rob, was what the church staff did, and what he had had to do himself maybe a couple of times. He had to do a bit of it back when they had the pastor who was big on knocking on doors, and then once when he went as a chaperone on the youth choir trip and a couple of the boys had some questions about what it meant to be baptized and join the church—so he had talked to them about it.

Actually, Rob himself had never joined the church, but most people probably didn't even realize that. He would go through periods of more involvement and periods of less involvement. Sometimes he would be there every Sunday for a year and then other times he wouldn't be there for a month, two months, three months; and, honestly, he kind of liked it that way. He was able to pick and choose the things he wanted to get involved with. After all, joining the church had always seemed to him like giving someone a blank check.

And then there were the problems a few years back when his daughter in the choir had been taught some things by someone at church that he thought were just crazy. Why, if they had gone on, his daughter could even have ended up as a foreign missionary or something! So he had forbade her to go to choir, youth group, Bible study, or even church for a while, and he didn't go himself for the better part of a year. He wasn't too worried about it, though, because he knew that he believed "once saved, always saved," and he knew that he had been saved because he remembered praying that prayer with Sarah and Shawn, so he didn't really have anything to worry about.

Besides, at that time they had had a pastor with whom he just didn't get along very well, and, to be honest, he just figured he would wait him out. He had seen pastors come and go. Some of the new things this pastor wanted to do really bothered him. He wanted to give a lot more money to missions when there was plenty of work that needed doing on their own building. He talked about the church changing things like having elders; he even talked about "church discipline" (which to Rob sounded scary, judgmental, and un-Christian). Rob knew that most pastors didn't last long, especially if Rob let it be known that he was avoiding church involvement for a while because of that pastor being there.

Would it surprise you if I told you that Rob wasn't really growing as a Christian? And, more than that, that it didn't really bother him that he wasn't growing as a Christian?

Even if Rob isn't so concerned about growth as a Christian, pollster George Barna tells us that many others today are. At the end of 1998, Barna reported that the percentage of people who feel the need to experience spiritual growth had grown an astounding 24 percent (from 58 to 82 percent) in just four years. I read in another recent survey that the percentage of those who said they have given a lot of thought during the previous two years to the basic meaning and value of their lives has jumped 11 percent. Barna suggests that such findings are a further indication of a surge of interest in spirituality and a search for meaning in life, as we enter the new century.

Well, what do you think about that? Four questions:

1. Are such desires for spiritual growth biblical? Or can we as believers be settled, comfortable, and secure like Rob was?
2. If we do want to grow spiritually—as individuals and as a church—how do we do that?
3. Is spiritual growth really so important?
4. What if we don't grow?

A healthy church is characterized by a serious concern for spiritual growth on the part of its members. In a healthy church, people want to get better at following Jesus Christ.

A BIBLICAL THEOLOGY OF GROWTH

First, is the desire for spiritual growth biblical, or is it merely an example of modern American progress-mania—we worship progress in everything and so we just import it into our understanding of Christianity? Or is all this talk about spiritual growth perhaps just some kind of spiritual self-centeredness where we become Christian-narcissists, overly concerned about our own spiritual virtues? What do you think?

In looking through Scripture, we find that spiritual growth is not merely a concern of forward-looking Americans; it is a concern of the Bible as well.

In the very beginning of the Bible, you find in the very first chapter that God commands the creatures of the land and sea to multiply: "God blessed them and said, 'Be fruitful and increase in number and fill the water in the seas, and let the birds increase on the earth . . .'" (Gen. 1:22). And of course He gave that command, and more, to Adam and Eve just a few verses later: "God blessed them and said to them, 'Be fruitful and increase in number; fill the earth and subdue it. Rule over the fish of the sea and the birds of the air and over every living creature that moves on the ground'" (v. 28).

A few chapters later, after God had wiped out the world in judgment with the Flood, what was the first thing He commanded the sons of Noah to do? "Then God blessed Noah and his sons, saying to them, 'Be fruitful and increase in number and fill the earth'" (Gen. 9:1).

As you keep reading through Genesis, you see that God promised Abraham that the number of his descendants would be great and would increase. When the children of Israel went down into Egypt in captivity, they multiplied and increased in number. That was a sign of God's blessing. God blessed them again when they went into the Promised Land. Even when they were taken into exile in Babylonia, what happened? The Lord instructed them through Jeremiah: "Marry and have sons and daughters; find wives for your sons and give your daughters in marriage, so that they too may have sons and daughters. Increase in number there; do not decrease" (Jer. 29:6).

God does not subscribe to E. F. Schumacher's idea that small is beautiful! Though it may be sometimes, smaller is not necessarily better. I'm not saying that God is from Texas—simply that He seems to view abundance as a blessing. One of the ways God encourages righteousness in the Old Testament is by the abundance of blessings He pours out in growth and prosperity. So we read in Psalm 92:12-13:

> The righteous will flourish like a palm tree,
>   they will grow like a cedar of Lebanon;
> planted in the house of the LORD,
>   they will flourish in the courts of our God.

And in the Proverbs, God gives instructions on how we can grow in this way. Basically we're told to increase strength by increasing wisdom, and to increase wisdom by being with the wise (Prov. 24:5; 13:20).

Of course we're not to seek the wrong kind of growth. We're not to be too impressed by the growth of physical things such as wealth and possessions. As Psalm 49:16 warns:

> Do not be overawed when a man grows rich,
>   when the splendor of his house increases;
> for he will take nothing with him when he dies.

Death garners from us all the possessions we accumulate in this world. So we shouldn't be too impressed by them.

One thing we learn from the Bible about growth is that the kingdom of heaven will grow. This was prophesied in the Old Testament, and Jesus promised it as well. We sing that prophesy around Christmastime each year from Isaiah 9:7, in which the Lord promised that the kingdom of His Messiah would grow:

> Of the increase of his government and peace there will be no end.

He will reign on David's throne and over his kingdom,
establishing and upholding it with justice and righteousness
from that time on and forever.
The zeal of the LORD Almighty will accomplish this.

The Lord Jesus Himself speaks of how His kingdom will grow
in fulfillment of this prophecy. He says it will grow from the smallest seed to the largest plant in the Garden: "Though it is the smallest
of all your seeds, yet when it grows, it is the largest of garden plants
and becomes a tree, so that the birds of the air come and perch in its
branches" (Matt. 13:32).

The Seed, of course, did fall to the ground and die. But though
Jesus was crucified and buried, He was raised again, and the kingdom
of God that He began to build did exactly what He prophesied it
would do. It began to grow. If you read through the book of Acts
you'll find that refrain again and again:

In those days when the number of disciples was increasing. . . . the Word of God spread. The number of disciples in
Jerusalem increased rapidly, and a large number of priests
became obedient to the faith (Acts 6:1, 7).

But the word of God continued to increase and spread
(Acts 12:24).

The word of the Lord spread through the whole region
(Acts 13:49).

In this way the word of the Lord spread widely and grew in
power (Acts 19:20).

So, we find numerical growth going on in the New Testament
just as in the Old Testament. But the growth that we find talked of
and urged and prayed for in the New Testament isn't simply numerical growth. If your church is more crowded with people now than it

was a few years ago, does that mean that yours is a healthy church? Not necessarily. There is another kind of growth. In the New Testament we find the idea of a growth that involves not just more people but people who are growing up, maturing, and deepening in the faith. So we read in Ephesians 4:15-16:

> Instead, speaking the truth in love, we will in all things grow up into him who is the Head, that is, Christ. From Him the whole body, joined and held together by every supporting ligament, grows and builds itself up in love, as each part does its work.

How does such growth happen? Ultimately, it happens by God's work. We grow as the body of Christ as God causes growth. So we read in Colossians 2:19 about Christ being "the Head, from whom the whole body, supported and held together by its ligaments and sinews, grows as God causes it to grow."

It is not finally the preacher who causes a church to grow. God may use a preacher; that's up to Him. Paul wrote to the Corinthian Christians about this very point. They were particularly prone to worship eloquent preachers. So Paul wrote to them, reminding them that, "I planted the seed, Apollos watered it, but God made it grow. So neither he who plants nor he who waters is anything, but only God, who makes things grow" (1 Cor. 3:6-7).

In writing like this, Paul was a good disciple of Jesus. Jesus Himself had taught that the growth of the kingdom of God comes from God and is not dependent finally on us. Jesus told the story in Mark 4 about the kingdom of God being like a crop growing in a field, that grows while the farmer sleeps; whether the farmer gets up or not, the crop continues to grow. Jesus' point there isn't that we should be lazy and indolent, but that the growth of the kingdom of God does not finally depend on us. God Himself is committed to ensuring the growth of His church. "Night and day, whether he [the farmer] sleeps or gets up, the seed sprouts and grows, though he does not know how" (Mark 4:27). God causes the growth.

This is why, when Paul writes to the Thessalonians, he doesn't so much congratulate them on their growth—"Oh, you've grown so well!"—but rather thanks God for it. Growth doesn't have to produce pride. Growth can cause humility and recognition that it is God who gives growth:

> We ought always to thank God for you, brothers, and rightly so, because your faith is growing more and more, and the love every one of you has for each other is increasing (2 Thess. 1:3).

This is why, when Paul wants a congregation to grow, one of the things he does is pray for them. He realizes that growth comes from God. Look back one letter, to Paul's first letter Paul to the Thessalonians. There he prays,

> Now may our God and Father himself and our Lord Jesus clear the way for us to come to you. May the Lord make your love increase and overflow for each other and for everyone else, just as ours does for you. May he strengthen your hearts so that you will be blameless and holy in the presence of our God and Father when our Lord Jesus comes with all his holy ones (1 Thess. 3:11-13).

Turning to Colossians, we find Paul once again praying that his readers will grow spiritually:

> We pray this in order that you may live a life worthy of the Lord and may please him in every way: bearing fruit in every good work, growing in the knowledge of God. (Col. 1:10).

Now, I don't mean to suggest that we have nothing to do with our own spiritual growth. The fact that I've even bothered to write about this in a book means I must believe that we as Christians have something to do with our own spiritual growth. In 2 Peter 3:18, Peter finishes his letter with an exhortation to "grow in the grace and

knowledge of our Lord and Savior Jesus Christ." It is an imperative.
"Grow!" he says.

We should want to grow spiritually. But how do we do it? In the
first chapter of this letter, Peter says,

> For if you possess these qualities in increasing measure, they
> will keep you from being ineffective and unproductive in
> your knowledge of our Lord Jesus Christ (2 Pet. 1:8).

What qualities? Go back to verse 5:

> For this very reason, make every effort to add to your faith
> goodness; and to goodness, knowledge; and to knowledge,
> self-control; and to self-control, perseverance; and to perse-
> verance, godliness; and to godliness, brotherly kindness; and
> to brotherly kindness, love. For if you possess these qualities
> in increasing measure, they will keep you from being inef-
> fective and unproductive in your knowledge of our Lord
> Jesus Christ (vv. 5-8).

So we should want to grow. And we grow by cultivating these
qualities.

Elsewhere Peter emphasizes the importance of knowing God's
Word. If you want to grow, he says, do this:

> Like newborn babies, crave pure spiritual milk, so that by it
> you may grow up in your salvation, now that you have tasted
> that the Lord is good. As you come to him, the living Stone—
> rejected by men but chosen by God and precious to him—
> you also, like living stones, are being built into a spiritual
> house to be a holy priesthood, offering spiritual sacrifices
> acceptable to God through Jesus Christ (1 Pet. 2:2-5).

So, we see, spiritual growth is a solidly biblical concept. It isn't
only Americans who are concerned about growth; it isn't just some-

thing about our national culture. It is an idea that's in the Bible and that seems to be there even from creation itself.

A BIBLICAL PRACTICE OF GROWTH

A second question, then: How do we grow as Christians? What kind of church will cultivate such discipleship among its members? In one sense, that's what we've been considering throughout this whole book. But in a more specific sense, how do each of the eight other "marks" considered in this book affect our growth—individually and corporately—as Christians?

Expositional Preaching

A church in which there is expositional preaching will be a church that is encouraging Christian growth—as we listen to God speaking from His Word into our lives. God's Word is what we need if we are to grow. But we won't learn that basic fact by looking to the culture around us to tell us what we most need. We can't even look into our own hearts for such knowledge. Os Guinness has written that,

> The exaggerated half-truth about the church's "needing to meet needs" . . . breeds unintended consequences. Just as church-growth's modern passion for "relevance" will become its road to irrelevance, so its modern passion for "felt needs" will turn the church into an echo chamber of fashionable needs that drown out the one voice that addresses real human need below all felt needs. After all, if true needs are a first step toward faith and prayer, false needs are the opposite. As George Macdonald observed . . . , "that need which is no need, is a demon sucking at the spring of your life."[1]

To learn what we most need in our lives, we finally need to turn to God Himself. We need to hear His Word—all of it—preached expositionally, so that we don't just hear selective themes. There are things in the Bible that we want to avoid. None of us is so holy and perfect and well-shaped spiritually that we happily welcome every word in God's book. God save us from being in a church where the Word is preached selectively. We should pray that God will provide His church with preachers who will preach all of His Word.

As we study God's Word, we see His help and His care for His own throughout history. We become aware of the beauty of God's plan. We see the glory of the Gospel. We see how He corrects us. In a funny way, when we hear expositional preaching we become less dependent on the preacher. We're more concerned about the Word of God. And so, if your pastor is away, if God calls him somewhere else or if he's gone and someone else is in the pulpit, that's okay. We love our minister, but more than that we love the Word of God. That's what we want to hear. That's what the church is built on: hearing God's Word speak to us as His Holy Spirit uses it in our hearts. Through His Word, we come to know more of God and of His character than you or I could ever guess or suppose.

Be very careful before you ever join a church that does not stress expositional preaching, or help to call a preacher who is not an expositional preacher, who is not committed to preaching all of God's Word, regardless of how uncomfortable parts of it may be.

Biblical Theology

A church built on biblical theology is a church that will help its members grow as Christians.

We grow as we understand more of the truth about God and about us. We grow as we understand more of His care and His character. We grow as we read the biblical record of His choosing a people and then working with them through very difficult circumstances. We are encouraged by seeing the big picture, the plan, the meaning. We see more of God's character. We begin to grow in our knowledge of Him. We begin to trust Him more.

How do you grow in your ability to trust God? You grow in that ability partly through the difficulties God allows you to go through. But experience is only half of it. That's what gives you the opportunity to trust. But why trust Him? We trust Him because He has shown Himself perfectly trustworthy. God's revelation of Himself throughout the Word, throughout history, shows Him to be worthy of our trust for anything He would send our way.

A Biblical Understanding of the Gospel
A church that promotes a biblical understanding especially of the Gospel is a church that will help us grow as Christians.

As we realize more and more the depth of our need, we are trained to rely on Christ. John Newton, the author of "Amazing Grace," wrote a poem about trusting Christ and about trying to grow as a Christian:

> I asked the Lord that I might grow
>   In faith, and love, and every grace,
> Might more of his salvation know,
>   And seek more earnestly his face.
>
> I hoped that in some favoured hour
>   At once He'd answer my request,
> And by His love's constraining power
>   Subdue my sins, and give me rest.
>
> Instead of this, He made me feel
>   The hidden evils of my heart;
> And let the angry powers of hell
>   Assault my soul in every part.[2]

When we begin to have a more biblical understanding of our state as humans, though we're grievously saddened by tragedies that may happen in Kosovo or at Columbine High or Wedgewood Baptist, we can't say that we're finally shocked in the way that a non-Christian would be. We understand something of our tremendous capacities as image-bearers of God and how terribly, terribly wrong those capacities can go when we don't use them in submission to God. As we begin to understand more of our own brokenness, of our own sinful rebellion, we—strange as it may seem—begin to understand more of His love. Sometimes the distinction is made in the popular mind between "hellfire" preachers on the one hand and preachers that understand God's love on the other. But that distinction is no more than a caricature. The preachers who talk only about God's love talk about it less and less with every sermon they preach, because there is less and less in their own mind that God loves us in spite of. There's less and less of a problem that has been dealt with. There's less and less weight that Christ has carried. There's less and less of an extent to which He has gone in His love for us.

When, on the other hand, we begin to understand the reality of our sinful rebellion against God, then we begin to understand more of God's love for us in Christ.

A church that is clear on the Gospel will help you grow as a Christian. It will help you grow in confidence as you know the love of God. Indeed you cannot help but grow as you understand more and more what God has done for you in Christ. Do you want to grow as a Christian? Meditate on Charles Wesley's great hymn, "And Can It Be?" Return to being amazed at the Gospel.

A Biblical Understanding of Conversion

A biblical understanding of conversion will help you to grow as a Christian.

As you realize your own spiritual state and realize your dependence on God for your own Christian life, rather than becoming indifferent, you become grateful—profoundly and deeply thankful to God that He has had mercy on you and on so many others. As you do so your hope becomes more certain, because you realize your hope isn't finally based on your own faithfulness but on God's faithfulness. That's a tremendous encouragement to anyone who knows himself to be a sinner. God loves us out of His own nature of love.

As we begin to recognize our own salvation as the fruit of God's work in our lives, we're not even tempted to feel the wrong kind of pride in our own spiritual life, because we have understood from the

Bible what conversion is. We have understood more of what a true
Christian is, and how we become one—by the grace of God.

A Biblical Understanding of Evangelism
The lack of spiritual growth in people who call themselves
Christians is often an evidence that they have been wrongly evangelized. We have taught people who are not Christians to think of
themselves as though they are. One church-growth consultant
recently claimed that "'five to ten million baby boomers would be
back in the fold within a month' if churches adopted three simple
changes: 1. 'Advertise' 2. Let people know about 'product benefits'
3. Be 'nice to new people.'"[3] That's it? Advertise, put the product
benefits up front, and be nice to new people, and we would see five
to ten million people back in the churches within a month? Perhaps
so. But I don't know if we would see them converted.

Don't misunderstand me. It's not as though I want to take
down the signs and not advertise. It's not that I don't want to tell
people any of the good things about being a Christian and just keep
it a secret to myself. It's not that I want us to be mean to new people when they come in. But we have to understand that evangelism
is something more than all those things. The church is not finally
a booster organization. We're telling people a serious message
about their condition before God, and about the tremendous news
of the new life God is offering them in Christ. And we're inviting
them to enter into that life by dire and desperate means—repentance and faith.

When we begin to understand more of what the Bible teaches
about evangelism, we will begin to trust God in helping us to spread
the Good News. We will feel more like obeying Him as we realize
that it is not our duty to convert anyone but simply to faithfully tell
the news. There is a wonderful freedom in that. I don't have to feel
that I have to answer every person's every question. I just have to tell
them the truth about Jesus, and love them and pray for them. I'm
called simply to be faithful in the message, and that brings a wonder-

ful freedom. As I more fully understand God's work in regeneration, it encourages me to trust God.

A Biblical Understanding of Church Membership

A biblical understanding of church membership also helps people to grow as Christians. Living the Christian life means being committed to each other. It entails being part of a community that is centered around Jesus Christ. By dealing with each other, we are forced to deal with areas of our lives that we would otherwise avoid; because of our committed love to each other, we pray and reflect on those areas and repent. Through our commitments and responsibilities as church members, we learn more of what true Christian love is all about. We're encouraged as we see God's work in other people's lives. We're encouraged by seeing the older members cared for, and encouraged by seeing newer Christians maturing. Even if things in our lives are not going so well, we can be encouraged by the work of God in other people's lives. That's how it is supposed to be. That's one of the reasons why God doesn't call us to run this race alone. Being rooted in a church also encourages accountability. It helps us in so many ways to grow as Christians.

A Biblical Understanding of Church Discipline

A biblical understanding of church discipline also helps us to grow. One of the unintended consequences of a church's neglect of proper discipline is that it gets much harder to produce disciples. In an undisciplined church, examples are unclear and models are confused.

"Oh, Mr. So and So has been a member of the church for forty years, but look what he does."

"Well, yes, but he's on all the committees."

Weeds are undesirable. No gardener sets out to grow weeds. They can have bad effects on the plants around them. God's plan for the local church does not encourage us to leave weeds unchecked. He intends, for His own glory, that the church be composed of imperfect people; but He intends that these imperfect people should be people who love Him and in whose lives He can work—to make them more holy.

For the good of the one disciplined, for the good of other Christians as a warning, for the health of the church as a whole, for the good of our witness to non-Christians, and for the glory of God, we will be helped to grow as we practice church discipline.

A Biblical Understanding of Church Leadership

We'll also be helped as Christians by a biblical understanding of leadership. As God brings people into our lives whom He has called to be spiritual leaders, we gain practical role models and godly vision.

These are some of the ways that our eight other "marks of a healthy church" contribute to our spiritual growth as Christians.

HOPES FOR GROWTH

Before discussing the *importance* of spiritual growth, let me share with you some of my hopes for my own ministry—for my own life and my own church—in this matter of spiritual growth.

Pastoral Visitation

In my role as a pastor, I hope specifically that, slowly but surely, I'll be able to do regular pastoral visitation in a way that was standard in years gone by. To that end, I am slowly but surely working my way back through the membership list, to meet with members of my congregation who were already in the church when I came. Since coming to this church, I have personally interviewed all new members about their understanding of the Gospel and about their own testimony of becoming and being a Christian. I am now trying to have that conversation with *all* the members in the church. I'm hoping to gain an understanding of these people that goes beyond what can be gained by the brief times I have with each of them—sometimes only at the church door on Sunday morning. Ultimately, I hope to have a regular visitation schedule whereby I or maybe some of the other elders meet with each member for prayer and to ask them about their lives. I would probably ask questions such as the following, shared with me by another pastor:

- In what particular way have you grown in your understanding of the Christian life since we last met?
- In what particular way have you grown in your practice of the Christian life since we last met?
- In what particular way do you feel that you need instruction?
- In what particular way are you disappointed in your own pursuit of holiness?
- How, specifically, can I pray for you?

This is what I would like to see in the church I serve, and I pray that it will become more typical of your church as well.

Growth Together as a Church

I hope that, more and more, we at Capitol Hill Baptist Church will live out what we have pledged to God and to each other in our church covenant—which reads as follows:

CHURCH COVENANT

Having, as we trust, been brought by Divine Grace to repent and believe in the Lord Jesus Christ and to give up ourselves to Him, and having been baptized upon our profession of faith, in the name of the Father and of the Son and of the Holy Spirit, we do now, relying on His gracious aid, solemnly and joyfully renew our covenant with each other.

We will work and pray for the unity of the Spirit in the bond of peace.

We will walk together in brotherly love, as becomes the members of a Christian church; exercise an affectionate care and watchfulness over each other and faithfully admonish and entreat one another as occasion may require.

We will not forsake the assembling of ourselves together, nor neglect to pray for ourselves and others.

We will endeavor to bring up such as may at any time be under our care, in the nurture and admonition of the Lord, and by a pure and loving example to seek the salvation of our family and friends.

We will rejoice at each other's happiness, and endeavor with tenderness and sympathy to bear each other's burdens and sorrows.

We will seek, by Divine aid, to live carefully in the world, denying ungodliness and worldly lusts, and remembering that, as we have been voluntarily buried by baptism and raised again from the symbolic grave, so there is on us a special obligation now to lead a new and holy life.

We will work together for the continuance of a faithful evangelical ministry in this church, as we sustain its worship, ordinances, discipline, and doctrines. We will contribute cheerfully and regularly to the support of the ministry, the expenses of the church, the relief of the poor, and the spread of the gospel through all nations.

We will, when we move from this place, as soon as possible, unite with some other church where we can carry out the spirit of this covenant and the principles of God's Word.

May the grace of the Lord Jesus Christ, and the love of God, and the fellowship of the Holy Spirit be with us all. Amen.

This covenant expresses the idea that growth as a Christian is not just the responsibility of the individual. And it is not only mine as the pastor. Members of the church are to teach each other. That's part of what knits us together as the body of Christ. And as you read our church covenant, you see what we as a church pledge to do to help each other grow as Christians. We'll do it imperfectly—there's no doubt about that. Nevertheless, this is my hope: that we in our church (and you in your church) will increasingly work and pray together, walk together, not forsake the assembling of ourselves, endeavor to bring up those that the Lord gives us in His will and ways, rejoicing and sorrowing with each other, seeking to live carefully, working together in ministry, contributing to the expenses, contributing to the needs of the Gospel throughout all nations, knowing that when we move from this place we'll unite with another church where we can continue to do these things. These are what we pledge for each other, to help each other to grow as Christians.

THE IMPORTANCE OF GOOD GROWTH

Is growth important? Yes, to grow as a Christian is very important. This is how we give testimony to God. When we see a church composed of members growing in Christlikeness, who gets the credit? We've already seen the answer in Scripture: "God made it grow" (1 Cor. 3:6). As Peter writes, "Live such good lives among the pagans that, though they accuse you of doing wrong, they may see your good deeds and glorify God on the day he visits us" (1 Pet. 2:12).

Peter was obviously remembering Jesus' words from the Sermon on the Mount: "Let your light shine before men, that they may see your good deeds . . ." and surely here it would be natural to fall into the trap of self-admiration, but Jesus continued, ". . . and praise your Father in heaven" (Matt. 5:16). Working to promote Christian discipleship and growth is working to bring glory not to ourselves but to God. This is how God will make Himself known in the world.

A healthy church has a pervasive concern with church growth—not simply growing numbers but growing members. A church full of growing Christians is the kind of church growth I want as a pastor. Some today seem to think that one can be a "baby Christian" for a whole lifetime. Growth is seen to be an optional extra for particularly zealous disciples. But be very careful about taking that line of thought. Growth is a sign of life. Growing trees are living trees, and growing animals are living animals. When something stops growing, it dies.

Growth may not mean that you negotiate this rapid in half the time you negotiated the last; it may simply mean that you are able to continue in the right direction as a Christian, regardless of the adverse circumstances. Remember, it is only the things that are alive that swim upstream; the dead things all float along with the current.

Paul hoped the Corinthians would grow in their Christian faith (2 Cor. 10:15). The Ephesians, he hoped, would "grow up into him who is the Head, that is Christ" (Eph. 4:15; cf. Col. 1:10; 2 Thess. 1:3). It is tempting at times for pastors to reduce their churches to manageable statistics of attendance, baptisms, giving, and membership, where growth is tangible, recordable, demonstrable, and comparable. However, such statistics fall far short of the true growth that Paul describes in these verses, and that God desires. Rather than thinking of growth as a linear graph, recording mounting or declining measurements—totals of services attended, dollars given, books read—perhaps it is better to think of Christian growth as a sort of video game where each day you are given a fresh challenge to live that day as a Christian.

In his *Treatise Concerning Religious Affections*, Jonathan Edwards suggested that true growth in Christian discipleship is not finally mere excitement, increasing use of religious language, or a growing knowledge of Scripture. It is not even an evident increase in joy or in love or concern for the church. Even increases in zeal and praise to God and confidence of one's own faith are not infallible evidences of true Christian growth. What, then, *is* evidence of true Christian growth? According to Edwards, while all these things may be evidences of true Christian growth, the only certain observable sign of such growth is a life of increasing holiness, rooted in Christian self-denial. The church should be marked by a vital concern for this kind of increasing godliness in the lives of its members.

Good influences in a covenanted community of believers can be tools in God's hand for growing His people. As God's people are built up and grow together in holiness and self-giving love, they should improve in their ability to administer discipline and to encourage discipleship. The church has an obligation to be a means of God's growing people in grace. If instead our churches are places where only the pastor's thoughts are taught, where God is questioned more than He is worshiped, where the Gospel is diluted and evangelism perverted, where church membership is made meaningless, and a worldly cult of personality is allowed to grow up around the pastor, then one can hardly expect to find a community that is either cohesive or edifying. Such a church certainly will not glorify God. So Peter's final benediction to those early Christians he wrote to was a prayer couched in the imperative: "Grow in the grace and knowledge of our Lord and Savior Jesus Christ. To him be glory both now and forever! Amen" (2 Pet. 3:18).

Of all the "nine marks" covered in this book, this is the one I first became concerned about. How many of us have seen large churches with thousands of members who never come, and hundreds of those who do attend seeming not really to care much about God? In any church there will be many very nice people who have lived moral lives; but then there will be some who seem especially to love the Lord, and they will usually "stick out" from all the rest—they will seem different from the rest of the church. For probably twenty years or more I have been wondering why churches are like this. What has gone on in our churches, when people who really live like Christians seem unusual, even compared to other church members? In this book, I have been tracing back those things that I have noticed in this regard, finally getting back to the fount of God's activity among us—His Word.

If we are to grow as individual believers and as churches, we must sit under the Word. We must pray for the Holy Spirit to plant and to weed the gardens of our hearts. This spiritual growth is not optional; it is vital, because spiritual growth indicates life. Things that are truly alive, grow. That's just the way it is.

WHAT IF WE DON'T GROW?

Finally, what if we don't grow spiritually? What about Rob? Why was Rob apparently not growing in his Christian life? Was Rob perhaps not a Christian at all?

You may think, *Now, that's a little harsh. Maybe Rob's just one of those "carnal" Christians that Paul talks about somewhere in the Bible.*

Yes, in 1 Corinthians Paul uses the expression "carnal Christian." He writes, "Brothers, I could not address you as spiritual but as worldly ["carnal," KJV]—mere infants in Christ" (1 Cor. 3:1). But who are these people? Are these carnal Christians a "middle category" of people who have Jesus in their life but not on the throne? It sounds like a strange idea, doesn't it? On the one hand, you've got Christians who have Christ as Lord, with Him on the throne. Then, on the other side, you have non-Christians. But, it is argued, you also have this interesting middle category where Christ really is in the person's life but He's not on the throne. These are the "carnal" Christians. Well, that's one way you could read this verse.

I think a more natural way to read the verse is that Paul is shaming his readers by speaking of these self-confessed Christians as worldly. In calling them "worldly" or "carnal," Paul is intentionally using an oxymoron. An oxymoron is the joining of two words not meant to go together. In that sense, a carnal Christian would be like hot ice. It's just not supposed to make any sense. By writing in these terms, Paul is basically telling his readers, "Get off the fence! You are living differently than you are professing. You cannot do that. Those horses go in opposite directions—so jump on one or the other!" That's what Paul is saying.

Many people, by a wrong use of this verse, have been convinced that they are some kind of truly saved person, some kind of real Christian, even though they have not really repented and believed. No wonder the Christian lives of so many are such messes, if the churches of which they're a part are so confused on such a basic matter.

Consider what it means to be a Christian. It's not that you're perfect, but that your heart does intend to seek the Lord. If you are a Christian, it is because God, by His own gracious action in your life, has grown a desire in you to live a life that pleases Him more and more. Such growth is a sign of true spiritual life, and another mark of a healthy church.

WHAT'S COMING UP . . .

MARK NINE:
BIBLICAL CHURCH LEADERSHIP

The Congregational Context of Church Leadership

The Biblical Qualifications for Church Leadership

The Charismatic Nature of Church Leadership

The Christlikeness of Church Leadership

    Boss

    Out Front

    Supply

    Serve

The Relationship of Church Leadership to God's Nature and Character

MARK
NINE

BIBLICAL CHURCH LEADERSHIP

"All animals are equal but some animals are more equal than others."
With that line in the last chapter of his tale *Animal Farm*,[1] George
Orwell delivered his summary critique of Karl Marx and the Soviet
Russian government. The story is a well-known one: animals rise up,
organize, displace the Joneses (the human owners of the farm) and
begin to run the farm for their own benefit—thus the name "Animal
Farm"—run by animals for animals, so the story goes.

Of course, being after the Fall, this Utopian experiment is bound
to fail, and it does. In the end, a new ruling class emerges—the pigs—
and by the book's conclusion, they're putting up those signs: "All animals are equal but some animals are more equal than others."

Rather than abuse of authority being merely a part of a pre-com-
munist economy as Marx had taught, Orwell said that the problem
was really further in—in the nature of human relationships, of reality, of the human heart.

Orwell's critique of authority seemed penetrating and biting
when it first appeared more than fifty years ago. Today it seems obvious. We've become accustomed to thinking about abuse and power
in the same sentence, and about authoritarianism whenever we think
about authority.

Whatever the reason, there is a latent suspicion of authority in
our society. Perhaps it has to do with the fact that our national government was established in revolt against the claims and demands of

220 NINE MARKS OF A HEALTHY CHURCH

the Parliament in London. Perhaps it has to do with the fact that for many Americans, the government that now works to ensure their equal opportunity was the same government that in the past worked to make sure they had none. Perhaps it has to do with a vision of human nobility—the American optimism that believes people are so good that, if we merely leave them to themselves, "we, the people" will be the best we can possibly be.

Or perhaps the explanation for our anti-authoritarianism is more simple. Perhaps it has to do with selfishness.

Christianity has always recognized the need for authority in society, in the home, and also in the church, and that last one is our topic for this chapter: biblical church leadership. This is our last "mark of a healthy church." It is particularly important, given the increasingly poor models of authority we seem to have all around us today.

What does the Bible say about authority and leadership in the church? In answering that question we'll focus on five aspects of church leadership:

1. its congregational context
2. its biblical qualifications
3. its charismatic nature
4. its Christlikeness
5. its relationship to God's nature and character

In this chapter we'll be investigating the "plumbing" of the church, if you will, but our study should bear fruit for us if we hang in there.

THE CONGREGATIONAL CONTEXT OF CHURCH LEADERSHIP

The first topic we need to consider when discussing biblical church leadership is the role of the members, the congregation. The Bible's discussion of church leadership always assumes a congregational context.

Previous decades and centuries of the church's life have been spent in controversy over exactly whom God has intended to have the final say in what is taught and done in churches. Some have said it is to be the bishops. Others have even said it should be one bishop in particular. Still others have said it is to be the ministers or some body representing them. Still others have said it should be the local pastor or some specially gifted leader whom God raises up.

We can understand the confusion. If you start looking in the New Testament for how we should organize as a church, you won't find a straightforward manual of church government; there is no ideal constitution for a church. But that doesn't mean that the Bible has nothing to say about how we are to organize ourselves. One of the most important passages about church life is Matthew 18:15-17, where Jesus said,

> "If your brother sins against you, go and show him his fault, just between the two of you. If he listens to you, you have won your brother over. But if he will not listen, take one or two others along, so that 'every matter may be established by the testimony of two or three witnesses.' If he refuses to listen to them, tell it to the church; and if he refuses to listen even to the church, treat him as you would a pagan or a tax collector."

Notice to whom one finally appeals in such situations. What court has the final word? It is not a bishop, a pope, or a presbytery; it is not an assembly, a synod, a convention, or a conference. It is not even a pastor or a board of elders, a board of deacons or a church committee. It is, quite simply, the church—that is, the assembly of those individual believers who are the church.

In Acts 6:2-5 we read of an event in the life of the early church that is important to this discussion. There was a problem, apparently, over the distribution of the church's resources, and this problem was evidently requiring a good bit of the apostles' attention:

> So the Twelve gathered all the disciples together and said, "It would not be right for us to neglect the ministry of the Word

of God in order to wait on tables. Brothers, choose seven men from among you who are known to be full of the Spirit and wisdom. We will turn this responsibility over to them and will give our attention to prayer and the ministry of the Word."

This proposal pleased the whole group.

Luke goes on to name those whom the church chose for this ministry.

One of the complexities of using the New Testament as a guide to how we are to structure our church life is the presence of the apostles in these churches. How much can we later, post-apostolic elders, pastors, and overseers assume the apostles' practice as a guide for our own? Can we define doctrine, delineate error, or recall the words of Christ as these could who had been with Jesus throughout His earthly ministry, who were taught by Him and instructed by Him and who were specially commissioned by Him to be the foundation of His church? Will the names of those of us who are elders today be inscribed on the foundations of the New Jerusalem, as are the names of the apostles (Rev. 21:14)? The answer to all of these questions is obviously no.

Our problem with the model of the apostles is that, in following it, we present-day church leaders might ascribe too much authority to ourselves, without deserving such authority. Yet here in Acts 6, we see these very apostles handing over responsibility to the congregation; it almost seems that they were recognizing in the church assembly the same kind of ultimate authority, under God, that Jesus had recognized in His statement in Matthew 18:15-17.

Finally, to learn more from the New Testament about church life, let's turn to the letters of Paul. Here we find a continuation of Christ's teaching and of the practice of the apostles. In Paul's letters we see that the discipline and doctrine of a local church is ultimately held in trust, under God, by the congregation. The discipline and doctrine is finally the responsibility under God of the congregation.

On the question of the responsibility for discipline, for

instance, look at how Paul exhorts the *whole congregation* at Corinth in 1 Corinthians 5:4-5:

> When you are assembled in the name of our Lord Jesus and I am with you in spirit, and the power of our Lord Jesus is present, hand this man over to Satan, so that the sinful nature may be destroyed and his spirit saved on the day of the Lord.

Paul instructs the whole church—not just the leaders—to take action. Indeed, he is upset with the whole church—not just the leaders—that they haven't already taken action and had been tolerating such sin.

In 2 Corinthians 2:6 we see something of how this church responded to Paul's directives. Apparently the man who was in such heinous sin (presumably the same man referred to in 1 Corinthians) had repented. But notice how Paul described the decision they had made: "The punishment inflicted on him by the majority is sufficient for him" (2 Cor. 2:6). The word in Greek literally seems to presume there would have been some definite number of people and that the greater part of that set number of people would have made the decision. Perhaps you've heard people say there are no church votes recorded in the New Testament. Yet here in this passage, there does seem to be a vote (a "majority") in view. Paul knew that this congregation in Corinth was competent to discipline itself.

Paul believed that individual church congregations had the final responsibility even for the teaching they heard. In Galatians, Paul basically says hello, offers a brief prayer for his readers (vv. 1-5), and then says,

> I am astonished that you are so quickly deserting the one who called you by the grace of Christ and are turning to a different gospel—which is really no gospel at all. Evidently some people are throwing you into confusion and are trying to pervert the gospel of Christ. But even if we or an angel from heaven should preach a gospel other than the one we

preached to you, let him be eternally condemned! As we have already said, so now I say again: If anybody is preaching to you a gospel other than what you accepted, let him be eternally condemned! (Gal. 1:6-9).

Throughout this whole letter to the Galatians, Paul is telling them that they are responsible for judging the correctness of the message being presented to them by others. Paul says that the message they have been hearing is not really the Gospel. Therefore, says Paul, they must assume the responsibility of rejecting that message and those who are delivering it.

It is significant that, in combating this false Gospel, Paul didn't simply write to the pastor or the elders, to the presbytery, to the bishop or the conference, to the convention or the seminary. No, Paul wrote to the churches. He wrote to the Christians who composed the churches and who knew in their own lives the power of the Gospel. He appealed to them and made it quite clear that not only are they competent to sit in judgment of a message presented as the Gospel, but they *must* do so. Anytime someone came and presented something else and called it "the Gospel," the congregation would have a decision to make. They had an inescapable duty to judge even those who claimed to be apostles.

Paul made this point even more clearly in 2 Timothy, where he counseled Timothy, the pastor of the church in Ephesus, on how to deal with false teachers. As Paul described the coming tide of false teachers in the church, he didn't just mention the teachers themselves: He particularly blamed those who, "to suit their own desires . . . gather around them a great number of teachers to say what their itching ears want to hear" (2 Tim. 4:3). If you are in a church where the Gospel is not being preached, I hope you gain from this verse a strong sense of the responsibility you have. Whether in selecting teachers or paying for them, in approving of their teaching, or in simply consenting to listen to them repeatedly and happily, the congregation that Paul envisioned here was culpable for the false teaching that they endured and sponsored. They were to be held as guilty as those who actually did the false teaching. Once again we see that final responsibility rested with the congregation itself.

Have you ever listened to a sermon that was so bad you wanted to walk out? I have walked out on a sermon once, and I walked out loudly, because I thought what was being said was so terribly destructive of the Gospel that it should not be tolerated. I didn't want my bodily presence, with me sitting there with my mouth shut, to encourage anyone to listen to the speaker. (He was directly contradicting the doctrine of original sin.)

If you sit and listen to trash being presented as the Word of God, you will be held responsible. Indeed, if you sit and listen to *my* teaching, you will bear some responsibility for it.

Every local church in Christendom, from Greek Orthodox to Pentecostal, from Roman Catholic to Baptist, from Episcopalian to Lutheran, from Presbyterian to Methodist, is congregational in nature. They exist only as the people continue to participate in their activities. When the people vote—whether at a congregational meeting or (where that's not allowed) with their funds or their feet—the leaders of the congregation must listen. They don't have to agree, but they must listen. The congregation will have their say. That's a simple fact. It is like gravity. It is just a matter of the way things work.

Beyond the simple inevitability of congregationalism, however, the congregation has a wonderful responsibility that should be recognized and encouraged and cultivated. As a congregation, we are responsible to see that we have sound teaching. In our church covenant at Capitol Hill Baptist, we pledge that we will work to make sure that a faithful, evangelical ministry continues in our midst. We have a responsibility to make sure that God is honored among us by having His Word rightly preached, His commands obeyed, and His character reflected in our lives together. This is the responsibility of our church and of every other local church around the world.

As church congregations today, we must make decisions together even as the early disciples did about discipline and about doctrine. Does this mean that congregationalism is democracy? Perhaps in some ways, in that the *demos,* the people, make decisions. But there are dissimilarities, too. A church is not just straightforward democracy, for in churches there is a common recognition of our fallen state, of our tendency to err, and, on the other hand, of the *in*errancy of God's Word. So the members of a church congregation are democratic, perhaps, only in the sense that they work together as a congregation to try to understand God's Word.

I certainly do not believe in the inerrancy of congregational votes. Before I came to be their pastor, I spoke very openly to the congregation where I now serve, telling them that if I were to be their pastor I needed to know that I would ultimately not be working for them but for God. They could instruct the pastor to do this or that, but the pastor must not mistake such congregational input as, necessarily, divine guidance.

As leaders and congregation, we strive for the unity of the Spirit in the bond of peace; we work together for what we believe would be best for the church. And we work together so long as our understandings of God's Word and His will are sufficiently in line—"in sync" with each other—in order for us to do so.

Is congregationalism democracy? Though congregationalism and democracy have some important similarities and common principles, the simple answer must be no, not entirely. Perhaps the Cambridge Platform of 1648 put it best:

> This Government of the church, is a mixt Government (and so hath been acknowledged long before the term of Independency was heard of): In respect of Christ, the head and King of the church, and the Sovereaigne power residing in him, and exercised by him, it is a Monarchy: In respect of the body, or Brotherhood of the church, and power from Christ graunted unto them, it resembles a Democracy: In respect of the Presbytery and power committed to them, it is an Aristocracy (X.3).[2]

For you as an individual, this means that you are to take an active part in your church not simply by attending, by praying, and by giving (though you should do all those things); more than such things, you should actively be getting to know your church family. You should be praying through the list of those other people with whom you have covenanted to serve God. You should listen as other members of the body tell about what God is doing in their lives or about their concerns—and then pray with them. You must realize that part of your obligation and privilege as a member of the church is to get to know other believers and to make yourself known to them. Study God's Word together. Learn to think as a church about God's Word. You should be growing in grace yourself, and in the knowledge of God's Word, in the knowledge of your own heart and of the hearts of your brothers and sisters, and in awareness of the opportunities God is putting in front of your church.

God does not, however, leave us merely to operate all the time as a "committee of the whole." We need to trust that God gives particular people gifts to serve as church leaders. We should therefore desire to see in our church the right balance of authority and trust. It is a serious spiritual deficiency in a church either to have leaders who are untrustworthy or to have members who are incapable of trusting. As individual members, we must be able to thank God for the leaders He puts among us, to recognize those so gifted, and to trust them. In Ephesians 4, Paul speaks of such leaders as God's gifts to His church. We should cultivate a church culture in which such leaders are honored and esteemed.

At the end of Hebrews 13 there is a passage that sounds very strange to our modern ears. Pray that God will help us understand it and to apply it well to our own hearts:

> Obey your leaders and submit to their authority. They keep watch over you as men who must give an account. Obey them so that their work will be a joy, not a burden, for that would be of no advantage to you (Heb. 13:17).

Think of the pastors you have had in your church. Have you worked in such a way that you have made their leadership of you and their charge of your soul a *joy* to them? Or have you made it a burden?

This passage contains some words we aren't used to hearing today—"obey . . . submit . . . obey . . ." They're words we don't hear very often, but they are part of God's Word. And they require from us a certain amount of trust.

It is often said that trust must be earned, and I understand what that means. When a new government administration comes in, when we get a new boss at work, or even when a new friendship begins, we want to see by experience how the person or people will weather the difficulties, how they will persevere, whether they will contribute to the well-being of all concerned. And so, we say, trust is earned. "Show me your competence to lead, and I will give you my trust by following."

But that attitude is at best only half true. Of course, when we recognize leaders in the church as in any other sphere of life, we want them to be people who seem capable of holding such responsibilities. Paul himself lays out some qualifications for elders and deacons when he writes to Timothy and Titus.

At the same time, however, the kind of trust that we are called to give to our fellow imperfect humans in this life, be they family or friends, employers or government officials, or even leaders in a church, can never finally be earned. It must be given as a gift—a gift in faith, in trust more of the God who gives than of the leaders He has given (Eph. 4:11-13).

That's the congregational context of biblical church leadership. Now we'll consider the leaders themselves.

THE BIBLICAL QUALIFICATIONS FOR CHURCH LEADERSHIP

We will now consider the biblical qualifications for being a church leader.

As a pastor, I pray regularly that God will provide us with good leaders in our own local church. I pray particularly that God will place within our fellowship men whose spiritual gifts and pastoral concern indicate that God has called them to be elders or overseers (the words are used interchangeably in the Bible; see, for example, Acts 20). If it becomes clear that God has so gifted a certain man in the church, and if, after prayer, the church recognizes his gifts, then he should be set apart as an elder.

All churches have had individuals who performed the functions of elders even if they haven't used that word for them. The two most common New Testament names for this office were *episcopos* (overseer) and *presbuteros* (elder). When evangelicals today hear the word *elder* many immediately think "Presbyterian," yet when congregationalists first arose back in the sixteenth century they stressed eldership as well. Elders could be found in Baptist churches in America throughout the eighteenth and into the nineteenth century. W. B. Johnson, the first president of the Southern Baptist Convention, wrote a book on church life in which he strongly advocated the idea of a plurality of elders in the local church.

Somehow that practice—never universal—fell out of use almost entirely among Baptists. Whether through inattention to Scripture or the pressure of life on the frontier (where churches were springing up at an amazing rate), the practice of cultivating such congregational leadership stopped among Baptist churches. But discussion of reviving this biblical office continued among Baptist publications. As late as the early twentieth century, Baptist publications were referring to leaders by the title of *elder;* but as the twentieth century wore on, the idea seemed to vanish, until today it has become very unusual for a Baptist church to have elders.

Today, though, there is a growing trend to go back to this biblical office—and for good reason. It was needed in New Testament times, and it is needed now.

The Bible clearly models a plurality of elders in each local church. Though it never suggests a specific number of elders for a particular congregation, the New Testament refers to "elders" in the plural in local churches (e.g., Acts 14:23; 16:4; 20:17; 21:18; Titus 1:5;

James 5:14). When you read through Acts and the Epistles, there is always more than one elder being talked about.

Probably the single most useful thing for me in my pastoral ministry has been the recognition of a group of men in our church as elders. It has helped me immensely in my pastoral work, knowing that these are men that the congregation has recognized as gifted and godly. We meet and pray and talk over matters and, by so doing, they greatly supplement my wisdom. So my own experience attests to the usefulness of following the New Testament practice of having, where possible, more elders in a local church than simply a lone pastor—and of their being people rooted in the congregation, not simply church staff hired from outside.

This does not mean that I don't have any distinctive role as the pastor, but I am fundamentally an elder, one of the people God has gifted to lead the church together. How do we find such leaders in our church? We pray for wisdom. We study God's Word, especially 1 Timothy and Titus. We see who meets those qualifications. We don't just look for people who are influential in the local community.

In the New Testament, we find hints of the main preacher being distinct from the rest of the elders. There are a number of references in the New Testament to preaching and preachers that would not apply to all the elders in a congregation. For example, in Corinth Paul gave himself exclusively to preaching in a way that non-staff elders in a church could not. Probably the church could only support a limited number of elders full-time (cf. Acts 18:5; 1 Cor. 9:14; 1 Tim. 4:13; 5:17). Preachers seemed to move to an area expressly to preach (Rom. 10:14-15), whereas elders seemed to be already part of the local community (Titus 1:5).

We must remember, however, that the preacher (or pastor) is also fundamentally one of the elders of his congregation. This means that many decisions involving the church yet not requiring the attention of all the members should fall not to the pastor alone but to the elders as a whole. While this is sometimes cumbersome, it has the immense benefits of rounding out the pastor's gifts, making up for some of his deficiencies, supplementing his judgment, and creating congregational support for decisions, leaving leaders less exposed to unjust criticism. It also makes leadership more rooted and permanent and allows for more mature continuity. It encourages the church to take more responsibility for the spiritual growth of its own members and helps make the church less dependent on its employees.

Many modern churches have tended to confuse elders with either the church staff or the deacons. Deacons, too, fill a New Testament office, one rooted in Acts 6. While any absolute distinction between the two offices is difficult, the concerns of the deacons are the practical details of church life: administration, maintenance, and the care of church members with physical needs. In many churches today, deacons have taken some spiritual role, but much has simply been left to the pastor. It would be to the benefit of the church to again distinguish the role of elder from that of deacon.

When you think of a church leader today, what comes to mind? Os Guinness, in *Dining with the Devil,* laments so many churches having fallen prey to secularizing influences in the way they choose their leaders. He writes,

> In distinct contrast to the widespread conservative fallacy of the eighties, the sharpest challenge of modernity is not secularism, but secularization. Secularism is a philosophy; secularization is a process. Whereas the philosophy is obviously hostile and touches only a few, the process is largely invisible and touches many. Being openly hostile, secularism rarely deceives Christians. Being much more subtle, secularization often deceives Christians before they are aware of it, including those in the church-growth movement. How else can one explain the comment of a Japanese businessman to a visiting Australian? "Whenever I meet a Buddhist leader, I meet a holy man. Whenever I meet a Christian leader, I meet a manager."[3]

Instead of searching for leaders with secular qualifications, we are to search for people of character, reputation, ability to handle the Word, and who display the fruit of the Spirit in their lives. Those are the kinds of people we should recognize and into whose hands we should commit the responsibility of leading a congregation.

Part of finding good church leaders is finding those whom we can trust and who can trust us as a congregation—who can have enough faith in the congregation's decisions and commitments that they feel that they can work with us and with each other.

That, I think, is why Paul in 1 Timothy 3 emphasizes how the elder deals with his family—because that reveals so much about him and how he would actually work as an elder. It is also interesting to note how many of these qualifications have to do with giving oneself in service for others. Elders are to be other-centered. They are to be irreproachable, particularly in their observable conduct. They are to have an exemplary marriage and family life, to be temperate in all things, "self-controlled, respectable, hospitable, able to teach," not violent or quarrelsome or greedy, not a recent convert, and well respected by those outside the church.

Deacons too are to be blameless, exemplary in their family life, temperate in everything, not greedy but respectable, not liars but people who honestly hold the "deep truths of the faith."

Such must be the case of those who would be shepherds of the church of God. As good shepherds, they are not to fleece the flock in self-interest but to tend and care for each one of the sheep.

That's something of the biblical qualifications of church leaders.

THE CHARISMATIC NATURE OF CHURCH LEADERSHIP

Third, we should note the charismatic nature of biblical church leadership. By "charismatic" I do not mean a particular supernatural experience such as speaking in tongues. The Greek word *charisma* (plural *charismata*) simply means a gift of grace—a gift of God's grace. In the Bible, it is clear that God's Spirit gives His church gifts in order to build us up in the faith. Even our salvation as Christians is referred to as such a grace gift, a *charisma*. The gifts of the Holy Spirit are specific examples of God's grace, whether our very salvation or any of God's other gifts to His children. Paul speaks of the gift of Christ's righteousness (Rom. 5:17) and of the gift of eternal life in Christ (6:23). The righteousness of Christ is God's *charisma* to us.

But we also read of more specific examples of God's gifts. In Romans 11 Paul speaks of the gifts God gave specifically to His people Israel (Rom. 11:29; cf. 9:4-5). In Romans 12:6-8 he mentions some specific gifts of God to the church:

> We have different gifts, according to the grace given us. If a man's gift is prophesying, let him use it in proportion to his faith. If it is serving, let him serve; if it is teaching, let him teach; if it is encouraging, let him encourage; if it is contributing to the needs of others, let him give generously; if it is leadership, let him govern diligently; if it is showing mercy, let him do it cheerfully.

(Notice that all of these gifts are for the benefit of *others*.)

In 1 Corinthians Paul refers to teaching, encouraging, giving generously, leadership, showing mercy, all as grace gifts. He addresses the Corinthian Christians as those who have been "enriched in every way" and who "do not lack any spiritual gift" (1 Cor. 1:5, 7). When we read through this letter, we find a number of these spiritual gifts mentioned. In 7:7 Paul even called celibacy and marriage spiritual gifts.

In fact, one of the reasons Paul wrote this letter was to instruct these Christians on "spiritual gifts," as he said in 12:1. He then goes on in this chapter to give a list (beginning at v. 7). This is a list of "extraordinary gifts," as the seventeenth-century Puritan writer John Owen called them. As Paul says in verse 11, "he [the Spirit] gives them to each one, just as he determines." In verses 27-31 Paul gives another list of spiritual gifts, then concludes by instructing the Corinthians to "eagerly desire the greater gifts."

In 2 Corinthians 1:11 Paul refers to his physical deliverance as a *charisma*, a grace gift. In 1 Timothy 4:14 and 2 Timothy 1:6 he refers to Timothy's calling to the ministry as a gift. As he said to the Ephesians, we have "every spiritual blessing in Christ" (1:3).

I hope you have noticed that all of these gifts have a shared goal. In Romans 1:11-12 we see that Paul understood spiritual gifts to be given for encouraging each other and building each other up. In 1 Corinthians 12:4-7 we see clearly that these gifts are given "for the common good."

The most obvious teaching on the purpose of spiritual gifts is found in 1 Corinthians 14. Look particularly at 14:4, which is very often misunderstood: "He who speaks in a tongue edifies himself, but he who prophesies edifies the church." Some take this as a neutral statement, as if Paul is merely commenting that there are two different kinds of good edification—if you want self-edification, you should seek to speak in tongues or pray in tongues; if you want church edification, then you should seek to prophesy. But I don't think that's what Paul means here. Look at 14:1. He encourages these Christians to desire especially the gift of prophecy. Then down in verse 12, he says, "Since you are eager to have spiritual gifts, try to excel in gifts that build up the church." Then down in verse 19 he says, "But in the church I would rather speak five intelligible words to instruct others than ten thousand words in a tongue." Paul is saying that you have to be able to understand something in order to be edified by it. Intelligibility is necessary for edifying the church! And that, he says, is the goal of spiritual gifts.

The one thing that does not change every time the word *charisma* is used in the New Testament is that these gifts are given for the building up of the body. Whether it is an escape of Paul from a shipwreck or the gifts he writes about in 1 Corinthians 14, they are all *charismata* and they are always for building up the church in some way.

The goal of all of these spiritual gifts, Paul states clearly, is the "strengthening" of the church (1 Cor. 14:26). That's why the Spirit gives these gifts in the church. So, to return to 1 Corinthians 14:4, Paul isn't merely mentioning two different kinds of edification. He is criticizing any kind of self-serving use of gifts, and he is redefining the goals for these gifts, realigning the Corinthians' purposes with the Spirit's purpose, which is the building up of the church.

As John Calvin said, commenting on 1 Corinthians 14:12: "The more anxious a person is to devote himself to upbuilding, the more highly Paul wishes him to be regarded."[4] As Peter writes in 1 Peter 4:10, "Each one should use whatever gift he has received to serve others, faithfully administering God's grace."

If edification is the goal of the spiritual gifts Christ has given to His church, what does that mean for us and our churches? It means that we are especially to value the gifts that clearly build up the churches. Furthermore, this is a call to us to realize how important a part of our Christian life the upbuilding of the church is to be—not merely organizationally, but to build up each other in our love and concern and prayers for one another. We are all called to initiate involvement in each other's lives. As I have mentioned, at Capitol Hill Baptist we covenant together to work and pray for unity, to walk together in love, to exercise care and watchfulness over each other, to faithfully admonish and entreat one another as occasion may require, to assemble together, to pray for each other, to rejoice and to bear with each other, and to pray for God's help in all this.

Imagine two congregations, one with a lot of people speaking in tongues, the other with scores of young people attending the funeral of an older man whom they had come to know as a fellow church member. That second church seems to me to be more "charismatic" in the biblical sense of that word. That second church looks more like what I understand the New Testament to be calling a church to be— a community in which people have learned to love and to care for each other. That's the new society that God is calling us as Christians to be a part of.

Christianity isn't a merely individualistic decision to come to church to see what I can get out of it. "I'll use the preacher as a public lecturer, as my own personal spiritual trainer, and insofar as he benefits me I'll have a better life." That's not quite Christianity. That might be close in some ways, but Christianity in the New Testament has very much to do with your reactions to the people sitting around you. The care and the concern you take as a covenanted group, your willingness to make a commitment to God fleshed out in your commitment to each other—that seems to be the issue as we look at the New Testament.

The charismatic nature of the church means God's Holy Spirit working among us so that we will love and care for each other. It is a grace gift (a *charisma*) for some to get up and lead worship. It is a grace gift for others to go and read Scripture to those in the hospital. It is a grace gift to take minutes at the church meetings. It is a grace gift to teach Greek. It is a grace gift to phone your pastor and tell him that you're praying for him. Those things, according to the New Testament, are charismatic gifts. Paul never intended to give an exhaustive list of *charismata* in the seventeen gifts listed. Whenever the church is working by the power of the Spirit for the upbuilding of the body, there the Spirit's gifts are present. Any understanding we have of biblical church leadership must be seen in that context.

As a church, leadership is exercised in a covenanted congregational context that is specially equipped by God. That is the charismatic nature of biblical church leadership.

THE CHRISTLIKENESS OF CHURCH LEADERSHIP

Have you ever noticed the Christlikeness of biblical church leadership? I've come up with a mnemonic device so that you can remember more easily four aspects of Christ's leadership. The mnemonic device is "BOSS," and it can be represented by the drawings of four triangles pointed in different directions that you see on the facing page. "BOSS" represents four roles that Jesus filled as a leader and that He calls those of us who are leaders to fill:

BOSS: FOUR ASPECTS OF LEADERSHIP

B = Boss

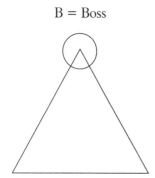

O = Out Front

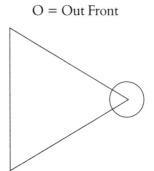

S = Supply

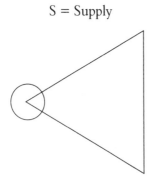

S = Serve

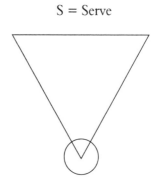

While these aspects of leadership may be true in many walks of life, I mention them now particularly with reference to being a Christian and exercising leadership in a congregational context.

Boss

Christ Himself commanded many things. For instance, He commanded us to instruct others (Matt. 28:20). Paul, too, commanded. He told Christians to tell others what to do. He instructed elders to decide what should be taught, though to do this with gentleness (2 Tim. 2:24-25) and with patience and endurance (2 Tim. 4:2). We who are elders must teach carefully, because God will hold us responsible for how faithful we have been to His Word (see James 3:1). Clearly, church leaders—like any leaders—must sometimes command, making decisions and taking the responsibility.

Some today are uncomfortable with this. But Jesus clearly commanded, and He instructed His followers (and that includes us) to do the same—to teach, to give instructions, to be willing to exercise authority when He calls us to do so. This kind of leadership should not be avoided. Though such authority may be abused, authority itself is a good thing, and we can help to recover a godly respect for authority by exercising it carefully.

Out Front

If you look at the figure marked "Out Front," you see a triangle pointing to the right, with the right-most tip circled. This represents another part of leadership—to be the one who is out front, who takes the initiative and sets the example. Much of leadership is in example-setting and initiative-taking. Probably the most feared general in all of World War II was the German tank commander Rommel, the "Desert Fox." When a battle involving his forces would begin, the word would go out, "Rommel in the lead!" That message would galvanize the troops to follow him. Good leaders take the initiative.

Another part of biblical leadership is that of setting an example. Jesus said in John 13:34, "As I have loved you, so you must love one another." Paul wrote, "Your attitude should be the same as that of

Christ Jesus" (Phil. 2:5). Peter exhorted some early Christians to remember that, "Christ suffered for you, leaving you an example, that you should follow in his steps" (1 Pet. 2:21). To the Corinthian Christians, Paul wrote, "Follow my example, as I follow the example of Christ" (1 Cor. 11:1). And he specifically told the Thessalonian believers that he had labored to make himself a model that they could follow (2 Thess. 3:7-9). He deliberately worked to live a model life— not a perfect life, but still an exemplary one. Paul offered his own life as the example, leading out in front to show how it is to be done.

And this is what we're to do. As part of our leadership, we're to be examples (see John 13:15; Phil. 3:17; 1 Tim. 4:12; Titus 2:7; James 5:10).

Supply

Looking now at the figure titled "Supply," you see another triangle, only this one is pointing to the left, with the left-most tip circled. This figure reminds us that another part of leadership is supply.

Consider an army with a vital supply line stretching out to the frontline troops. Much of what is done in good leadership is strategically working to give shape and focus and freedom to the work that others are called to do. Leaders direct the traffic of the church, cutting up ministry into bite-sized bits that others will be able to do.

If we are called to be suppliers, we go back behind the lines and give people the tools they need in order to go on out themselves. Jesus in Luke 9 and 10, having prepared His disciples, sent them out. They failed in Luke 9, but then He sent them out again in Luke 10 and they succeeded. Jesus, in this example, was back behind the lines, supplying and equipping others.

Of course we're a bit different, because we can't go with the people we send out, as Jesus can by His Spirit. So our situation is a bit more like Paul's when, in his last letter, he instructed Timothy to teach those who can teach others (2 Tim. 2:2). Paul understood that he could greatly multiply his ministry as he supplied the resources for others to do their own ministries.

Serve

Finally, look at the figure titled "Serve." This triangle is pointing downward, with the lowest tip circled. This represents the role of service. This is the second *S* in *BOSS*. This is perhaps the most distinctly Christian kind of leadership. We see it in Christ most fully as He gave Himself for us on the Cross, dying for us so that we might live to Him. Moving descriptions of this self-sacrificial service are found in each of the gospels, with further reflections throughout the New Testament. Philippians 2 and 1 Peter 2 are particularly clear and moving.

This is the example of leadership that Christ has left us. And this is especially the case if we are called to be leaders in a congregation. Peter writes,

> To the elders among you, I appeal as a fellow elder, a witness of Christ's sufferings and one who also will share in the glory to be revealed: Be shepherds of God's flock that is under your care, serving as overseers—not because you must, but because you are willing, as God wants you to be; not greedy for money, but eager to serve; not lording it over those entrusted to you, but being examples to the flock. And when the Chief Shepherd appears, you will receive the crown of glory that will never fade away (1 Pet. 5:1-4).

All four of those different aspects—the boss commanding, the out-front example, the supplying of what's needed, and then the serving—will be part of biblical church leadership.

THE RELATIONSHIP OF CHURCH LEADERSHIP TO GOD'S NATURE AND CHARACTER

As we conclude our look at church leadership, we should consider how the exercise of such leadership relates to God's nature and character.

Leadership is not finally just a matter of church politics. One time while I was in Cambridge, I was dining out with a friend and he was expressing his anger at a recent decision of the city council to sell off some land beside a school near his house. As he talked, I recalled how typical this was of my friend. He was always expressing anger about this or that thing that some authority had done. So I asked him a simple, direct, unqualified question: "Do you think authority is bad?" I thought he would give me a carefully crafted answer, shaded with subtle meanings. But I was shocked by his un-nuanced, simple, direct, unqualified answer: "Yes. Authority is bad."

Recognizing the fallen nature of human authority and the fact that authority can be abused is a good and healthy thing. Of course, power apart from God's purposes is always demonic. But a suspicion of all authority is also very bad. It often reveals more of the person questioning than of the authority being questioned. To live as God meant us to live, we must be able to trust Him, and we must be able to trust those made in His image.

This is not to say that godliness is simply gullibility, but it is to say that the capacity to trust is a crucial component of reflecting the image of God and of operating within the relationships of life in which that image is played out and expressed.

In Ephesians 3:14-21, as he prays for the Christians in Ephesus, Paul begins by telling them that he prayed to "the Father from whom his whole family in heaven and on earth derives its name." Paul's point is not simply that God is the Father of His church family, the church universal (though that's certainly true), but that God is the Creator who has made us in His image, and that even the very social structures of authority that we have in our families derive from Him and from His authority. So authority and leadership are not matters of indifference to us as Christians; they are matters of great concern, because they are part of the image of God that we are to reflect in our lives.

A world without authority would be like desires with no restraints, a car with no controls, an intersection with no traffic lights, a game with no rules, a home with no parents, a world with no God.

It could go on for a little while, but before long it would seem pointless, then cruel and unutterably tragic.

In their book *Authority: The Most Misunderstood Idea in America*, Eugene Kennedy and Sara Charles argue that, "The stabilizing character of healthy authority is what has been missing. Its return is what will make us more confident and less anxious in managing our lives."[5] They suggest that, "Healthy authority matches the needs and goals of serious intimate relationships, because its concern is not to overcome others but to fuel the growth of people who feel safe with each other."[6]

According to these authors, in movies such as *Pleasantville,*

> Greater sexual freedom, in and of itself, is viewed as the fruit of a noble rebellion against inhuman and repressive forces. Such a thing is validated in popular culture as an end in itself. Unqualified sexual liberation, that is, sex detached from human relationships, becomes a central tenet of the popular wisdom."[7]

And yet to take that intimacy outside of the structure of commitment, authority, submission, and covenant love is to uproot some of the most important lessons we can learn as creatures made in God's image—about how we are to relate both to each other and to God.

The family is supposed to be our training ground in this loving authority. It is a "ramping-up" place that God has given us to learn love, respect, honor, obedience, and trust, in order to prepare us for relating to others and ultimately to God Himself.

When we exercise authority in a good and proper way—through the law, around the family table, in our jobs, in the scout troop, in our homes, especially in the church—we are helping to display God's image to His creation.

Our conduct in the church in regard to this matter of leadership is to be such that the Gospel is not brought into disrepute but rather is held up to be the glorious light of hope and truth in the world. Our lives together are to be as pure as can be, so that God's heart of love for the world will shine clearly through us.

This is a tremendous call that God gives us, to recognize and respect godly authority in the church. This is a sign of a healthy church and of healthy Christians. This is our call. This is our privilege. And there is a world that needs to see people made in the image of God living out that image in this way. Let's pray that we can do that together in our churches—for our churches' health and for God's glory.

APPENDIX

ONE

TIPS FOR LEADING THE CHURCH IN A HEALTHY DIRECTION

✝

THE HEALTHY DIRECTION

When we can rightly assume that most of those within a church are regenerated and that they are committed to the church, then the New Testament image of the church as a body and as a family can become a living, vital reality.

In His goodness, God has called us to live out the Christian life together. In being part of a church I have grown as a Christian because of God's work through my brothers and sisters. I think that's normal. I don't think that's meant to be unusual. God intends to work on us by His Spirit through each other. Relationships imply commitment in the world; surely they imply no less in the church.

In the third commandment (Ex. 20:7; Deut. 5:11) God warned His people not to take His name in vain. By this He does not mean just avoiding profanity. More than that, He is saying, "Don't take My name upon yourself, don't claim to be My follower if you're not going to live like one of Mine." That, no less than profanity, would be taking God's name in vain.

That command is for us as a church as well. Many churches today mistake selfish gain for spiritual growth. We mistake mere excitement for true worship. We treasure worldly acceptance rather than living in a way that will incur worldly opposition (see 2 Tim.

3:12). Regardless of their statistical profiles, too many churches today seem unconcerned about the very biblical marks that should distinguish a vital, growing church.

The health of the church should be the concern of all Christians, because it does involve the spiritual life of everyone who is a Christian and a member of a church, especially of those called to be leaders in the church. Our churches are to display the glorious Gospel of God to His creation in an amazing variety by all the different personalities He puts in the church and the ways He allows them to relate together and to show His glory. That's what we're called to—we're called to display God and His character in a glorious way to His Creation (Eph. 3:10). We are to bring Him glory by our lives together.

TIPS FOR LEADING

I had thought of writing a book for pastors called "How to Get Fired ... And Fast!" I could sum up the basic idea of this unwritten book in one sentence of Pauline proportions: A pastor could go into a church members' meeting questioning the salvation of some of the church members, refusing to baptize children, advocating a priority of congregational singing over performed music, asking to remove the Christian and national flags and to stop any kind of altar calls, replace committees (even the nominating committee) with elders, ignore the secular rotation of Mothers' Day, Fathers' Day, Labor Day, Halloween, Veterans' Day, New Year's Day, Martin Luther King, Jr.'s birthday, Valentine's Day, Memorial Day, the local high school graduation and the Fourth of July, begin practicing church discipline, remove women from elder-like positions in the church, and state that he had theological opposition to multiple services on Sunday morning... Such a pastor might not get much farther than his next members' meeting.

While I could write such a book, I think that first I should take a more constructive approach. I fear that some may read this book and may immediately go into their churches impatient for radical change. But with a little wisdom, patience, prayer, careful instruction, and love we might be surprised how far we can get with our churches. The story of the persistent tortoise and the hurrying hare becomes a parable for pastors.

Here are four characteristics that you as a pastor should cultivate to help implement the changes you feel are needed in your church:

1. Be Truthful

Ask God to keep you faithful to His written Word. Never underestimate the power of teaching truth. Pray that you will have integrity within yourself, in your own thinking. Pray that you will be honest with all—in responding to questions, but even more actively, in working to help people get to know you.

2. Be Trustful

Rely on God rather than on your own gifts and abilities. Spend time in prayer privately, with others, and with the congregation. Be patient. Recall Paul's words to Timothy in 2 Timothy 4:2: "Preach the Word; be prepared in season and out of season; correct, rebuke and encourage—with great patience and careful instruction."

Give your ambitions to the Lord. Be willing to trust Him with your life; be willing to pray that God may leave you in your present place of ministry for the rest of your life. Longevity was factored in by God in bringing children to adulthood; such longevity has also characterized many fruitful ministries. The Puritan pastor William Gouge often said that the height of his ambition was to go from Blackfriars (his church) to heaven. Gouge was pastor of that same church from June 1608 until his death on December 12, 1653. He was pastor of the same church for forty-six years. Pray that God will increase your faith and help you see that His concern for His church is even greater than your own.

3. Be Positive

Pray that you neither be nor be perceived to be fundamentally a critic. Set forth a positive agenda. Clarify God's vision for His church, and your particular plans, in terms of both long-term goals and more

NINE MARKS OF A HEALTHY CHURCH

immediate goals. Pray that God will help you to build solid personal relationships. Pray particularly that God will help you to develop more leaders within the church (2 Tim. 2:2). Pray that God will make you a personal example of and a chief advocate for evangelism and missions. Pray that God will increase your zeal—and your church's zeal—for His glory.

4. Be Particular

Contextualize God's concern for His church. Use the good resources of your church's own history. Learn from older members about the history of your church. Be an ecclesiastical dendrologist. At Lincoln Cathedral, one tour guide told me that dendrologists (people who study trees) could take core samples from the forty-six-foot oak beams that have held up the cathedral's roof for centuries and figure out when the tree was planted and when it was harvested. The ones he showed us had been more than 150 years old when harvested, many having been planted in the 900s and harvested in the 1100s.

Become the chief student of your church's history. By doing this you show respect, and you learn.

May you become the agent for recovering what has been best in your church's past and the agent for leading your church into the great things God has for it in the future, as your church displays the character of God to His creation. This burden of display is our awesome responsibility and our tremendous privilege. May God make your church such a healthy church, and may He pour out His Spirit on churches across our land and around the world to do the same, for His own glory. And may God bless you in the attempt.

The Numerical Nineties and Beyond (2004)

Here, in outline form and in chronological order, is just a small sampling of prescriptions from various recent authors for the problems of the local church:

Kennon L. Callahan, *Twelve Keys to an Effective Church* (San Francisco: Harper & Row, 1987)

Twelve Central Characteristics of an Effective Church (p. 14)

 1. specific, concrete missional objectives
 2. pastoral/lay visitation in community
 3. corporate, dynamic worship
 4. significant relational groups
 5. strong leadership resources
 6. solid, participatory decision making
 7. several competent programs and activities
 8. open accessibility
 9. high visibility
10. adequate parking, land, and landscaping
11. adequate space and facilities
12. solid financial resources

George Barna, *The Frog in the Kettle* (Ventura, Calif.: Regal, 1990)

Ten Critical, Achievable Goals . . . for the 90s (p. 226)

1. win people to Christ
2. raise Bible knowledge
3. equip the Christian body
4. establish Christian community
5. renew Christian behavior
6. enhance the image of the local church
7. champion Christian morals
8. live by a Christian philosophy of life
9. restore people's self-esteem
10. focus on reaching the world for Christ

John MacArthur, *Marks of a Healthy Church* (Chicago: Moody, 1990)

Marks of an Effective Church (p. 23)

1. godly leaders
2. functional goals and objectives
3. discipleship
4. penetrating the community
5. active church members
6. concern for one another
7. devotion to the family
8. Bible teaching and preaching
9. a willingness to change
10. great faith
11. sacrifice
12. worshiping God

George Barna, *User Friendly Churches* (Ventura, Calif.: Regal, 1991)

Ten Things Successful User-Friendly Churches Don't Do

1. limit God
2. beat a dead horse

3. humiliate visitors
4. insulate themselves from the community
5. alienate those who are different
6. cold-call evangelism
7. apologize for seeking help
8. avoid confrontation
9. base staffing on precedent
10. take the safe route

Bruce Shelley and Marshall Shelley, *The Consumer Church* (Downers Grove, Ill.: InterVarsity, 1992)

Seven Vital Steps to Create a Healthy Blend of Effectiveness and Faithfulness (p. 226)

1. identify prevailing values and lifestyles in their ministry context
2. determine common values with people they would reach
3. design attractive programs to serve the people they would reach
4. these ministries must be viewed as significant spiritual steps toward the "common life" of the church
5. be sensitive and receptive to the unchurched
6. "charm" these seekers into a more mature and explicit expression of Christian discipleship in worship, membership, and outreach
7. reshape the values and lifestyles of new members and enlist them in outreach

George Barna, *Turn-Around Churches* (Ventura, Calif.: Regal, 1993)

Eleven Factors of Dying Churches Revived, or Restored to Wholeness (p. 42; actually he lists 14)

1. the presence of the Holy Spirit and an openness to His working
2. pastoral love of people; the pastor establishes a bond of trust with the congregation; pastor radically loves his people
3. a new pastor must be brought in to lead a revolution
4. release the past
5. intentionally define types of outreach the church will emphasize

6. equip the laity for effective, targeted ministry
7. pastor must be a strong leader
8. pastor must be hardworking
9. widespread and heartfelt prayer
10. their sermons were a cut or two better than what the congregation had received in the past
11. gaining an objective, outsider's perspective
12. having great staff members
13. having a core of supportive zealots in the congregation
14. long-term pastor

Thom Rainer, *The Book of Church Growth* (Nashville: Broadman & Holman, 1993)

Thirteen Principles of Church Growth (pp. 171-316)

1. prayer
2. leadership
3. laity and ministry
4. church planting
5. evangelism
6. worship
7. finding the people
8. receptivity
9. planning and goal setting
10. physical facilities
11. assimilation and reclamation
12. small groups
13. signs and wonders; evident spiritual power

Wayne Grudem, *Systematic Theology* (Grand Rapids, Mich.: Zondervan, 1994)

Twelve Signs of a More Pure Church

1. biblical doctrine (or right preaching of the Word)
2. proper use of the sacraments (or ordinances)
3. right use of church discipline
4. genuine worship

5. effective prayer
6. effective witness
7. effective fellowship
8. biblical church government
9. spiritual power in ministry
10. personal holiness of life among members
11. care for the poor
12. love for Christ

Ken Hemphill, *The Antioch Effect: Eight Characteristics of Highly Effective Churches* (Nashville: Broadman & Holman, 1994)
1. supernatural power
2. Christ-exalting worship
3. God-connecting prayer
4. servant leaders
5. kingdom family relationships
6. God-sized vision
7. passion for the lost
8. maturation of believers

Carlyle Fielding Stewart, *African American Church Growth* (Nashville: Abingdon, 1994)
Twelve Principles for Prophetic Ministry
1. celebrative worship
2. invitation in worship
3. informative worship
4. pastor as prophetic clarifier
5. pastor as creative confronter
6. pastor as prophetic restorer and comforter
7. investigative education
8. interpretive education
9. applied education
10. proclamation evangelism
11. propagation evangelism
12. participative evangelism

Thom Rainer, *Giant Awakenings* (Nashville: Broadman & Holman, 1995)

Nine Surprising Trends that Can Benefit Your Church

1. the great prayer movement
2. the rediscovery of the Bible and theology
3. the renewal of the Sunday school
4. the new understanding of culture
5. the new traditional church layperson
6. the new traditional church pastor
7. evangelistic renewal of the traditional church
8. the explosion of church planting
9. the acceptance of multiple worship styles

Rick Warren, *The Purpose Driven Church* (Grand Rapids, Mich.: Zondervan, 1995)

Lots of lists in the book; probably most important are his five purposes, which are also the five components of a purpose statement (pp. 103-107), and his program for church growth (p. 49)

1. worship: love the Lord with all your heart: church grows stronger
2. ministry: love your neighbor as yourself: church grows broader
3. evangelism: go and make disciples: church grows larger
4. fellowship: baptizing them: church grows warmer
5. discipleship: teaching them to obey: church grows deeper

Warren advocates that we . . .

1. define our purposes
2. communicate our purposes
3. organize around our purposes
4. apply our purposes

C. Peter Wagner, *The Healthy Church: Avoiding and Curing the Nine Diseases that Can Afflict Any Church* (Ventura, Calif.: Regal, 1996)

1. community around the church changes
2. community the church is in deteriorates

3. don't understand cultural barriers between us and those we would reach
4. substituting multi-church evangelism for local church evangelism
5. being spiritually self-absorbed navel-gazers
6. inadequate facilities
7. no spiritual growth
8. nominalism and formalism
9. the absence of the power of the Holy Spirit

C. Jeff Woods, *Congregational Megatrends* (Washington, D.C.: Albans Institute, 1996)

Seven megatrends happening in congregations, are shifts . . .

1. from mass evangelism to relational evangelism
2. from tribal education to immigrant education
3. from surrogate missions to hands-on missions
4. from reasonable spirituality to mysterious spirituality
5. from official leadership to gifted leadership
6. from segmented programming to holographic programming
7. from secondary planning to primary planning

Bill Hull, *Seven Steps to Transform Your Church* (Grand Rapids, Mich.: Revell, 1997)

1. seek renewal
2. develop principled leadership training
3. transform existing leadership
4. cast the vision
5. sacrifice forms for function
6. create community
7. truly do evangelism

Darrell W. Robinson, *Total Church Life* (Nashville: Broadman & Holman, 1997)

Twelve Components of Total Church Life Strategy (p. 4)

1. vision
2. commitment

3. leadership
4. unity
5. membership involvement
6. celebrative and joyful worship and praise
7. prayer
8. fellowship
9. organization
10. equipping
11. pastoral care and ministry
12. evangelizing

Mark Shaw, *Ten Great Ideas from Church History* (Downers Grove, Ill.: InterVarsity, 1997).
1. truth (Luther)
2. spirituality (Calvin)
3. unity (Burroughs)
4. assurance (Perkins)
5. worship (Baxter)
6. renewal (Edwards)
7. growth (Wesley)
8. love for the lost (Carey)
9. justice (Wilberforce)
10. fellowship (Bonhoeffer)

James Emery White, *Rethinking the Church* (Grand Rapids; Baker, 1997; 2nd ed., 2003)
1. rethinking evangelism
2. rethinking discipleship
3. rethinking ministry
4. rethinking worship
5. rethinking structure
6. rethinking community

George Barna, *The Habits of Highly Effective Churches* (Ventura, Calif.: Regal, 1998)
Highly effective churches . . .

1. rely on strategic leadership
2. are organized to facilitate highly effective ministry
3. emphasize developing significant relationships within the congregation
4. invest themselves in genuine worship
5. engage in strategic evangelism
6. get their people involved in systematic theological growth
7. utilize holistic stewardship practices
8. serve the needy people in their community
9. equip families to minister to themselves

Brian D. McLaren, *Reinventing Your Church* (Grand Rapids, Mich.: Zondervan, 1998)

Thirteen Strategies

1. maximize discontinuity
2. redefine your mission
3. practice systems thinking
4. trade up your traditions for tradition
5. resurrect theology as art and science
6. design a new apologetic
7. learn a new rhetoric
8. abandon structures as they are outgrown
9. save the leaders
10. subsume missions in mission
11. look ahead, farther ahead
12. enter the postmodern world—understand and engage it
13. add to this list

Christian A. Schwarz, *The ABC's of Natural Church Development* (Carol Stream, Ill. : ChurchSmart, 1998)

Eight Quality Characteristics of Growing Churches

1. empowering leadership
2. gift-oriented ministry
3. passionate spirituality
4. functional structures

5. inspiring worship service
6. holistic small groups
7. need-oriented evangelism
8. loving relationships

Leith Anderson, "Seven Ways to Rate Your Church," *Leadership* (Winter 1999)

What People Are Looking For

1. sensing the presence of God
2. others centered
3. understanding terminology
4. people who look like me
5. healthy problem handling
6. accessibility
7. sense of expectation

John Bisagno, "Five Characteristics of Successful Churches," (unpublished sermon, 1999)

1. they all are characterized by strong pastoral leadership
2. all successful churches are Bible churches, which preach inerrancy and inspiration
3. all successful churches are "good-time churches," emphasizing happiness and celebration
4. all are churches of unity that can't be split
5. all successful churches have an indomitable sense of unrest, an insatiable thirst for more in ministry

Dale E. Galloway, *Making Church Relevant* (Kansas City, Mo. : Beacon Hill, 1999)

Ten Characteristics of a Healthy Church, Plus One

1. clear-cut vision
2. passion for the lost
3. shared ministry
4. empowered leaders
5. fervent spirituality

6. a flexible and functional structure
7. celebrative worship
8. small groups
9. seeker-friendly evangelism
10. loving relationships
11. evaluation

Stephen Macchia, *Becoming a Healthy Church* (Grand Rapids, Mich. : Baker, 1999)
Ten Characteristics
1. God's empowering presence
2. God-exalting worship
3. spiritual disciplines
4. learning and growing in community
5. commitment to loving relationships
6. servant-leadership development
7. outward focus
8. wise administration and accountability
9. networking with the body of Christ
10. stewardship and generosity

Donald J. MacNair, *The Practices of a Healthy Church* (Phillipsburg, N.J. : Presbyterian & Reformed, 1999)
Three Vital Signs
1. individual members are growing in spiritual maturity
2. the church is actively seeking to help unbelievers come to Christ
3. the absence of major divisions

Six Healthy Practices
1. retain uncompromising commitment to holy Scriptures
2. engage in regular, vibrant worship of God
3. continually train and implement shepherd-leadership
4. mechanism for utilizing gifted member initiative with elder-accountability
5. continually modified vision and plan unique to that church

6. prayerfully seek the grace of God to build commitment to biblical health

Mark Dever, *Nine Marks of a Healthy Church* (Wheaton, Ill.: Crossway, 2000)
1. expositional preaching
2. biblical theology
3. biblical understanding of the good news
4. biblical understanding of conversion
5. biblical understanding of evangelism
6. biblical understanding of church membership
7. biblical understanding of church discipline
8. biblical understanding of church leadership
9. concern for promoting Christian discipleship and growth

Eddie Gibbs, *Church Next* (Downers Grove, Ill. : InterVarsity Press, 2000) (p. 52, citing *The Gospel and Our Culture* 10, no. 3 [1998])
Twelve Empirical Indicators of a Missional Church
1. proclaims the gospel
2. all members involved in discipleship
3. Bible is normative
4. church understands itself as different from the world because of its union with Christ
5. seeks to discern God's specific missional vocation for entire community and for all its members
6. behaves Christianly toward one another
7. practices reconciliation
8. people hold themselves accountable to one another in love
9. practices hospitality
10. worship is central
11. vital public witness
12. recognition that church is an incomplete expression of the reign of God

Herb Miller, "What Priorities Build a Healthy Church?" The MBA Connection, Parish Paper (2000)

Four Main Priorities

1. maturational growth
2. incarnational growth
3. systems growth
4. numerical growth

What Else Counts—Eight More Priorities

1. attitude
2. persistence
3. members who sense that nearby residents . . . are similar to themselves
4. members who strongly emphasize the building of positive relationships with outsiders
5. pastors and staff encouraged that their members understand the main priorities
6. vibrant, sincere prayer
7. numerically declining churches can be strong in incarnational ministries
8. some congregations grow in all four main areas simultaneously

Bob Russell, *When God Builds a Church: Ten Principles for Growing a Dynamic Church* (West Monroe, La. : Howard 2000)

1. truth: proclaim God's Word as truth and apply it to people's lives
2. worship: worship God every week in spirit and truth
3. leadership: develop Christ-centered leaders who lead by example
4. excellence: do your best in every area of service
5. faith: be willing to step out with a bold faith and take risks
6. harmony: maintain a spirit of harmony
7. participation: expect the congregation to participate in every ministry
8. fellowship: continually practice agape love for one another

9. stewardship: give generously of God's resources as a church and as individuals

10. evangelism: commit enthusiastically to evangelism as your primary mission

Report of the Eighteenth Plenary of the Consultation on Church Union (2000)

Nine Visible Marks of Churches Uniting in Christ

1. mutual recognition of each other as expressions of the one church
2. mutual recognition of members in one baptism
3. mutual recognition of ordained ministry
4. mutual recognition that each affirms the Apostles' and Nicene Creeds
5. provision for celebration of the Eucharist together with intentional regularity
6. engagement together in Christ's mission regularly and intentionally
7. intentional commitment to promote unity of all persons in church and society
8. ongoing process of theological dialogue
9. appropriate structures of accountability and for decision making

Robert Baake, "Ten Leading Indicators of a Healthy Church," EFCA *Beacon* (2001), p. 13

1. centrality of God's Word
2. passionate spirituality
3. fruitful evangelism
4. high-impact worship
5. mission- and vision-driven
6. leadership development
7. church planting
8. financial stewardship
9. intentional disciple making
10. loving relationships

Thom Rainer, "Nine Habits to Attract, Keep Unchurched" *Western Recorder,* April 17, 2001, p. 10.

1. intentionality
2. cultural awareness
3. high expectations
4. clear doctrine
5. risk taking
6. dynamic small groups
7. effective pastoral leadership
8. effective preaching
9. prayer

Ed Stetzer, "Prof Lists Ten Commandments for Postmodern U. S. Churches," *Western Recorder,* **February 27, 2001, p. 7.**
1. be unashamedly spiritual
2. promote incarnational ministry
3. worship experientially
4. preach narrative expository messages
5. appreciate and participate in ancient patterns
6. experience visual worship
7. engage in service
8. connect with technology
9. live community
10. promote team-based leadership

Waldo Werning, *Twelve Pillars of a Healthy Church* **(St. Charles, Ill.: ChurchSmart, 2001)**
1. empowering leadership
2. gift-oriented service/ministry
3. passionate spirituality
4. functional structures/administration/servant leadership
5. inspiring/high-impact/God-exalting worship services
6. multiplied small groups/intentional disciple making/growing in community
7. witnessing/fruitful evangelism/missions
8. loving relationships
9. centrality of God's Word/Gospel/grace
10. mission- and vision-driven

11. biblical financial stewardship
12. church planting

Andy Stanley and Ed Young, *Can We Do That? Twenty-Four Innovative Practices that Will Change the Way You Do Church* (West Monroe, La.; Howard, 2002)

1. Invest and invite: We partner with our regular attenders to reach the unchurched.
2. Targeting the unchurched: We focus on making the unchurched visitor feel welcome and comfortable.
3. Videotaped baptism testimonies: We videotape baptism testimonies and use them as an evangelistic tool during baptismal services.
4. Streaming video: We stream baptisms, dedication services, and sermons on the Internet.
5. Intentional marketing: We are intense about advertising our church to the community.
6. Making membership strategic: We make the membership process a strategic part of emphasizing the small-group, community aspect of church.
7. Closing the deal: We hold a Newcomers Class to give information about the church and prepare people to join.
8. Kidstuff: We provide a place where kids take their parents to learn.
9. Aligning student ministry: We understand and plan for the unique relational and ministry needs of junior high and high school students.
10. Welcome teams: We have four distinct teams that focus on specific areas of weekend hospitality.
11. Community groups: We emphasize small groups as a place to find real community.
12. Area fellowships: We utilize Area Fellowships to get people to begin to connect relationally.
13. Group link: We move people from Area Fellowships to Group Link, an environment designed to jump-start small groups.
14. The sports ministry: We have a full-blown athletics ministry without any permanent recreational facilities.
15. Church leadership: We are a staff-led church.

16. Ministry team representatives: What? No deacons?
17. Hiring the right people: We hire staff from within the church body.
18. Storytelling: We share ministry stories during staff meetings for inspiration and instruction.
19. Sermon planning: We make the message the first priority of the service—and of the pastor.
20. Preaching calendar: We are intentional and deliberate in the timing and topics of our sermon series.
21. Creativity: We creatively adapt the service and the worship center to enhance a creative message.
22. Teaching less for more: We gear our teaching for comprehension and meeting the listeners' needs.
23. Integrating vision: We constantly incorporate the vision of our church into our messages.
24. Personal evaluation: I watch the video of my message every weekend and evaluate my effectiveness.

Gary L. McIntosh, *Biblical Church Growth* (Grand Rapids, Mich.; Baker, 2003)
1. the right premise: God's Word
2. the right priority: glorifying God
3. the right process: discipleship
4. the right power: the Holy Spirit
5. the right pastor: a faithful shepherd
6. the right people: effective ministers
7. the right philosophy: cultural relevance
8. the right plan: target focused
9. the right procedure: simple structure
10. mix it right

Philip Graham Ryken, *City on a Hill* (Chicago: Moody, 2003)
1. making God's Word plain—expository preaching
2. giving praise to God—corporate worship
3. growing together in groups—fellowship
4. shepherding God's flock—pastoral care
5. thinking and acting biblically—discipleship

6. reaching the world—missions and evangelism
7. serving with compassion—mercy ministry
8. why the church needs the Gospel—repentance and renewal

Peter Scazzero, *The Emotionally Healthy Church* (Grand Rapids, Mich.: Zondervan, 2003)
1. look beneath the surface
2. break the power of the past
3. live in brokenness and vulnerability
4. receive the gift of limits
5. embrace grieving and loss
6. make incarnation your model for loving well

David Garrison, *Church Planting Movements* (Midlothian, Va.: WIGTake Resources, 2004)
1. extraordinary prayer
2. abundant evangelism
3. intentional planting of reproducing churches
4. the authority of God's Word
5. local leadership
6. lay leadership
7. house churches
8. churches planting churches
9. rapid reproduction
10. healthy churches

APPENDIX
THREE

MEDICINES FROM THE CABINET

✝

While I would not agree with everything in every book listed, here are a few suggestions for key books in each of the areas addressed in this book. They are listed by chapter.

MARK ONE: Expositional Preaching

Graeme Goldsworthy, *Preaching the Whole Bible as Christian Scripture* (Grand Rapids, Mich.: Eerdmans, 2000).

John Piper, *The Supremacy of God in Preaching* (Grand Rapids, Mich.: Baker, 1990).

John R. W. Stott, *Between Two Worlds* (Grand Rapids, Mich.: Eerdmans, 1994).

MARK TWO: Biblical Theology

Graeme Goldsworthy, *According to Plan: The Unfolding Revelation of God in the Bible* (Downers Grove, Ill.: InterVarsity Press, 2002).

J. I. Packer, *Knowing God* (Downers Grove, Ill.: InterVarsity, 1993).

John Piper, *The Pleasures of God* (Portland, Ore.: Multnomah, 1991).

MARK THREE: The Gospel

John Cheeseman, *Saving Grace* (Carlisle, Pa.: Banner of Truth, 2000).

Martin Luther, *Bondage of the Will* (Ventura, Calif.: Revell, 1990).

John MacArthur, *The Gospel According to Jesus* (Grand Rapids, Mich.: Zondervan, 1994).

C. J. Mahaney, *The Cross Centered Life: Experiencing the Power of the Gospel* (Portland, Ore.: Multnomah, 2002).

J. I. Packer, "Saved by His Precious Blood," chapter 8 of Packer, *A Quest for Godliness* (Wheaton, Ill.: Crossway, 1990).

Thomas Scott, *The Articles of the Synod of Dort* (Harrisonburg, Va.: Sprinkle, 1993).

John Stott, *Basic Christianity* (Grand Rapids, Mich.: Eerdmans, 1986).

MARK FOUR: A Biblical Understanding of Conversion

Jonathan Edwards, *Distinguishing Marks of a Work of the Spirit of God* (Temecula, Calif.: Reprint Services Corp., 1992). See also Archie Parrish and R. C. Sproul, *The Spirit of Revival* (Wheaton, Ill.: Crossway, 2000), which contains the complete modernized text of Edwards's *The Distinguishing Marks of a Work of the Spirit of God.*

Paul Helm, *Beginnings: Word and Spirit in Conversion* (Carlisle, Pa.: Banner of Truth, 1988).

John MacArthur, *The Gospel According to Jesus* (Grand Rapids, Mich.: Zondervan, 1994).

Ernest C. Reisinger, *The Carnal Christian* (Carlisle, Pa.: Banner of Truth, 1991).

Don Whitney, *How Can I Be Sure I'm a Christian* (Colorado Springs, Colo.: NavPress, 1994).

Don Whitney, *Ten Questions to Diagnose Your Spiritual Life* (Colorado Springs, Colo.: NavPress, 2002).

MARK FIVE: A Biblical Understanding of Evangelism

Will Metzger, *Tell the Truth* (Downers Grove, Ill.: InterVarsity Press, rev. 2002).

Iain Murray, *Revival and Revivalism* (Carlisle, Pa.: Banner of Truth, 1994).

J. I. Packer, *Evangelism and the Sovereignty of God* (Downers Grove, Ill.: InterVarsity Press, 1991).

Philip Graham Ryken, *City on a Hill* (Chicago: Moody, 2003).

Mack Stiles, *Speaking of Jesus* (Downers Grove, Ill.: InterVarsity Press, 1995).

MARK SIX: A Biblical Understanding of Church Membership

Mark Dever, *A Display of God's Glory* (Washington, D.C.: Center for Church Reform, 2001).

Mark E. Dever, ed., *Polity: Biblical Arguments on How to Conduct Church Life: Some Historic Baptist Documents* (Washington, D.C.: Center for Church Reform, 2000).

Josh Harris, *Stop Dating the Church!* (Portland, Ore.: Multnomah, 2004).

Don Whitney, *Spiritual Disciplines Within the Church* (Chicago: Moody, 1996).

MARK SEVEN: Biblical Church Discipline

Jay E. Adams, *Handbook of Church Discipline* (Grand Rapids, Mich.: Zondervan, 1986).

Dever, *Polity* (see MARK SIX, above).

Ken Sande, *The Peacemaker* (Grand Rapids, Mich.: Baker, 1997).

Gregory A. Wills, *Democratic Religion* (New York: Oxford University Press, 1996).

Daniel Wray, *Biblical Church Discipline* (Carlisle, Pa.: Banner of Truth, 1991).

MARK EIGHT: A Concern for Discipleship and Growth

Robert Coleman, *The Master Plan of Evangelism* (Grand Rapids, Mich.: Revell, 1994).

Kris Lundgaard, *The Enemy Within* (Phillipsburg, N.J.: Presbyterian & Reformed, 1998).

John Piper, *Don't Waste Your Life* (Wheaton, Ill.: Crossway, 2003).

John Piper, *Future Grace* (Portland, Ore.: Multnomah, 1998).

J. C. Ryle, *Holiness* (Moscow, Idaho: Charles Nolan, 2001).

Paul Tripp, *Instruments in the Redeemer's Hands* (Phillipsburg, N.J.: Presbyterian & Reformed, 2002).

Paul Tripp, *War of Words* (Phillipsburg, N.J.: Presbyterian & Reformed, 2000).

Edward Welch, *When People Are Big and God Is Small* (Phillipsburg, N.J.: Presbyterian & Reformed, 1997).

Donald S. Whitney, *Spiritual Disciplines for the Christian Life* (Colorado Springs, Colo.: NavPress, 1997).

Donald S. Whitney, *Spiritual Disciplines Within the Church* (Chicago: Moody, 1996).

One of the best contemporary resources for articles and books on biblical counseling is the official website of the Christian Counseling and Educational Foundation, *www.ccef.org*.

MARK NINE: Biblical Church Leadership

On elders:

Tom Ascol, ed., *Dear Timothy* (Cape Coral, Fla.: Founders, 2004).

Mark Dever, *A Display of God's Glory* (Washington, D.C.: Center for Church Reform, 2001).

David Dickson, *The Elder and His Work* (Phillipsburg, N.J.: Presbyterian & Reformed, 2004).

Phil A. Newton, *Elders in Congregational Life: A Model for Leadership in the Local Church* (Grand Rapids, Mich.: Kregel, 2005).

John Piper, *Biblical Eldership* (Minneapolis: Desiring God Ministries, 1999).

Alexander Strauch, *Biblical Eldership* (Littleton, Colo.: Lewis and Roth, 1995).

On congregationalism:

Mark Dever, *A Display of God's Glory* (Washington, D.C.: Center for Church Reform, 2001).

Dever, *Polity* (see MARK SIX, above).

NOTES

PREFACE

1. Cited in *The Complete Works of Richard Sibbes, D.D.,* ed. Alexander Balloch Grosart (Edinburgh: J. Nichol, 1862–1864).

INTRODUCTION

1. David Wells, *God in the Wasteland* (Grand Rapids, Mich.: Eerdmans, 1994), 213.

2. See appendix 2, "The Numerical Nineties," to see what a number of authors have suggested we should do about the problems in the local church.

3. John Stott, *Men with a Message* (Longmans: London, 1954), 163-164. Reprinted in the United States as *Basic Introduction to the New Testament* (Grand Rapids, Mich.: Eerdmans, 1964).

4. Edmund Clowney, *The Church* (Downers Grove, Ill.: InterVarsity, 1995), 101.

5. John Calvin, *Institutes of the Christian Religion,* trans. F. L. Battles (Philadelphia: Westminster, 1977), IV.ii.3, 1045.

6. One might compare this with Luther's various writings about aspects taken to constitute a true church. See, e.g., his "Against Hanswurst," a treatise defending the Reformation from attacks by Henry, Duke of Braunschweig/Wolfenbuttel, in which Luther lays out what he considers to be ten characteristics of churches that are "faithful to the true ancient churches." *Luther's Works* (Philadelphia: Fortress, 1966), 41:194-198.

7. Philip Melanchthon, *Loci Communes,* trans. J. A. O. Preus (St. Louis: Concordia, 1992), 137.

8. *Documents of the English Reformation,* ed. Gerald Bray (Cambridge, England: James Clarke, 1994), 296.

9. Cf. Calvin, *Institutes,* IV.i.xii, 1025-1026.

10. For an example of a modern popular treatment, see D. Martyn Lloyd-Jones, *The Church and the Last Things* (Wheaton, Ill.: Crossway, 1998), 13-18.

11. See A. C. Cochrane, ed., *Reformed Confessions of the Sixteenth Century* (Philadelphia: Westminster, 1966). So, too, the Scottish Confession (1560), Article 18: "The trew preaching of the Worde of God . . . . the right administration of the sacraments of Christ Jesus . . . . Ecclesiastical discipline uprightlie ministered." See James Bulloch, trans., *The Scots Confession of 1560* (Edinburgh: St. Andrews College Press, 1993).

12. Clowney, *Church*, 101. On pages 99-115, Clowney has a good summary of the marks of the church considered biblically, historically, and in current questions of distinguishing the church from the parachurch.

13. Carl E. Braaten, "The Gospel for a Neopagan Culture," in Carl E. Braaten and Robert W. Jenson, eds., *Either/Or: The Gospel or Neopaganism* (Grand Rapids, Mich.: Eerdmans, 1995), 19-20.

14. Os Guinness, *Dining with the Devil: The Megachurch Movement Flirts with Modernity* (Grand Rapids, Mich.: Baker, 1993), 49. For one interesting example of such unintentional secularization, see Samuel S. Hill, "Forum: Southern Religion," in *Religion and American Culture* 8, no. 2 (Summer 1998): 160-161.

15. Richard A. Muller, *The Study of Theology* (Grand Rapids, Mich.: Zondervan, 1991), xiii.

16. Carl Braaten, "The Gospel for a Neopagan Culture," 19. A later essay in the same collection expresses similar worries: "The church is tempted to become relevant to the people of this culture by using their wishes and criteria rather than those of the church. Evangelism is then driven by a market or consumer-oriented mentality. The church can 'meet people's needs' as people define their needs. Thus the people who may have little or no recent experience in the church develop the evaluation of the church and the church struggles to fulfill their expectations." James R. Crumley, "Setting the Church's Agenda," in Braaten and Jenson, *Either/Or*, 119.

17. John Broadus, "A Catechism of Bible Teaching," in Tom J. Nettles, *Teaching Truth, Training Hearts: The Study of Catechisms in Baptist Life* (Amityville, N.Y.: Calvary, 1998), 208.

18. Mark Ross, unpublished sermon notes.

19. My summary from his comments at a conference in Wheaton, Maryland, October 9, 1997.

20. David Hilborn, *Picking Up the Pieces: Can Evangelicals Adapt to Contemporary Culture?* (London: Hodder and Stoughton, 1997), especially 148-162.

MARK ONE: Expositional Preaching

1. Martin Luther, *Luther's Works* (Philadelphia: Fortress, 1959), 51:77.

2. Cited by Guinness, *Dining with the Devil*, 59.

MARK TWO: Biblical Theology

1. Karl R. Popper, *The Open Society and Its Enemies* (Princeton, N.J.: Princeton University Press, 1966).

2. C. S. Lewis, *The Last Battle* (New York: Macmillan, 1956), 183.

MARK THREE: The Gospel

1. Guinness, *Dining with the Devil*, 63.

2. See James Miller, *The Passion of Michel Foucault* (New York: Simon and Schuster, 1993), 375-385.

3. Westminster Confession of Faith, 2:2.

4. J. C. Ryle, *Holiness* (Grand Rapids, Mich.: Baker, 1979), 204.

5. B. B. Warfield, *The Divine Origin of the Bible,* reprinted in *The Works of Benjamin Warfield* (Philadelphia: Presbyterian Board of Publication, 1991), I.432.

6. Quoted in *Newsweek* (July 10, 1995), 8.

7. Fyodor Dostoyevsky, quoted in Jean Paul Sartre, *Existentialism and Human Emotions,* trans. Bernard Frechtman (New York: Philosophical Library, 1957), 22.

8. John Wesley, *Inspiration Three* (New Canaan, Conn.: Keats, 1973), 119.

MARK FOUR: A Biblical Understanding of Conversion

1. Robert W. Jenson, "The God-Wars," in Carl E. Braaten and Robert W. Jenson, eds., *Either/Or: The Gospel or Neopaganism* (Grand Rapids, Mich.: Eerdmans, 1995), 25.

2. Charles H. Spurgeon, "The Prayer of Jabez," *The Metropolitan Tabernacle Pulpit* (Pasadena, Tex.: Pilgrim, 1969), 17:320.

3. See O. C. S. Wallace, *What Baptists Believe: The New Hampshire Confession: An Exposition* (Nashville, Tenn.: The Sunday School Board of the Southern Baptist Convention, 1934).

4. A. W. Tozer, *Men Who Met God,* comp. and ed. Gerald B. Smith (Camp Hill, Pa.: Christian Publications, 1986), 83.

MARK FIVE: A Biblical Understanding of Evangelism

1. Will Metzger, *Tell the Truth* (Downers Grove, Ill.: InterVarsity, 1984).

2. J. Mack Stiles, *Speaking of Jesus* (Downers Grove, Ill.: InterVarsity, 1995).

3. Iain H. Murray, *Revival and Revivalism* (Carlisle, Pa.: Banner of Truth, 1994).

4. J. I. Packer, *Evangelism and the Sovereignty of God* (Downers Grove, Ill.: InterVarsity, 1991).

5. Joseph Bayly, *The Gospel Blimp and Other Stories* (Elgin, Ill.: David C. Cook, 1973), 11-12.

6. Robert Schuller, quoted in *Milk and Honey* (December 1997), 4.

7. Donald McGavran, "The Dimensions of World Evangelization," in *Let the Earth Hear His Voice,* ed. J. D. Douglas (Minneapolis: World Wide, 1975), 109.

8. John Stott, "The Biblical Basis of Evangelism," in ibid., 69.

9. Ibid.

10. John Cheeseman, et.al., *The Grace of God in the Gospel* (Edinburgh: Banner of Truth, 1972), 119.

11. Ibid., 122.

12. C. S. Lovett, *Soul-Winning Made Easy* (LaHabra, Calif.: The Lockman Foundation, 1959), 17-18.

13. Ibid., 50.

14. Charles H. Spurgeon, *The Metropolitan Tabernacle Pulpit* (Pasadena, Tex.: Pilgrim, 1974), 34:115.

MARK SIX: A Biblical Understanding of Church Membership

1. Don E. Eberly, *Restoring the Good Society* (Grand Rapids, Mich.: Baker, 1994), 38.

2. Jonathan Edwards, *Distinguishing Marks of a Work of the Spirit of God* (Temecula, Calif.: Reprint Services Corp., 1992). See also Archie Parrish and R. C. Sproul, *The Spirit of Revival* (Wheaton, Ill.: Crossway, 2000), which contains the complete modernized text of Edwards's *The Distinguishing Marks of a Work of the Spirit of God*.

3. O. C. S. Wallace, *What Baptists Believe: The New Hampshire Confession: An Exposition* (Nashville, Tenn.: The Sunday School Board of the Southern Baptist Convention, 1934), 89.

4. Robert Bolt, *A Man for All Seasons* (New York: Random, 1990), 141.

MARK SEVEN: Biblical Church Discipline

1. Theron Brown and Hezekiah Butterworth, *The Story of the Hymns and Tunes* (New York: George H. Doran, 1923), 434.

2. R. Albert Mohler, Jr., "Church Discipline: The Missing Mark," in John H. Armstrong, ed., *The Compromised Church* (Wheaton, Ill.: Crossway, 1998), 171-187.

3. Daniel E. Wray, *Biblical Church Discipline* (Carlisle, Pa.: Banner of Truth, 1978).

4. Gregory A. Wills, *Democratic Religion* (New York: Oxford University Press, 1996).

5. John L. Dagg, *Manual of Church Order* (Harrisonburg, Va.: Gano, 1982).

6. Mark Dever, *Polity: How Christians Should Live Together in a Church* (Washington, D.C.: Center for Church Reform, 2001).

7. Jay E. Adams, *Handbook of Church Discipline* (Grand Rapids, Mich.: Zondervan, 1986).

8. Dietrich Bonhoeffer, *Life Together* (San Francisco: HarperSan Francisco, 1993).

9. H. E. Dana, *Manual of Ecclesiology* (Kansas City, Kan.: Central Seminary Press, 1944), 244.

10. Wills, *Democratic Religion*, 32.

11. Ibid., 22.
12. Ibid., 10.
13. Ibid., 9.
14. *The Creeds of Christendom: With a History and Critical Notes* (Grand Rapids, Mich.: Baker, 1983), 419-420.
15. Os Guinness, *Dining with the Devil: The Megachurch Movement Flirts with Modernity* (Grand Rapids, Mich.: Baker, 1993), 38).
16. Wills, *Democratic Religion*, 33.
17. Dagg, *Manual of Church Order*, 274.

MARK EIGHT: A Concern for Discipleship and Growth

1. Os Guinness, *Dining with the Devil: The Megachurch Movement Flirts with Modernity* (Grand Rapids, Mich.: Baker, 1993), 67.
2. John Newton, quoted in J. I. Packer, *Knowing God* (Downers Grove, Ill.: InterVarsity, 1993), 251.
3. Guinness, *Dining with the Devil*, 38.

MARK NINE: Biblical Church Leadership

1. George Orwell, *Animal Farm* (New York: New American Library, 1963), 123.
2. Williston Walker, *The Creeds and Platforms of Congregationalism* (New York: Pilgrim, 1991), 217-218.
3. Os Guinness, *Dining with the Devil: The Megachurch Movement Flirts with Modernity* (Grand Rapids, Mich.: Baker, 1993), 49.
4. John Calvin, *Commentary on the Epistles of Paul the Apostle to the Corinthians,* trans. John Pringles (Grand Rapids, Mich.: Baker, 1981), 20:442-443.
5. Eugene Kennedy and Sara Charles, *Authority: The Most Misunderstood Idea in America* (New York: Free Press, 1997), 2.
6. Ibid., 35.
7. Ibid., 30.

GENERAL INDEX

SCRIPTURE INDEX

For more information about the ideas in this book, contact:

MARKS

MINISTRIES

God designed the church to be a display of His own glory and wisdom (Eph. 3:10), and we believe He has spoken clearly in the Bible regarding the purpose, leadership, organization, and methods of the local church.

9Marks Ministries is not here simply to point out all the problems with the church; nor do we intend to suggest an innovative approach to "doing church." Rather, our goal is to point the way back to healthy church life by calling attention to the timeless biblical priorities, principles, and methods that God has ordained for the maturity of the local church— God's work, God's way.

We serve pastors and other church leaders by **refocusing** attention on the value of healthy congregations. As we do this, we want to encourage leaders to **rethink** the biblical nature, purpose, and leadership structures of the church, and to **reconnect** careful biblical theology with responsible church practice.

9Marks Ministries provides an educational forum to examine and discuss the elements of a healthy local church. We also want to present a working model that is constantly being reformed by the Word of God. The four primary channels through which we seek to demonstrate this healthy church model include:

Media: downloadable web resources, audio interviews, e-newsletter, educational curriculum
Study: training weekends, conferences, internships, think tanks
Publishing: books, pamphlets, papers
Outreach: On-site visits, phone conversations
To learn more . . .

VISIT   www.9marks.org

or

CALL   888.543.1030

9Marks Ministries – the Word building the church